Maria Giannoula
Fragments of Solidarity

Social Movement and Protest | Volume 11

Maria Giannoula studied Political Sciences in Thessaloniki and completed her PhD at the Europa-Universität Viadrina in Frankfurt (Oder), Germany. Her ethnographic research focuses on uses and understandings of solidarity within an alternative community in Greece.

Maria Giannoula

Fragments of Solidarity

An Ethnography of an Alternative Community in Modern Greece

[transcript]

This book draws on my doctoral research which was conducted at the Faculty of Social and Cultural Sciences of the Europa-Universität Viadrina in Frankfurt (Oder) under the supervision of Prof. Dr. Werner Schiffauer, Europa-Universität Viadrina Frankfurt (Oder) and Prof. Dr. Michał Buchowski, Europa-Universität Viadrina Frankfurt (Oder), and Adam Mickiewicz University, Poznan and was defended and concluded on 14 June 2021.

Bibliographic information published by the Deutsche Nationalbibliothek
The Deutsche Nationalbibliothek lists this publication in the Deutsche Nationalbibliografie; detailed bibliographic data are available in the Internet at http://dnb.d-nb.de

Cover layout: Maria Arndt, Bielefeld
Printed by: Majuskel Medienproduktion GmbH, Wetzlar
https://doi.org/10.14361/9783839466988
Print-ISBN 978-3-8376-6698-4
PDF-ISBN 978-3-8394-6698-8
ISSN of series: 2701-0473
eISSN of series: 2703-1667

Printed on permanent acid-free text paper.

Contents

Acknowledgements

This book owes its existence to my friends. For me, it is foremost a book about relationships and emotions, both of which would lack any meaning in my life without my friends. From its very beginning, this study was conducted with the constant encouragement and support of Maria, Gogo, Michalis, Vanda, Stelios, Sophie, Marek and Zoe. They accompanied me throughout the research and writing process and each of them contributed to it in a variety of ways. I thank them from the bottom of my heart for their belief and trust that this book would one day achieve a final form.

Various versions of this study went through detailed discussions in the anthropological colloquium in the European University of Viadrina, Frankfurt (Oder). I am deeply obliged to my colleagues for all these fruitful exchanges, and I would especially like to express my gratitude to my supervisor, Prof. Dr. Werner Schiffauer for his patience and kindness while guiding me throughout this study and Prof. Dr. Michał Buchowski for all his insightful comments on my research. I would also like to acknowledge that the first year of research was accomplished thanks to the financial support of DAAD [Deutscher Akademischer Austauschdienst].

Dr. Luana Martin-Russu and Dr. Anika Keinz reviewed some of the latest versions of this text, and their comments were always a valuable source of inspiration. I thank them for their help, trust and their friendship.

Special thanks belong to Dr. Michael Vaughan for all the solidarity he presented throughout the proofreading and editing of this text, and for all the positive energy he shared with me throughout this strenuous task. He really taught me that the strength of a text probably lies in its simplicity.

I am also deeply grateful to the members of the group, who generously shared their time, and energy throughout this learning process.

However, this work was ultimately carried out until its very final end with the persistent urging of Ioanna and Nikos, who tirelessly and selflessly supported me with their feedback, comments and humour and filled my journey through the writing process with a lot of joy and constant reflection. I dedicate this book to them with love, as well as to Pawel who caringly tolerated me and my absences for a number of years until the last dot of this text was ultimately placed.

List of Abbreviations

ANEL	Anexartiti Ellines [Independent Greeks Party]
ANTARSYA	Antikapitalistiki Aristeri Synergasia gia tin Anatropi [Anti-capitalist Left Cooperation for the Overthrow]
DAP-NDFK	Dimokratiki Ananeotiki Protoporia- Nea Dimokratiki Fititiki Kinisi [Democratic Renewal Innovation- New Democratic Student Movement]
EAM	Ethniko Apeleftherotiko Metopo [National Liberation Front]
EAR	Elliniki Aristera [Greek Left]
EC	European Commission
ECB	European Central Bank
EDA	Eniea Dimokratiki Aristera [United Democratic Left]
EEC	European Economic Community
ELAS	Ethnikos Laikos Apeleftherotikos Stratos [National Popular Liberation Army]
ERT	Elliniki Radiofonia Tileorasi [Hellenic Broadcasting Corporation]
EU	European Union
FYROM	The Former Yugoslav Republic of Macedonia
IMF	International Monetary Fund
KKE (es.)	Kommounistiko Komma Elladas Esoterikou [Communist Party of Greece Interior]
KKE	Kommounistiko Komma Elladas [Communist Party of Greece]
KKE m-l	Kommounistiko Komma Elladas (Marxistiko-Leninistiko) [Communist Party of Greece (Marxist-Leninist)]
KNE	Kommounistiki Neolaia Ellados [Communist Youth of Greece]
ND	Nea Dimokratia [New Democracy Party]
PASOK	Panellinio Sosialistiko Kinima [Panhellenic Socialist Movement]
PASP	Panellinia Agonistiki Spoudastiki Parataxi [Panhellenic Militant Student Organisation]
SEK	Sosialistiko Ergatiko Komma [Socialist Workers Party]

SYN	Synaspismos ton Kinimaton, tis Aristeras kai tis Oikologias [The Coalition of the Left, of Movements and Ecology]
SYRIZA	Synaspismos Rizospastikis Aristeras [Coalition of the Radical Left – Progressive Alliance]

Introduction: Thessaloniki, 2009

It was Thursday, 10th December 2009. On the first floor of a building in the heart of Thessaloniki various groups had set up a social centre called the Sanctuary,[1] from which volunteers would run a number of initiatives to help migrants in the city. I observed the place from the opposite corner. I stood there rolling a cigarette, preparing to introduce myself to the people I was about to meet. I had found out about the Sanctuary from Joey, a good friend of mine, a couple of months earlier. I had told him I was thinking of starting a new research project and he had suggested that I check out this new place in the city. He even put me in contact with one of his acquaintances, Evdokia. She was a member of AuRA[2], one of the groups that had set up the Sanctuary, and Joey had arranged for her to meet me during my first visit there.

The Sanctuary was in an old historical building in the city centre. I made my way up to the grand staircase, not sure where I was going, and then I saw an open door, a first sign of the welcoming atmosphere of the Sanctuary. On entering, I saw there was a café, a small bar, and behind the bar a small kitchen. In front of the bar some tables and chairs were laid out. There were people talking in the corridor, some were sitting in the café, others working behind the bar. People greeted me nonchalantly, as if I was already acquainted with them, but I still felt a bit overwhelmed and tried to act casually, so as not to stand out. There were doors, and corridors going off in all directions. Not sure where to go, I went over to a table and looked at some pamphlets, thinking that I must look completely lost, but since I had to wait a while for Evdokia, I decided to take the opportunity to get to know the place a bit. I sat at the bar, ordered a drink and chatted a little to the people behind the bar, while also taking in the surrounding atmosphere.

As I understood it, most of the people who were around were teachers who had volunteered to give lessons to migrants. I thought some of them belonged to some of the groups who were affiliated with the Sanctuary, but at the beginning I was rather

1 In order to preserve anonymity all places' and members' names have been replaced with pseudonyms.

2 AuRA is the activist group under investigation, focussing on migrants' rights, anti-racist and anti-discriminatory projects.

clumsy when it came to the identification of who was who in the different groups that participated there.

Chatting to the people running the bar, I found out a bit more about the place. They explained to me that each day a different group was responsible for the running of the café and the kitchen. During the evenings, besides any lessons that were taking place, various assemblies were held to discuss the upcoming weekly issues. That evening the teachers' assembly was about to start, and later that night a social event was also taking place. There were three levels of language courses available, taught in both Greek and English, and many children along with women and men of all ages attended them. Nobody, however, could tell with certainty the exact number of the students attending the courses, as it grew on a daily basis – something the members were really proud of.

The collectives who participated in the Sanctuary paid a rent of 1,500 euros for the first floor and for a short period of time also "occupied" the second floor without paying, as the people at the bar put it. One of the members feared that "they were very likely to have problems with the owner in the future," despite the fact that their presence there served a "good cause." It was clear that nobody had expected the Sanctuary to be as successful as it was, and the occupation of the second floor resulted from there not being enough space on the first floor for all of the activities the place was hosting.

The Sanctuary opened every evening around 7pm. The weekly routine of the participants included attending the weekly general assemblies, attending the separate meetings of the various collectives and work-groups, putting on the language courses for migrants, providing legal aid for migrants, organising protests and hosting a range of night-time events, such as film showings, open discussions and music events. There was also help available for children with their schoolwork.

Between talking to the people at the bar, I also had time to flip through some of the pamphlets I had picked up, and I noticed some recurring words and phrases that drew my attention: "solidarity" and "not a political organisation." I wondered for a moment who might have written it. Who was actually in charge? Who decided how the place would present itself?

Before I visited the place, I had been rather anxious, as I used to live under the impression that such collectives usually form cliques who are suspicious of – if not resistant to – outsiders, thus making it difficult for anyone interested in their structure and way of functioning to gain access to them. I suppose this impression had largely been formed during my student years in Thessaloniki. In our small department there had been three or four main political positions. Besides the student youth groups of the two main political parties in Greece (the DAP-NDFK who were affiliated to Nea Dimokratia and the PASP who were affiliated to PASOK), there were also representatives of the KNE (Communist Youth Party). There were also one or two groups who were affiliated with the extra-parliamentary Left, but these – although they seemed to present more alternative ways of engaging in politics – were rather confusing and had an aura of detached intellectuality that I could never really grasp.

Thus, the idea of having "no clear political identity" as the pamphlets implied, seemed a bit unlikely to me, and made me wonder how things really were behind the scene. However, the aspiration of the Sanctuary and AuRA to stand in solidarity with migrants and unite broader political spaces provided a clue to the ideological orientation of the group which was all I needed for the time being. The Greek participants were members of broadly leftist collectives, parties, and environmental organisations. They came from a range of smaller groups who were willing to be united under principles that were formulated within the common frame of the Sanctuary.

Before too long, Evdokia arrived. Polite and enthusiastic, she emitted a particular energy that already seemed familiar to me as a characteristic of the place. I followed her as she moved freely through the Sanctuary, sometimes checking that a door was locked or that something was in the right place, greeting her friends, and checking in with people about the various tasks that had to be accomplished during the evening. She gave the impression that she was somehow 'in charge.' She was certainly committed to what she was doing. We had a brief chat about her studies and her participation in AuRA and the Sanctuary. She seemed rather impressed by the success of the Sanctuary.

Stratos, a friend of Evdokia, and another member of AuRA with whom I had spent some time before her arrival, joined our discussion as well. He asked me exactly what I was looking for and, as I felt hesitant about revealing my interest in studying AuRA, I said something brief and vague: "I was thinking of starting a study about places that support migrants in Greece." Stratos immediately started giving me all kinds of relevant information; who I should talk to, what the situation is with migrants in Thessaloniki, how their participation in some areas is limited, as well as how similar projects emerged in Athens some years ago (where things seemed to be more "organised") but with quite different intentions from the ones that guided the Sanctuary. He also asked Emanuel, an older participant who happened to be nearby, to come and meet me. Emanuel immediately started giving me even more information, before talking about what he understood to be a real necessity of establishing a more coherent ground of communication between various organisations in Thessaloniki, something that he felt they should insist on more.

Evdokia also commented on the importance of engaging more people, not only in the language courses but also in the overall life of the Sanctuary. She had the sense that many migrants did not feel comfortable joining in with activities that were not clearly defined or connected to their specific needs. For example, they might attend a language class, but did not find it easy to join the members of the collectives for a drink at the café bar afterwards. She described how the Afghan women who attended the language courses had a tendency to isolate themselves and were hesitant about socialising with other people, preferring to stay with each other in a separate room while waiting for their children to finish the language course.

AuRA was one of the main things that had drawn my attention to the Sanctuary before actually visiting the place. The group emerged in the anti-racist scene in Thessaloniki in the early 2000s and seemed to have a steadily growing presence in issues regarding anti-discrimination and anti-racism. A main contribution of the group, and one that made it quite well known in the city, was its provision of the language lessons for migrants, which it had already been offering at the group's previous location since the mid-2000s. The Sanctuary, however, as a place which hosted a variety of groups, was something new in the city. It was a place where various activities could take place – not only a practical place of learning and information, and of political education – but also a social space where its various members could spend time without attending specific classes or activities.

The meeting with Evdokia, Stratos and Emanuel lasted for a couple of hours. I was so focussed on our conversation that I hardly noticed how crowded the place became with students, teachers, migrants and members of various groups. During this time (we had started off at a table in the café, then moved to the computer room where we spent most of this time, and ended up on a bench in the corridor), people had already re-organised the tables in the café and joined the event that was taking place there. Some members together with visitors were cooking, some were sitting at the bar and at the tables waiting to try the food, while on the wall of the café a documentary film was being projected.

Evdokia and Stratos asked me to stay and join them, and I accepted their invitation, curious to see how the night would evolve. People continued to arrive, and the Sanctuary continued to fill up. When the teachers' assembly finished, I was surprised to see that my own teacher from high school was there. We found a corner to sit and spent some time catching up. She told me that she had visited the Sanctuary a few times as she was interested in volunteering in the language lessons, and she was still working out exactly how she fitted in there. While we were swapping stories from the eight years since we had last seen each other, another old acquaintance of mine came in and, surprised to see me, immediately came over to greet me. Paul and I had studied together at the university and he too seemed to be familiar with the place and its members. I promised my teacher we would keep in touch, and along with Paul I re-joined Evdokia and the others. We spent the rest of the night all together. It was about 2 am by the time I realised how late it had got and decided it was finally time to leave.

Returning back home, I was thinking about how my first visit had turned out to be far more interesting and enjoyable than I had expected, and how once you have been in the place, it is probably not that easy to disentangle yourself from it. Without intending to, I had become part of a large coterie that night: I had met some old acquaintances and some new ones, I had had some interesting conversations, and by the end of the night I had started moving freely throughout the place myself, as if it was not my first visit there at all. But what exactly I was looking for?

The AuRA group and this new experiment called the Sanctuary had caught my attention. AuRA's robust presence in the anti-racist scene in Thessaloniki gave this group (and the creation of the Sanctuary) a distinctive character. From my very first moments in the Sanctuary, and throughout my meeting with the members of AuRA who so enthusiastically engaged in our discussion, certain questions kept coming into my mind: how did people make the decision to set up a place like the Sanctuary? What were the reasons that had led them to join the AuRA group in the first place? How did they interact with the other people and groups there? What was AuRA's specific contribution to the Sanctuary? What was so distinctive about this group? How did the members feel about their participation in it? And most of all... where did all this enthusiasm come from?

In its beginnings then, this study started with the aspiration to try and answer these questions by looking at life in the Sanctuary and the way its members understood and worked towards their egalitarian vision. Over the years, however, the project took various forms and shapes as new questions were constantly born out of it, a fact that made the research process an open field of constant reflection and elaboration.

Outline of Chapters

In Chapter One, I will review some of the decisions that led me to engage in this research project, with reference to both my own research interests and also to the breadth and complexity of the field I have chosen to investigate. I will also look at some of the basic ideas and concepts I have used to guide myself through this research.

In Chapter Two, I will delve into methodological issues, reflecting on how this research has been conducted, and considering certain dilemmas that were raised with reference to 'the researching self.' Starting from a conceptualisation of reflexivity, the chapter thematises the processes through which the research product takes its actual form. This will involve looking at issues of power, at the insider/outsider status of the researcher, and at the role of ongoing relationships and friendships as a tool in the research field, all of which constitute fragments of the actual research process. I will also look at the ways in which researchers deal with their multiple emotional and ethical dilemmas. The main questions that the chapter looks at are who is the writing subject and in what kind of relation do they stand towards the research subject and the individuals participating in it?

In Chapter Three, I will look at the social and political context of the emergence of AuRA, and we will go back to the decades of the 1980s and 1990s in an attempt to identify the conditions for the formation of AuRA through the stories of some of its protagonists. This will shed light on the broader context within which various activist initiatives were undertaken in this period. Starting from its origins in a very small group that resisted the intense nationalism and racism of the 1990s, we will observe how AuRA came into existence and how the idea of the Sanctuary was formed. What were the political and social conditions that allowed or necessitated this emergence and what principles guided the members in this new venture?

Chapter Four focuses on the atmosphere created in the Sanctuary, on its culture and on the principles that its members followed in their daily interactions. We will look in detail at the functioning of the Sanctuary, and in particular its weekly assemblies at which all important decisions were made, as well as at the preparations that went into organising its annual festival. We will see that many of the processes that played a pivotal role in the group's practical organisation also had an equally important role in the group's bonding and its participants' experience of togetherness. In the second part of the Chapter we will ask what the Sanctuary means to its participants, and what relevance solidarity has in their discourse. What kind of feelings accompany people's participation in the Sanctuary and in AuRA? What do the participants say about solidarity? Why did they become part of the Sanctuary and what keeps them together? At the same time, we will observe how the vision of its founding members started to be realised within the new setting that the Sanctuary created.

Chapter Five will examine how the principles and overall vision of the group are held together through the individual roles and activities that its members fulfil. Who are the sub-groups that support the ideal of solidarity and what kind of relationships do they have with each other and with the collective as a whole? The typology I present of the roles of different members will reveal certain power relations that were formed in the group, and how these related to the ideological underpinnings of the endeavour. The 'types' I identify can provide insights into the organisation of the group, and also illustrate the members' emotional commitment to the movement's unified purposes. Ideas of solidarity emerge from different genealogies of participation, as well as from the different roles that people took on within the group, and as such they will shed light on the different tendencies of solidarity that emerged in the group.

Chapter Six will focus on the last period of my research, which coincided with a demanding period for the group. The impact of the financial, political and social crisis in Greece was by now obvious and we will see the members of the group give a detailed account of the problems that arose and the possible solutions (in terms of solidarity) that would bring back to the Sanctuary the sustainability and enthusiasm that had been waning due to a lack of resources, internal fatigue and personal exhaustion. The group emphasised the importance of solidarity in three different areas when addressing the problems they were faced with: an emphasis on external coalitions, on internal bonding and inter-spaces, and on relationships and inter-betweenness.

In the Conclusion, I will consider what emerged from my research as the defining characteristics of the Sanctuary. We will look at the characteristics that made the formation of the Sanctuary distinctive, and we will take a last glimpse at what characterised AuRA's alternative nature. I will also reflect on the idea of "unlearning" by conducting research, a process that proved fruitful both for my research and for me personally. The book will end as it started, with a reflection on going back to the field.

1. In Search of Meaning

Influences

The initial impetus for this research came from my previous preoccupation with the notion of *utopia*. This interest in utopia developed as I was finishing my masters studies, when something about the idea seemed to persistently demand that I engage in a more rigorous study of it. My theoretical background in sociology and political science helped me to guide myself through the field of utopian studies, but I became increasingly aware that without a concrete field of research it would be very difficult to understand how people actually engage in the passionate pursuit of a better world. What is it that leads people to pursue a better world? How do they go about it? How do they feel about their action? What lies behind their ideals? What kind of spiritual reservoir helps fuel their plan, and can it be exhausted? One of the main reasons I engaged in this project was the necessity of going beyond the literature and engaging in an actual field of research in a more ethnographic way in order to answer questions such as these. When I made this decision in early 2009, I realised that the scholarly tradition I had been part of throughout my studies, and the kind of theoretical positions that I was forming on the subjects that interested me, would have to be re-negotiated, reviewed or even abandoned if I was to be able to look at particular phenomena from a more engaged perspective. However, coming from this background, I could not encounter the Sanctuary as a tabula rasa, and it is worth considering some of the theoretical works that had informed my thinking up to this time.

Early on, the works of Hannah Arendt and Martin Buber made a great impression on me,[1] and gave me the impetus for a more serious study of the classical texts by Weber, Durkheim, Simmel and Schutz.[2] My own perspective on this material was twofold: on the one hand, I was greatly interested in the theoretical meaning of so-

1 Arendt 1970, 1986, 1990/1963, 1998/1958, 2006; Buber 1996/1970, 1996, 2002.

2 Weber 2002, 2007a; Weber 2005, 1949; Schutz 1972, 1976; Wolff, Kurt, H. 2012; Durkheim 2008.

cial action and agency, and on the other hand I was constantly looking for the significance and contribution of social research to the study of contemporary life.[3]

One text that provided me with a kind of compass at this time was Berger and Luckmann's *The Social Construction of Reality*.[4] The way in which this text presented the world as constituted in a dialectical relationship between society and individuals – or between the objective and subjective worlds within which we acquire experience, mature and take action – seemed to me to at least partly solve some of social theory's classical problems.[5] While we are in society, as Berger writes, society is also 'in us,' a fact that produces a certain space of autonomy within which individuals can decide how they want to live in society by accepting, adjusting to, or as he puts it, "internalising" its main principles.[6] Berger and Luckmann's claim to bring the crucial issues of social theory together in a theory that would answer the question of how individuals develop 'know-how' about the world they live in is an ambitious one, and the theory they develop is not without its problems. Firstly, while their analysis of the "subjective production of meaning" and the construction of reality at this level is well established and leaves space for further interpretation, their arguments regarding the "objectivity of the social world" remain rather underdeveloped.[7] Secondly, by placing society "inside the head" of individuals, as Craib might have put it,[8] one feels that a dual determinism appears inescapable. If society "constructs" the reality that individuals find in the social world, and if the individuals in turn reproduce these "objective" social norms and institutions, then a kind of vicious circle of the "predictability" of non-autonomous-being-in-the-world emerges. At the same time, by overemphasising the subjective factors of this dialectical relationship, that is to say by focusing solely on the subjective and emotional side of the dialectic, Berger and Luckmann may also be underestimating the role of power relationships and structures.[9]

Sometime later, when the idea for this project was starting to take its shape, I realised that my sociological background would not suffice, and that I would need some support from a field that greatly inspired me, but to which I only had a distant relationship, namely anthropology. By delving into the ethnographic approach, the kind of frame that I was looking for gradually emerged. As Geertz puts it, the aim of ethnography is "to draw large conclusions from small, but very densely textured

---

3 Weber 1949; Weber 2004b.

4 Berger and Luckmann 1991.

5 Berger and Luckmann 1991; Craib 1993.

6 Berger 2011, see especially Chapter Four and Five, on "Man in Society" and "Society in Man". As Berger and Luckmann write: "Man's self-production is always, and of necessity, a social enterprise." Berger and Luckmann 1991, 69.

7 Ritzer 1998, 303–4.

8 Craib 1993, 101.

9 Craib 1993; Hjelm 2019.

facts; to support broad assertions about the role of culture in the construction of collective life by engaging them exactly with complex specifics."[10] By diving into a field at a microscopic level through "thick description"[11] and participation, the focus can be placed on what participants themselves have to say about their own principles, interrelations, and how they themselves make meaning out of their action. My own approach was to try and remain as close as possible to members' own assessments about what life within the group means to them. As such, I remained focussed on the anthropological requirement to take seriously the "research practices" that members of groups themselves advance, and to follow them in the production of their own findings and results, which are based on their own fields of interest and the knowledge they acquire within the group's frame.[12] A number of scholars have noted that the knowledge, experiences, stories and ideologies that make the world meaningful to the individuals concerned should all be taken seriously by social researchers.[13] Although I cannot but agree with Katz and Csordas' comment that "the culture as lived is never quite the same as the culture as represented,"[14] in this book I at least attempt to keep the phenomenological and interpretive viewpoint as close as possible to the culture I examined, while reviewing all the ambivalences that such an approach may reveal.

Having said this, I was not opposed to the use of theory where it seemed to shed some light on what I was observing, or on what the members of the group themselves were saying. Indeed, to a great extent, theory functions as complementary both to my interlocutors' ideas and to my own interpretations of them. For example, Arendt's conceptualisation of action as the human ability to "act in concert"[15] was one idea that seemed to be directly related to what I was observing, while Buber's emphasis on in-between relationships and on the priority of human affairs constantly reminded me of what my interlocutors themselves foregrounded as important in their own participation in the group.[16] In this way, my theoretical background helped to guide me during the initial stages of my participation in the research group. The extent to which those influences also defined the theoretical aspect of this research would be difficult to disentangle and remains part of the reflective negotiation that takes place throughout this study. This negotiation between the theoretical aspect and the actual field research will also be looked at in particular in Chapter Two.

10 Geertz 1973, 28.
11 Ibid, 3–30.
12 Casas-Cortés, Osterweil, and Powell 2008; Hirai 2015; Zavos and Biglia 2009.
13 Casas-Cortés, Osterweil, and Powell 2008, 21.
14 Katz and Csordas 2003, 285.
15 Arendt 1998/1958, 179.
16 Buber 1996/1970, 2002.

Throughout the conducting of this research two main things were important to me. First, and to the extent that this was possible, I tried to focus on the micro-level of the daily reality and to see through the participants' own eyes, so to speak, by observing the production of shared meanings and the formation of relationships in the group's evolution. A second concern was the interdisciplinary character of this study, which I would like to believe offers possible interpretations of the phenomena I analyse and does not attempt to reduce them to a unified theoretical project. In this sense, I hope that my job as a researcher, which is to say as an intermediary, bears fruits by shedding some new light on the topics here discussed.

In what follows, I will first give a brief idea of the social context within which this research project developed, looking in particular at the different understandings of solidarity that occurred in response to the Greek financial crisis. I will then introduce three useful perspectives from which one might explore the Sanctuary and AuRA, before concluding this chapter by presenting some specific theoretical notions that characterised this research.

Solidarity in Context

These theoretical preoccupations did not distract me from keeping track of the wider context within which my study was taking place. Namely, a rapidly changing social and political context that gave rise to the peculiar feeling that one was experiencing one of those moments at which history is being made. The financial crisis in Greece could be said to be the most general context within which my research developed. Although my focus is not solely on solidarity in relation to the crisis, it will be necessary to take a look at some of the changes it brought about in the activist endeavours of the time.

When I started my research, 'solidarity' was a rather neglected analytical category and an even more neglected issue. We might say that it was as restricted and neglected as the collectives who employed the term. But very soon afterwards, in the period of austerity that followed in the wake of the financial crisis, solidarity started to grow in popularity. It began to appear in both public and academic discourses as an overall term for collective action, collectives, and movements.[17]

What has come to be known as the financial crisis in Greece was a long period of recession and economic turbulence that started in 2009 and led to a series of measures being introduced in order to mitigate its effects.[18] The case of Greece was just the tip of a financial iceberg that would affect many countries in the eurozone in

17 Arampatzi 2018; Hadjimichalis 2018; Papataxiarchis 2016; Rakopoulos 2014a, 2014b, 2015, 2016; Rozakou 2016, 2018; Theodossopoulos 2016. See also Tsilimpounidi and Walsh 2014.

18 Hadjimichalis 2018; Sakellaropoulos 2014.

the following years, and which reflected the global developments of the late 2000s. During this period, however, a growing interest was to be observed, not only in the global economic developments as they affected more and more countries, but in the kinds of qualities and virtues that countries did or didn't possess, and which were held to be responsible for their financial decay.[19]

In Greece a heated debate arose which located the origins of the crisis in the culture of the Metapolitefsi.[20] The Metapolitefsi was the long period that started with the restoration of democracy in 1974 following the military junta of 1963–1974 and lasted until the 1990s (or for some scholars until much later).[21] The critique of the political and social culture that emerged during this period was characterised by a general scrutiny of social and political life during the 1980s and 1990s in order to detect those elements that led to the crisis.[22] One such element was the enthusiasm for financial growth and for participation in the European Community that characterised the early years of the Metapolitefsi in the 1980s, the wisdom of which was publicly re-examined in light of the crisis. In retrospect, many people claimed that the country had not been ready to join the European Community, and that there were certain aspects of Greek politics that made its adoption of European principles problematic.[23] This re-examination of the 'culture of the Metapolitefsi' revealed what was claimed to be a cultivated moral decay that had developed over the past twenty years and which was now evident in retrospect as a condition of the crisis.[24]

The popular discourses on the crisis encouraged unspoken hierarchies and cultural divisions that presented Europe and Greece (among other countries) as two opposite sites. Although European and international institutions were promoting the idea of supporting financially the southern countries, at the same time those countries were blamed for Europe's financial decay.[25] Something that Costis Hadjimichalis identified as the emergence of a perceived cultural division in Europe be-

---

19 Hadjimichalis 2018, 139–81.

20 Avgeridis, Gazi, and Kornetis 2015a, 15; Sakellaropoulos 2014, 32–33. For the idea of the political culture see Demertzls 1995.

21 Scholars have provided a wide range of different periodisations see indicatively Voulgaris 2002; Voulgaris 2008. See also Avgeridis, Gazi, and Kornetis 2015a, 15–18.

22 Avgeridis, Gazi, and Kornetis 2015a, 15. As these scholars observe, there is a new historical reading which questions even those aspects of social and political life that were previously considered as an achievement.

23 See also the argument about Swallow Europeanism ("Ρηχός Εξευρωπαϊσμός") in Balabanidis 2015.

24 For an overview of articles and themes related to this period see Avgeridis, Gazi, and Kornetis 2015b; Kouki and Liakos 2015. For two characteristic examples of different aspects of this critique see: Kathimerini, April 18, 2012; Böll, Sven, Böcking David, May 18, 2011.

25 Herzfeld 2016a, 2016b. Michael Herzfeld observed the kind of "European moralism" that was suggested in the case of the Greek crisis in particular among other southern European countries.

tween (what was claimed to be) the "bad south" and "the good north," with the former being characterised by a model of economic and ethical avoidance, while the latter were striving to save Europe as a whole from the former's recklessness.[26] As Hadjimichalis puts it, the perpetuation of "asymmetrical imaginations" about this recklessness of the southern countries was part of a long tradition of Mediterranean orientalism.[27] Kalantzis came to a similar conclusion, describing how the national and international press of the time represented the Greeks as the 'deviant children' of a European family, a representation which formed a recurring motif in accounts of the interplay between Greeks' infantilism ("παιδικότητα") and their consequent need for protection and hegemony ("ηγεμονία").[28] This emphasis on the alleged 'moral crisis' was also discussed in terms of a constructed pretext for the "asymmetrical social relations" of world capitalism, and for embedded systemic problems on a global level.[29]

In this search for the origins of the crisis, a whole complex of discourses emerged on the various European 'mentalities,' with views being put forward from all sides of the spectrum: political parties, the national press, the foreign press, official bodies, governments, and European institutions all seemed to have an opinion. Despite the range of the debates about Greece and its own 'moral decay,' however, it may be useful to identify two main aspects that seemed to be particularly characteristic: First, there was the largely historical aspect that the social and political conditions of the past decades were holding Greece back and preventing the country from becoming synchronised with European standards (a fact that was thought to have its roots in the ethno-patriotic and populist disposition of the politicians and the general 'backwardness' of the social and political life of the 1980s and 1990s).[30] Second, there was a more 'ontological' aspect that identified a kind of collective self-indulgence that was peculiar to Greece and was responsible for the country's narcissism, arrogance, and financial unaccountability.[31] What both aspects ultimately suggested though, was

26 Hadjimichalis 2018, 144–45.

27 Hadjimichalis 2020, 83; See also Said 1996a. See also Panagiotopoulos and Sotiropoulos 2020.

28 Kalantzis 2015a, 370. The term "παιδικότητα" that the writer originally uses, refers to an immaturity that was allegedly evident in the Greeks' inability to take care of their finances and themselves, and to respond to their obligations. See also Kalantzis 2015b.

29 Gkintidis 2017, 41.

30 Tsoukalas 2017/1993; Pappas 2010. Reading these scholars, one senses an evaluation in terms of delay, progress, and backwardness which overlooks the fact that terms like these are "ideologically charged," born out of specific historical contexts, and tied to specific politico-ideological narratives. See Lipovats 1995, 122. For an overview on this topic and the idea of a failed transition to modernity see Kouki and Liakos 2015.

31 A very interesting article that captures the atmosphere of entertainment locales in Greece and focuses on the consumption of whiskey and its connection to the process of modernisation is: Bampilis 2015. Panagiotopoulos identified how the affluence of the previous decades

that in the financial crisis Greece was finally 'paying the price' for its carefree past. The cultural myths and stereotypes about Greece during this period all revealed the same thing: that the Metapolitefsi lacked any responsible approach to financial issues; a lack which revealed the 'Mediterranean temperament' to be one of cunning, laziness and unaccountability.[32]

Faced with a crisis in their core value system, the European institutions gave prominence to 'solidarity,' and in particular to financial and ethical support for the countries that had lost their 'moral orientation' (Greece was not the only case of this).[33] Austerity plans were instigated not only to re-establish financial stability but even more importantly to provoke a return to consistency, responsibility, economic adjustment and rationalisation. In other words, a return to moral order.

These debates and criticisms seemed to me to take on an evaluative tone that could very easily lead the discussion towards cultural essentialism, and even towards racism, with their over-simplistic descriptions of much more complicated phenomena. At the same time, they were avoiding the more crucial issues of global economic developments, the nature of capitalism, and the growing distance between institutions and citizens.[34] Moreover, this retroactive damnation of a 'sinful past' that had led to the crisis, which was very often accompanied by an obsessive self-criticism and self-punishment, did not constitute a critical self-assessment, nor did it offer a productive ground for society to confront itself on.

Alongside the simplistic and exaggerated response to the crisis that was formulated in politics and the media, another response to the crisis was being formed from below, by movements and individuals that presented a high degree of readiness to intervene where help was needed. These grassroots networks of communication and action not only revealed the consequences of the crisis at the tangible level of people's everyday lives and their living conditions, but also an increase in self-awareness, and a growing tendency towards social and political mobilisation with the aim of making a real difference in the deteriorating financial, social and political conditions.[35] General strikes, riots and demonstrations, the emergence of multifarious local movements, and an emphasis on self-organisation and collective action were

had cultivated a narcissistic culture along the lines of western paradigms. Panagiotopoulos 2015, 353.

32 About stereotyping perspectives in the media, see Kalantzis 2015a; Hadjimichalis 2020, 94–107; See also Herzfeld 2016a, 10; Herzfeld 2016b. See also Gkintidis 2017.

33 The so-called Piigs (Portugal, Italy, Ireland, Greece, Spain), although Cyprus belongs to the formation as well. Hadjimichalis 2020, 119–22. See also Hadjimichalis 2018; Herzfeld 2016a.

34 Hadjimichalis 2018, 248.

35 Arampatzi 2018.

the main characteristics of activism and political engagement during this period.[36] All of these activities were aspects of a general demand for solidarity that was constantly growing in popularity. It seemed that the demand for solidarity was a collective response not only to the irresponsibility and unaccountability of a corrupt political system, but also to the indifference and passivity of a weak civil society that was claimed to have prevailed during the previous years.[37]

As the demands for solidarity as a remedy to the crisis multiplied after 2010, it took on a number of very different forms and shapes. Solidarity could be seen as a symbol of resistance, a symbol of people's readiness to defend their rights and to refuse to submit to the unjust regulations that were proposed by the European institutions and the government.[38] It also marked people's ability to realise their responsibilities and transform themselves into sensitised citizens who could have a real effect on their present situation and envision a better future. This capacity for self-reflection and the cultivation of a collective empathy through a range of initiatives formed a distinctive part of the collective response to the moral and political crisis. The explosion of a wave of practices under the banner of solidarity required that people make the effort to renegotiate their collective identity.[39]

Thus, a new political and ethical subject, one who recognises what was lacking in previous practices and attempts to address this by participating in the public realm, emerges through this intense engagement in local practices of solidarity.[40] However, these transformations were not only taking place in the public sphere; many studies focus on the transformations that took place in the private realm as well. Consumption can serve as an example. As consumption was linked to the ethical failings that led to the crisis, action was undertaken by individuals in order to achieve a feasible kind of austerity-management at home and in their private lives.[41] As Souliotis has observed, the shift in the way people perceived their past consumption patterns was accompanied by a tendency to view them in moral terms, and often to condemn them altogether, while at the same time seeking to cultivate a better, more cautious character, one that refrains from desiring unnecessary material wealth.[42]

Alongside the obvious reduction in consumption that this involved, there was also the development of alternative modes of exchange that were appropriate to an

---

36 See especially Rakopoulos 2014a, 2014b, 2015; Vradis and Dalakoglou 2011; Theodossopoulos 2013, 2016; Simiti 2016; Tsilimpounidi and Walsh 2014 Karyotis and Rüdig 2018. See also Leontidou 2015.

37 There was in general this argument about the weak civil society in Greece, see Sotiropoulos 2004. See also Leontidou 2010.

38 For an overview of the functions of solidarity-spaces, see Arampatzi 2018.

39 Douzinas 2011, 224–29.

40 Ibid, see also Hadjimichalis 2018, 281–286; 283.

41 Souliotis 2016. See also Emmanouil 2016; Alonso, Rodríguez, and Rojo 2015.

42 Souliotis 2016, 290–98.

alternative economy without intermediaries. Spaces of ethical and green consumption were also flourishing.[43] As Rakopoulos notes, these extensive networks of solidarity economy provided a way into political education "rather than just a moral economy of food consumption."[44] In addition to fleshing out the meaning of solidarity in concrete terms, these alternative economies became a counterexample, leading the way to a renewed political engagement.[45] At the same time, they fostered an anti-hegemonic discourse that stood in strong contrast to the prevalent discourse of the debt crisis and its neo-liberal foundations.[46]

There were multiple, diverse, and fragmented moments at which solidarity appeared as a demand for further action on a local level (in neighbourhoods, squares, and new alternative spaces) and also as an ethical principle to guide that action. Collective kitchens, alternative economies, the provision of help to homeless people, 'don't pay' initiatives, and ecological initiatives were just a few instances where the importance of solidarity was emphasised.[47] In these spaces the prerequisite of the reconstruction of a collective identity was based on new moral pledges. Solidarity became a symbol for standing against exploitation and injustice; and unlike the 'solidarity' that accompanied the austerity measures and was pledged by European institutions, it did not resemble a financial transaction.[48] Under the new ethical imperative of solidarity people united themselves in all kinds of smaller and large-scale events and projects that appeared during this period.

The idea of solidarity as a principle guiding voluntary organisations to take the initiative in all kinds of areas is not without precursors in Greece. Already in the late 2000s, Rozakou's research on voluntary organisations allowed her to discuss different conceptualisations of the 'ethical citizen' who participates in them.[49] However, the ethical citizen of the crisis seemed to take things a step further; no longer content to help out with already established initiatives, people were now taking situations into their own hands, self-organising and starting new initiatives. In this context, the ethical citizen ceases to be an amenable volunteer and becomes a self-conscious, responsible citizen in the service of both self-transformation and social change. Rozakou was among the first to observe a "boom in solidarity" which had already started in the first years of the crisis and had reached its peak with the refugee

43 Chatzidakis, Maclaran, and Bradshaw 2012.
44 Rakopoulos 2014a, 315. See also Rakopoulos 2014b.
45 Hadjimichalis 2018; Arampatzi 2018; Rakopoulos 2014b.
46 Rakopoulos 2014a, 313.
47 For an overview see Hadjimichalis 2018, 230–76.
48 At the time, the discourses about the corrupted south that spent money and the prudent north that borrowed money were quite heated. See Hadjimichalis 2018, 179–80.
49 Rozakou 2018. On the notion of the volunteer as an ethical citizen see pp. 19–22.

crisis of 2015.[50] It was at this time that the adjective 'solidarious' ("αλληλέγγυος") began to be heard more and more often.

I want to pause here to provide a brief note about this word and my use of it in this book. When I started writing the book, I was using the word solidarious as an adjective to characterise all the activities, sentiments and everything that my interlocutors described as related to solidarity. When a good friend of mine, and a native English speaker, informed me that the word does not exist, I started researching the issue and in particular whether I would be forced to abandon what was a very meaningful term for many of my interlocutors. I was encouraged to find that at least one scholar, Sara Koopman, had made a similar investigation, noting that solidarious – which she derived from the Spanish *solidario* – is actually a useful invention to convey what both the Greek and Spanish terms try to conceptualise.[51] As such, I decided to retain the word solidarious in exactly the same sense as the Greek *αλληλέγγυος*, and thus also retain the way my interlocutors repeatedly used it to describe any person or action that stands in solidarity with others. Hence, throughout the book such persons or actions will be referred to as solidarious.

The extensive use of the term solidarity in the broader culture, and the number of different perspectives from which it was approached (political, ideological or academic), raised a number of questions for me. First of all, as Papataxiarchis has eloquently stressed, the condition of crisis through which solidarity was approached often seemed to act like a kind of prism, distorting the analysis of certain phenomena.[52] This did not only apply to the idea of solidarity. Notions of resistance and even of the crisis itself were also among those blurred analytical categories.[53] In this sense, the term solidarity occupied a cloudy landscape, within which its analytical value was difficult to determine. In a way, its use and understanding remained within the entanglements that were born out of the epoch that produced it.[54] Solidarity to a great extent becomes a metaphor that progressively exhausts itself and loses its value, as it remains entangled in various ideologically and politically embedded discourses.[55] If this is true, we may ask why we should bother with solidarity any longer?

What I often found to be lacking in the literature on the crisis, with its emphasis on solidarity and austerity, was a more situated understanding of solidarity and even a genealogy of it within concrete groups and organisations that existed before the crisis. How did all these developments affect the organisations that already had

50 Rozakou 2016, 197.
51 Koopman 2015.
52 Papataxiarchis 2017, 203.
53 Papataxiarchis 2017, 203–4; Cabot 2015, 4.
54 Ibid.
55 Papataxiarchis 2017; Papataxiarchis 2016, 207. See also Ricœur 1978, 153–54.

for their focus more marginalised groups? How did they change, for better or for worse during this time of increased solidarity? There was also the question of how the emerging crisis affected my research into AuRA and the Sanctuary. My main impression was one of a rapidly changing socio-political landscape where the density of the political events, and the general atmosphere of an always shifting situation did not allow me to easily adopt a fixed position regarding my findings.[56] However, we should bear in mind that my field of research did not emerge either during the crisis or because of it. AuRA was initiated during the 2000s in response to the demands of that time, as we will examine in detail in Chapter Three. And even the Sanctuary's emergence in 2009 did not fully coincide with the experience of the crisis, which would not become fully evident until much later.

In this sense, due to the long-term nature of my research, and the variety of changes that took place over this period, I was able to gain a better insight into the nature of solidarity as my interlocutors experienced it in the different stages of the group's development.

In calling this book 'fragments of solidarity' what I mean to indicate is both the numerous moments, actions and episodes in which solidarity was active and evident, as well as the multifaceted understanding of solidarity that was held by the group. Thus, while the idea of fragments resists the notion that there could be a universal, all-encompassing understanding of solidarity, this does not mean that it therefore implies that solidarity is somehow dysfunctional, broken or 'in pieces.' The inspiration for the title stemmed from Barthes' use of the phrase "fragments of discourse" to describe what he calls "figures": "These fragments of discourse can be called *figures* [...] not in its rhetorical sense, but rather in its gymnastic or choreographic acceptation."[57] For Barthes – who was concerned here with a quite difficult topic, namely love – the "figure" is "the lover at work."[58] By analogy, then, what we are looking at here is 'solidarity at work,' and it is in this sense, that I talk about solidarity as fragmented; that is to say, as a multifaceted, dispersed and always shifting notion, yet one that is central to the self-understandings of each participant and of the collective as a whole.

56 Knight and Stewart 2016. See in particular their comments on the difficulty of drawing conclusions in a fast changing landscape. See also Tsilimpounidi 2014.

57 Barthes 2002, 3–4. Emphasis in original.

58 Ibid, 4.

Theoretical Underpinnings

Having provided some context for the much-discussed idea of solidarity I will now look at some of the main theoretical choices and perspectives that underlie this study. The rapidly changing socio-political landscape within which the Sanctuary and AuRA evolved made the choice of a single theoretical lens through which to approach them inappropriate. Due to the Sanctuary's experimental character – as a place that would unite a variety of persons, groups, and activities – I had to identify at the beginning of my investigation which approaches were most relevant to research that focussed on its changing character. In the end, I drew inspiration from three approaches that I could use to investigate the way the Sanctuary and AuRA functioned over this long period of time: the first, drawing on new social movements theory, looks at the group in terms of collective action and collective identity, the second looks at the group as a community that offers its members the potential for individual transformation, and the third looks at the Sanctuary as an 'open space' of social and political participation. Let us briefly look at some of the characteristics that made these approaches a valuable source of guidance, before then going on to consider the distinctive elements of my own approach to the study of AuRA and the Sanctuary.

The first approach that I kept in mind when I started to look at the Sanctuary and AuRA was to analyse them as part of a broader movement that strives for equality and human rights. Focussing on this context allowed me to look more closely at what differentiates their action from some older forms of collective action and participation. Melluci's understanding of collective action is particularly useful here. He defines it as:

> the product of purposeful orientations developed within a field of opportunities and constraints. Individuals acting collectively *construct* their action by defining in cognitive terms these possibilities and limits, while at the same time interacting with others in order to 'organize' (i.e., to make sense of) their common behaviour.[59]

This idea of collective action allowed me to not only approach AuRA as the end product of politically-oriented aims, but also to delve into the values and beliefs that its members share and which are evident in their vision of a new world that they are working towards bringing about. In this sense, although anti-racism forms a first field of action for AuRA, we will observe how the group's identity is not solely defined by or limited to anti-racism but is also constructed in practical day to day interactions between its members. Indeed, anti-racism itself takes on different forms as the group evolves, and as the content of the group's action is continually remoulded

59 Melucci 1989, 25. Emphasis in original.

through dynamic social and political processes which redefine issues of discrimination and inequality. Such ideas are not based on a definition of social movements as a "unified empirical object" but emphasise instead what Melucci described as the "relative and transitory nature" of new social movements.[60]

From this perspective, some of the basic characteristics of the new social movements would be the formation of extended networks, an emphasis on self-reflexivity and interdependence, and their adaptability to the changing nature of the issues they address.[61] In this sense, the new movements not only seek to intervene in political problems, but also have a symbolic function, or in Melucci's terms they "challenge dominant cultural forms."[62] By placing the emphasis on the cultural elements of a movement, and on the symbolic aspect or the production of meaning,[63] Melucci is able to consider forms of action that might look straightforwardly political as actually being both "pre-political" and "meta-political"; this means that "political forces can never represent them completely,"[64] since the minutiae of everyday life experience also plays a significant part in determining the forms they take. Expanding on this point, and rather than abandoning a political analysis for something more existential, I will explore the ways in which political demands are inextricably intertwined with processes of both personal and collective transformation in day to day life.

A related idea that is also helpful for dealing with issues of subjectivity and agency is that of collective identity.[65] Polletta and Jasper have defined collective identity in the following terms:

> [It is an] individual's cognitive, moral and emotional connection with a broader community, category practice or institution. It is a perception of a shared status or relation, which may be imagined, rather than experienced directly, and it is distinct from personal identities, although it may form part of a personal identity.[66]

In addition to these qualities, Melucci's definition of collective identity also includes the "opportunities and constraints"[67] that serve as a compass for individuals who share certain qualities and direct their action according to them. In his view, collective identity is a process constituted in at least three ways:

60 Melucci 1989, 42.

61 Melucci 1989, 73–79; Melucci 1996a. See also Della Porta and Diani 2006; Psimitis 2006.

62 Melucci 1989, 74; Melucci 1996a, 164.

63 Psimitis 2006, 164.

64 Melucci 1989, 72.

65 Polletta and Jasper, James, M. 2001; Melucci 1989, 30–36; Melucci 1996a; Melucci 2015; Della Porta and Diani 2006; Psimitis 2006, 156–58; Jasper 2015/1997, 85–90.

66 Polletta and Jasper, James, M. 2001, 285.

67 Melucci 1989, 34.

> [...] collective identity involves at least three fundamental dimensions which are in reality closely interwoven: first, formulating cognitive fieldworks concerning the goals, means and environment of action; second, activating relationships among the actors, who communicate, negotiate and make decisions; and third, making emotional investments, which enable individuals to recognize themselves in each other.[68]

What is of particular interest to me here is the emphasis on the cultural and symbolic dimension of a group's action. That is to say, although they oppose certain social and political practices and make demands for rights or reforms, they do not operate solely at this level, but also maintain a practical day to day life, and it is at this level of "activating relationships" and "emotional investments" that much of the collective identity is developed.

It is clear then, that to review the action of the group by only taking into consideration its political character would not be adequate. This is a fairly common point, and one that Peyman Vahabzadeh puts very well in his conceptualisation of social movements and the meaning of the political. In his view, a conceptualisation of social movements that does not take into account their own contribution to the "reshaping of contemporary societies" – which affects the social through the political – deprives us of a full understanding of them.[69] As he puts it, their action should not solely be conceptualised as "reactive" but also as "proactive."[70] In terms of how this figures in the actual research, I will pay close attention not only to what the members themselves define as the social and political problems that they seek to address (and the practices through which this is to be accomplished), but also to their accounts of the experiences that led them to participate in the way that they do. This is a point that we will continually return to throughout the text, not only with reference to the political and social aspects of the group itself, but also with reference to the understanding and interpretation of such groups (especially in terms of their creative production) in the social sciences.

The second approach that seemed appropriate to the study of a group which continued to evolve and change over the period of research was to consider them as a community. This approach foregrounds the importance of the elements of integration and re-socialisation in the Sanctuary, and the potential it offered for individual and collective transformation. Community is a much-discussed notion that has a rich theoretical background.[71] One of the earliest accounts is found in the classical work of Ferdinand Tönnies, who distinguished between society in general as "public life" (*Gesellschaft*) and the more specific community (*Gemeinschaft*) which is a more

68 Melucci 1989, 35.

69 Vahabzadeh 2001, 628.

70 Vahabzadeh 2001, 628–29.

71 For an overview see Delanty 2003.

"intimate, private and exclusive living together."[72] Distinguished in this way from modern society, the idea of community soon came to connote a more secure and stable entity of belonging and became a compass for the formation of a better future.[73] Thus, the idea of community is central to the ideological and utopian propositions of the nineteenth and twentieth centuries.[74] As one scholar observes, although community was used by different (and even contradictory) theoretical traditions, it always indicated a search for solutions to social problems and sought to restore social integration.[75] At the core of the idea of community were feelings of safety, stability and shared values, as opposed to the estranged living conditions found in the modern metropolis.[76]

Indeed, modern understandings of community were often formed as a response to feelings of alienation,[77] or to the feeling of not having a 'home' in the universe, as Berger might have put it.[78] This was seen in the 1960s and 1970s with the expansion of what was previously considered to belong strictly to the personal realm into the political. The women's movement, the new left, and other groups were all beginning to demand the reconciliation of their political and their personal needs, and even to question the very definition of a political that would exclude the personal.[79] This time, the idea of community highlighted the possibility of alternative ways of being with others, away from the notions of commercialism, capitalism, and oppression that dominated much of society.[80] Following this direction, we arrive at something like Passerini's comment that community (understood here as a space "based on affective and cognitive choices") realised utopia through the "direct communication" that takes place in everyday life.[81]

---

72 Tönnies 1963, 33.

73 Andriakaina 2005, 139; Delanty 2003, 15–20.

74 Delanty 2003, 19–20; Löwy 2002; Lekkas 2016.

75 Andriakaina 2005, 139.

76 For an overview of issues on the idea of modernity, see Giddens 2001; Melucci 1996b; Hall, Held, and McGrew 2003. See also Giddens 1991, 47–55.

77 Berger 1990/1967, 81–101; Lekkas 2012, 51.

78 Berger, Berger, and Kellner 1974, 77: These scholars bring to the fore the idea of the "homelessness mind" to discuss processes of modernisation and the altered nature of modern man's condition.

79 Zaretsky 1986, 89. For Zaretsky this very need sprung out of the socialist failure to define the meaning of "production" in an inclusive way, that is to say, one that would include household and private life and as such it would lay outside the understanding of economy as "restricted to the sphere of commodity production and exchange." Zaretsky 1986, 62. For some recent interesting studies about utopias, see Hansen 2010; and about communities, see Silos 2003. For this period and the counterculture, see Suri 2009.

80 Andriakaina 2005, 140–47.

81 Passerini 2002, 23.

Leon Gomez provides a number of examples of contemporary "utopian communities."[82] In such communities, the members construct a new life in which affection, fidelity, and togetherness allow for a "mystical experience of love and union" in such a way that "both group and individual become one."[83] Could the same be said of AuRA, or the Sanctuary? We will see when we look at solidarity as it was 'lived' from day to day in the Sanctuary (in Chapters Four, Five and Six) that there was certainly an emotional, and perhaps even what could be described as a spiritual bond between its members.

The third useful approach was to look at the Sanctuary as an open space of social and political engagement, that relies on the idea of a free space. As Polletta has shown, the idea of "free spaces" within movements and activist settings aspired to unite both cultural and structural characteristics and functioned as another site of mobilisation within the frame of broader movements.[84] These places, run by what she called "prefigurative groups," not only offered a space for services or activities (providing education, food, etc) to the people who used them, but also provided those people with the opportunity to participate themselves through the relationships that they were forming in the space. In this way, social centres, places where people met with each other, and even more mainstream locations such as pubs could function as a pole of attraction for further mobilisation. However, what was characteristic in these kind of spaces was that despite the "dense ties" they allowed their participants to form, they could neither guarantee a successful integration of members that could lead to more coherent action or social intervention, nor could they create long-term sustainability.[85]

A similar characterisation used by scholars in the context of Greek austerity that of "alternative spaces,"[86] spaces that aspired to intervene at a certain level of social and daily experience and which challenged the idea of a weak civil society, that was thought to prevail in Greece.[87] Social pharmacies, social clinics and alternative economic structures stressed the priority of producing tangible results at the level of people's everyday life and played a kind of intermediary role between society and the state.[88] This approach, then, can be useful when charting AuRA's development within the context of the alternative projects that flourished during this period, the kind of relationships it formed with them, and how they may have influenced it.

---

82 Gómez 2019.

83 Gómez 2019, 5.

84 Polletta 1999, 1–5.

85 Polletta 1999, 13.

86 Kavoulakos and Gritzas 2015; Gritzas and Kavoulakos 2016.

87 Sotiropoulos 2004. For more on this discussion see also Leontidou 2010.

88 Kavoulakos and Gritzas 2015; Gritzas and Kavoulakos 2016. See also Rakopoulos 2014b; Chatzidakis, Maclaran, and Bradshaw 2012; Theodossopoulos 2016; Cabot 2016. See further Hadjimichalis 2018, 262–76.

In AuRA and the Sanctuary one can identify elements of all these approaches which in their interplay may capture something of the experimental character and the alternative nature of the group's endeavours. Any attempt to restrict the analysis to one of these approaches (or to any other similar approaches) would be too selective and would not reflect the complex reality of the group or the Sanctuary. Instead, throughout this book I would like to explore those elements that make the Sanctuary and AuRA distinctive in the eyes of their members: that is to say, the *alternativity* of the endeavour is to be explored as an open field of experimentation. This is not to suggest a simple opposition between 'mainstream' versus 'alternative.' Rather, I am following the way in which the members themselves defined as alternative those elements that differentiated the group not only from past endeavours but also from current ones. As such its alternative character is to be examined at every moment of the group's development. It is contextualised as it appears within specific historical contexts and, as we will see, it includes competing values that are synthesised in the broader experimental character of the group. Let us now look at some of the key characteristics of this alternative nature of the Sanctuary and AuRA.

WE-NESS While I did take into consideration the idea of *collective identity* when researching the group, at the same time I focussed more on what we might call feelings of *we-ness* – differentiated feelings of belonging that were stressed by the members of the group themselves. The purpose of this was to preserve the emphasis on various individual standpoints in their construction of a common ground upon which the various groups and individuals would meet and work together. This idea of we-ness as expressed both by the individuals and the groups required a different understanding of identity from that of a more homogenous collective identity. Brubaker's and Cooper's suggestion of an alternative vocabulary could prove useful here.[89] Entering into the debate on identity, they have claimed that the term has become blurred due to its use in various heterogeneous contexts.[90] They suggest that fixed and often ideologically embedded ideas of identity should be replaced by the terms "identification and self-understanding" when it comes to describing processes of self-realisation and becoming. They also suggest using the terms "commonality, connectedness and groupness" to describe the various ties and developing bonds and affections that keep people interacting with each other.[91] These terms can also help us to understand how the affinities between people go beyond the single shared cause of political devotion and orientation. Conversely, the idea of we-ness does not necessarily imply an affinity or compatibility between the individuals that meet for a specific shared purpose.

---

89 Brubaker and Cooper 2000.

90 Brubaker and Cooper 2000, 6–14.

91 Brubaker and Cooper 2000, 19–21.

In order to understand AuRA, and by extension the Sanctuary, we need to pay close attention to the way in which the members seem to present themselves as a kind of 'differentiated unity,' and it is this that the notion of we-ness can help to recognise. It is worth noting that in psychological research the term "we-ness" is sometimes employed to express mutuality, and a common ground of communication.[92] This ground allows for differences to be explored through "we-stories" that people construct about their relationships to others, thus expanding the knowledge that each person in a relationship has of that relationship, leading to what Skerrett calls "wisdom."[93] It is a useful way of exploring the fragmented and shifting self-understandings that are interwoven into creative and spontaneous expressions of togetherness, as we will see in Chapter Four. By extension it also allows us to explore the existential grounding of the notion of solidarity, paying attention to the members' self-identifications, and remaining open and flexible enough to allow for subjective interpretations of collective belonging which the more homogenised concept of identity effaces.

TRANSFORMATION Closely connected to the idea of we-ness are certain processes of transformation that affect both the individuals, as participants in the group, and the group itself in its entirety. I will first examine the processes through which a gradual integration into the group occurs, and here I will rely on the ideas of socialisation and internalisation as they are presented in Berger and Luckmann's *The Social Construction of Reality*, before examining what is involved at certain life changing moments of re-socialisation in terms of 'plausibility structures.' Berger and Luckmann define socialisation as "the comprehensive and consistent induction of an individual into the objective world of a society or a sector of it."[94] Internalisation follows as "the objectivated social world is retrojected into consciousness in the course of socialization."[95] The importance of internalisation consists in the interpretation of events and actions which become meaningful to people and help them integrate into what is considered to be the 'social reality' or the objective structures of society (such as institutions, customs or ethics). Individuals are integrated into the social environment and gradually become acquainted with the world through the learning and repeti-

92 Skerrett 2016.

93 Skerrett 2016, 52.

94 Berger and Luckmann 1991, 150.

95 Berger and Luckmann 1991, 78. The idea of a "social life world" stems from Schutz's phenomenology. As Berger, Berger and Kellner put it: "*all social reality has an essential component of consciousness*. The *consciousness* of everyday life is the web of meanings that allow the individual to navigate his way through the ordinary events and encounters of his life with others. The totality of these meanings, which he shares with others, makes up a particular *social life-world*." See Berger, Berger, and Kellner 1974, 18. Emphasis in original.

tion of the standardised patterns (roles) provided within a social context.[96] As Berger and Luckmann understand it, the attitudes people adopt and the roles they assume are constituted socially, and the self is essentially 'produced' by society through the processes of socialisation and internalisation of the outer world.[97]

However, this socialisation process also involves all sorts of personal interactions, as it is through the people surrounding us that we learn about the things we take for granted in our everyday life. As Berger argues, our acceptance (or internalisation) of the objective world may not have been so easy if people around us did not confirm the correctness of doing so.[98] These people, primarily our parents during the first stages of the "primary socialisation process," are the "significant others" who help us integrate into what we recognise as the outer world.[99] However, this is not something that only happens once, when we are young. As Berger and Luckmann point out, these processes of socialisation are "never complete" as people constantly remould themselves and their biography, adding new elements to what they considered themselves to be and what they see themselves become, assuming socially available roles, and thus becoming companions, professionals, religious believers, right wingers and so on.[100] It is with reference to these changes in biography and in the life of individuals that I will try to shed light on the new world that the Sanctuary and AuRA constituted for its members.[101]

We should also note that while the process of socialisation is ongoing, there are also certain salient moments that stand out amongst the common daily experiences of the individual and spark a "change-of-life" process. Berger and Luckmann describe these significant changes in a person's life course in terms of "alternation," a process similar to the primary socialisation involving trust, strong emotional bonds and profound identification with significant others, along with the integration into a radically new reality, often entailing a total redefinition of the individual's identity and the conditions of their life.[102] Alternation is defined as "the perception of oneself in front of an infinite series of mirrors, each one transforming one's image in a different potential conversion."[103] Another important idea that is related to the process of alternation is that of "precariousness": as individuals stand in front of a variety of choices, their freedom consists not only in their ability to choose, but also

96 Berger and Luckmann 1991, 91; 151–152.

97 Berger and Luckmann 1991, 89–96; 68–69.

98 Berger and Luckmann 1991, 149–57; see also Mead 2015.

99 Berger and Luckmann 1991, 151–52. On the notion of the "generalised other," see Mead 2015, 197–210.

100 Berger and Luckmann 1991, 166; See also Berger 1961, 23–48

101 Berger 1983/1963, 69–82; Berger and Luckmann 1991, 176–82.

102 For a more extensive analysis of alternation, see Berger and Luckmann 1991, 176–80; Berger 1961, 8–47; Berger 1983/1963, 69–82.

103 Berger 2011, 90.

in their ability to assume responsibility, take action and transform both their world and themselves.[104] It is this "general proneness to be uncertain of one's position and to be ready to change" which gives the impetus for alternation and change.[105] Making use of Kierkegaard's idea of the "leap of faith," Berger concludes that any "intellectual and existential jump from one *Weltanschauung* (worldview) to another" can be actually achieved or at least attempted at each individual stage of becoming.[106] In this sense, alternation has been closely connected to both political and religious conversion.[107]

For our purposes, alternation, then, can be identified with the possibility and probability of change that is accompanied by individual flexibility and that is followed by shifts in attention in one's individual life course. From this point of view, alternation has a liberating effect, yet it ultimately avoids the connotations of religious conversion. Instead, it can be understood in terms of a "plausibility structure" within which processes of alternation take place and which provides a kind of "social base" that offers a degree of stability within change and which serves as "the 'laboratory' of transformation."[108] It is in this sense that people affirm and understand each new 'social world' they enter into. In our own research, we may be able to get an angle on the particular 'devotions' which are to be observed in AuRA if we see daily life in the Sanctuary as providing its members with something like a plausibility structure in this sense. Hence, while the analogy with religious conversion could to some degree prove conducive to our comprehending the zeal, the sense of commitment and the devotion with which participants construct a new life in the group, we must treat the analogy with caution, and in particular we must avoid the idea of blind faith in a pre-ordained set of values and emphasise instead the members' active participation in the development of the very group they believe in.

COMMUNITY To call the Sanctuary a 'community' is not without problems, but some key characteristics of community do apply to it. First it is what Cohen described as an 'entity of belonging,' which is more "immediate than the abstraction we call society," and which forms a wider space where one "learns and continues to practice how 'to

---

104 The idea of "precariousness" was recently thematised by Butler in an effort to draw attention to the generating and creative function that this "precariousness" (which is closely tied to the notion of "vulnerability") involves in terms of initiating action. See Butler 2018. Also relevant to this account is the work of Hannah Arendt. See Arendt 1998/1958. Especially illuminating in this respect is Arendt's idea about freedom. See Arendt 2006, 143–71.

105 Berger 1961, 17.

106 Ibid, 17.

107 Berger and Luckmann 1991, 177–78.

108 Berger and Luckmann 1991, 177. For the idea of "plausibility structure" see Berger 1990/1967, 45.

be social.'"[109] One of the fundamental characteristics of the community understood in these terms is that it includes both sameness and difference and it is recognisable by its "boundaries," the boundaries in this case being those signs or symbols that allow the members of the community to commonly recognise what is their community and their identity, even though they may experience it differently.[110] As Cohen puts it, "the reality of community lies in its members' perception of the vitality of its culture. People construct community symbolically, making it a resource and repository of meaning, and a referent of their identity."[111]

On a more existential level, the idea of community also applies to AuRA and the Sanctuary in the sense of a *communitas*. Turner has described *communitas* as "a community of men in their humankindness," which unfolds in the whole man's "relation to other whole men" and functions here as a spiritual impetus, showing the way to interrelatedness, togetherness, mutuality and being in the world with others.[112] Turner's *communitas* is inspired by Buber's writings and also Bergson's ideas about the open society.[113] In developing the notion of *communitas*, Turner drew heavily on Buber's idea of community, an idea that Buber contrasted to that of *collectivity*:

> Collectivity is not a binding but a bundling together: individuals packed together, armed and equipped in common, with only as much life from man to man as will inflame the marching step. But community, growing community [...] is the being no longer side by side but *with* one another of a multitude of persons. And this multitude, though it also moves towards one goal, yet experiences everywhere a turning to, a dynamic facing of, the other, a flowing from I to *Thou*. Community is where community happens.[114]

However, for Buber community surpasses an aggregate of feelings that get synchronised within a specific location. Rather it is a relationship. As he puts it "a community is built upon a living, reciprocal relationship, but the builder is the living, active centre."[115]

In a similar sense, Turner presents communitas as a counterpoint to social structure understood as the institutionalisation of social life, the space where norms, laws and organisation govern.[116] *Communitas* is to be found, or to put it better, *communitas happens* 'at the edges of structure,' or what Turner calls "in liminality."[117] Liminality

---

109 Cohen 2015/1985, 6; Guibernau 2013, 35–39.
110 Cohen 2015/1985, 7–10.
111 Cohen 2015/1985, 109.
112 Turner 1977/1969, 127–128.
113 Bergson 1977; Buber 2002, 1996/1970.
114 Buber 2002, 37. Emphasis in original.
115 Buber 1996/1970, 94.
116 Turner 1977/1969, 126.
117 Turner 1977/1969, 128.

could be considered a transitory phase in the life of an individual (related here to life changing events).[118] Another aspect of liminality is linked to what Turner terms "structural outsiderhood," a condition that is mostly connected to his argument that *communitas* is to be experienced at the margin of the structure, (although it cannot happen independently of it, as the two have a dialectical relationship).[119] However, these ideas concern us only to the extent that liminality is understood within the frame of what we might call 'creative marginality,' a condition that allows individuals to experience the potentiality of their creativity and imagination.[120] In this respect, we will stay closer to Buber's conceptualisation of community as a "spontaneous emergence" that "happens between people."[121] Indeed, this was one of the ideas that first inspired me to take this angle in exploring both AuRA and the Sanctuary.

These ideas of community and *communitas* can provide us with some valuable insights into the ways in which people in the group experienced not only their new life in the group, but also their continual participation in the creation of that new life. This interplay between the way in which the community allowed people to re-construct themselves on the one hand, and their own contribution to the construction of that community on the other, are central themes of both Chapter Four and Chapter Five.

IDEOLOGY, METAPHOR AND VOCABULARY It is no doubt already evident that a religious analogy permeates my idea of AuRA and the Sanctuary, and it will become more evident as the book progresses. However, the function of the religious analogy and the metaphors I employ throughout this text should not be understood as having an evaluative character, nor should they be seen as being ideologically charged. The religious metaphor and affiliated vocabulary allowed me to bring to the surface many of the qualities, values and other aspects of the group's culture by detecting and shedding light on a variety of alternative understandings of solidarity that I encountered. In particular the kind of spiritual aspiration that accompanied their action and which was often referred to by my interlocutors. In this sense, the religious metaphor is to be understood as 'a vehicle to the unknown horizons of meaning.'[122] However, as such analogies and metaphors could also lead to a certain amount of confusion, I would like to clarify how I understand and use them by briefly looking at the components of the analogy.

---

118 Van Gennep first used the concept 'liminal rites' to describe rites of transition. See van Gennep 2019, 10, 39.

119 Turner 1977/1969, 134.

120 Turner 1977/1969, 128.

121 Buber 2002, 37.

122 This phrase came to mind whilst reading Rasmussen's study of metaphors in the work of Hans Blumenberg, Rasmussen 2009, 24.

The ideological phenomenon has often been approached within a religious framework, and the comparison of the two systems has served various objectives.[123] One may easily identify religious elements in ideology, and ideological elements in religion, as they are both all-encompassing systems, that identify problems and suggest solutions.[124] Most relevant to my discussion here is the stable, safe and coherent world that religion and ideology alike offer to their members, and which can be considered as a point of departure for their comparison.[125] The similarities between the two systems are not limited to symbols and rituals.[126] Most importantly, both provide a coherent justification on how the world is and how it should be; that is to say, they unite a normative with an ethical agenda,[127] and they generate an effect of 'certainty' for their members.[128] Their all-encompassing coherent suggestions on how the world should be and their systematic effort to persuade their members about the plausibility of their agendas while they promise a change of either a secular or a religious character is another point where the two systems meet.[129]

My understanding of the ideological phenomenon is here framed by Geertz's ideas. He understands ideologies mainly as "maps of problematic social reality and matrices for the creation of collective conscience."[130] As such, ideologies present a similar function to religions, in so far as they provide both "a template or blueprint for the organization of social and psychological processes" and meaning and orientation to their members.[131] But we are not concerned here with institutionalised versions of religion, nor with specific ideologies. Rather we are concerned with their function as a "worldview" that provides a compass for how people believe they could

123 For an overview see Lekkas 2016, 2012. For the ideological phenomenon in the congruence with religion, see Buchowski 2001; Kolakowski 1997. For the issues of politics and faith, see Fuller and Oakeshott 1996; Löwy 2002. For ideology and utopia, see Jacoby 1999; Manuel 1973/1966.

124 On the function of religion and its legitimisation see Berger 1990/1967, 29–51; On ideology and religion see Lekkas 2012, 49, and on the elements of convergence/divergence of the two systems see ibid, 41–55.

125 Berger 1990/1967, 42–48.

126 Lekkas 2012, 48; Lekkas 2016, 164. See also Buchowski 2001.

127 Lekkas 2012, 49. See also Geertz 1973, 113.

128 Lekkas refers to an elitism of certainty ("ο ελιτισμός της βεβαιότητας") Lekkas 2012, 47; Lekkas 2016 ; See further Berger 1990/1967, 44–48.

129 Berger 1990/1967, 42–47. There is a broad literature about the meeting point of religious and ideological phenomena. For the religious phenomenon, see Weber 2007b; Durkheim 2008; Gauchet 2011; Berger 1990/1967, 2004, 1969, 1961. For the ideological phenomenon, see Geertz 1973; Lekkas 2012, 2016, 1996; Kolakowski 1997; Buchowski 2001; Fuller and Oakeshott 1996.

130 Geertz 1973, 220.

131 Geertz 1973, 216.

better live their own lives.[132] Relevant here is what Fassin (following Gauchet) refers to as the "ultimate victory of religion."[133] That is to say, the persistence of those non-identifiable invisible religious instances, that are intrinsic to the way we experience the world we inhabit and the ideas we comprehend, and which make 'religiosity' in a broad sense a fruitful field of experimentation. In this sense, both religion and ideology are seen in terms of how they influence, guide or affect the people who choose to believe in them.[134] There is a broad debate nowadays about how *religiousness* or *spirituality* is to be understood or experienced outside the institutionalised context of official religions, and I have a similar concern with the topic. Departing from the social-psychological idea that religion is "a cognitive and normative structure that makes it possible for man to feel 'at home' in the universe,"[135] I kept wondering what the 'religious instances' are that fill in the world of the movements with meaning for its members today.

In social movements research similar analogies have to a certain extent served to draw attention to the intensity of feelings and the way people engage in political movements.[136] However, the analogy usually entails a danger, either because it is perceived as having an evaluative character (often because the people who make the comparison have an opposing ideological stance and they use metaphors in order to try and discredit someone else's position), or because it can be misunderstood by the people who participate in political and social endeavours, raising concerns that the comparison detracts from the seriousness of their political action, and that it does not do them overall justice. Indeed, for many activists the comparison of their ideology to religion would be anathema, and they could only understand such a comparison as an insult. However, it is not uncommon when we refer to certain ideological aspects, to resort to a religious vocabulary and to draw a parallel between the effects that the two systems have on the life of the individuals who take part in them. Interestingly enough, despite the great distance between religious and ideological beliefs within the movement one frequently hears jokes and comments that highlight their affinity: one "speaks like a priest," or he "preaches," it is "time for catechesis," or everything is done "in the name of the people," instead of in the name of God. I found this broadly religious imagery very interesting. These images seemed to be reproduced through what Ricoeur referred to as the "iconic world" that the metaphors

132 Berger 1990/1967, 32; See also Geertz 1973, 87–125; 193–233.

133 Fassin 2012, 249; See also Gauchet 2011.

134 Berger 1990/1967; Lekkas 2012, 2016; Geertz 1973. See also Kristeva 2011.

135 Berger, Berger, and Kellner 1974, 75.

136 Jasper 2015/1997, 14.

create and that allow us to "reproduce further meaning" on the subjects of our investigation.[137]

In this sense, I do not claim that the members of the Sanctuary underwent a kind of "religious conversion" beyond the limits of the metaphors and the analogies that I use. Rather, through these metaphors, I have tried to recapture some aspects of the members' reality in the Sanctuary and of the aspirations of AuRA in a way that allows the reader to recognise the sort of enchantment that members experienced. In this sense, the metaphors used in the book constitute a 'vehicle' that allow broader issues of political and social engagement, solidarity, and commitment to be conceptualised by creatively thinking about them. How successful the use of such metaphors was is for the reader to decide.

137 The concept of the icon stems from Charles Sanders Peirce: Ricœur 2003/1978, 222–24; Ricœur 1976, 52; Ricœur 1978, 149.

2. Methodology

Conceptualising Reflexivity

The term reflexivity, while often used, tells us little about an individual's actual research. The term is used excessively and habitually, in such a way that it stands in for, rather than describing, the actions it refers to. This means that the subjective interpretation of what is happening when someone claims to be self-reflective or doing research self-reflectively often remains underdeveloped. While this fact is broadly acknowledged by scholars,[1] it is still rare that the thorny issue of the researcher's personal experience in the field is analysed in any depth. And while the researcher's personal experiences, anxieties and problems all decisively belong to the research process, they are rarely documented in the writing process. This became clear following a discussion with a friend who was conducting anthropological research in a similar field to mine, and whose work I greatly admired. Hearing him speak of the tumultuous nature of his relation to the field was strangely reassuring, since at the time of our meeting I thought I was the only one encountering difficulties in the field. The idea of reflexivity highlights the importance of the constant re-examination of the constitutive elements of research that we usually take for granted, yet which really affects both the activity and the outcomes of research. By looking more closely at how we come to know ourselves and others, we would better understand how this is reflected in the knowledge that is produced.

I have already discussed the idea of alternation in relation to my research into AuRA and the Sanctuary, but I would now like to clarify the relevance of the concept from a methodological perspective and note how it is linked to the notion of reflexivity. In Berger's *Precarious Vision*, the idea of alternation assumes a broader sense as a process of transformation, which is highly relevant to reflexivity.[2] Alternation has an obvious consequence beyond the underlying assumption that individuals are free to choose and capable of transformation. In a common-sense understanding, it

---

1 Denzin 1997, 2016; Bourdieu 2006; Giddens 1991; Plummer 2001, 206–15; Coffey 1999.

2 Berger 1961. Berger's work and influence are evident in my work and my conceptualisation of reflexivity.

signifies the individual's ability to pass through different life stages, with different circles of acquaintances, friends, colleagues, and thus different communities, preferences, lifestyles, various commitments and distinct belongings. As such, it allows us to view and re-assess previous experiences in the light of present reality.[3] When recalling fragments of these experiences, we tend to wonder about what it was that made past choices, actions or ideas even possible back then. Sometimes this can create a feeling of shame or guilt about our past, and invokes questions as to what kind of self it was who acted in such a way. Part of this process is characterised as self-reflective, and it may indeed be considered a reflexive re-assessment of previous experiences. And yet reflexivity goes much further. A reflexive disposition means being able to follow and observe ourselves throughout all the distinctive moments or stages of life, from the outside as well as from the inside. It means being able to recall in great detail both who we were, and what our beliefs were back then, as well as the processes through which we have acquired new beliefs, the conditions under which they were activated, and the probable reasons we acted in a certain way.

Although this puzzle of past actions and beliefs may be rather complicated and indeed very selective, our usual tendency is to judge 'what we were' in the light of 'what we have become.'[4] However, in my understanding reflexivity is entailed in the very process which seeks to embrace the past in terms of understanding and meaning-making.[5] It allows us to question why something happened, what the reasons behind our actions and decisions were, which factors might have been catalytic, what helped and what hindered us in making or not making certain decisions, what our motives were, and how we understood what was taking place.

Importantly, reflexivity is a means of questioning ourselves and our disposition as researchers, without seeking an evaluation in moral terms. Instead, it reveals an advanced curiosity, that is devoid of excessive emotionality and that enables an internal dialogue about multiple genealogies and different stages of life. In this way a 'coherent' narrative emerges from a multiplicity of life moments; yet it is one which preserves an implicit doubt about how those moments were in reality, and thus remains partial and elliptic in character.[6] It is a disposition linked to the production of new knowledge in the present, a knowledge that often appears to stem from a seemingly unified past. For an alternating researcher who is immersed in an evolving research field reflexivity is an essential tool, shedding light on the path we have

3 Berger 1961, 17–22.

4 Ibid. Berger describes through a variety of examples this process of evolving and transforming oneself according to the environments one meets and the different life conditions one is faced with.

5 Clifford 1983, 128; Bourdieu 2006, 47.

6 Clifford 2010, 7.

taken and the choices we have made, and becoming more detailed and more elaborate with every single re-assessment.[7] It opens up our cognitive arsenal and allows for the construction of a continuity amidst the multiplicity of perspectives we pass through; a continuity which, however, retains all the discontinuous fragments of a real lived history. In this sense, this reflexive knowledge is not to be confused with a linear, evolutionary narrative of our life history. Rather, it shows the actual path we followed, in a way that preserves all the shifts and changes that attended it and that constituted its reality. In research, then, reflexivity can make us more aware of our relationship with ourselves, the society, and the subjects under investigation, as Bourdieu suggested in his "Participant Objectivation."[8]

There are multiple histories behind our actions and decisions which we should not treat solely in psychological terms. Detached from its psychological or any metaphysical sense, and in purely biographical terms, this reassessment of past experiences has a lot to reveal about our choices, actions, and motives. It serves as a treatise in understanding. We progressively realise that no matter what position we find ourselves in, the thing that actually changes is the "audience," "the front" and "the back region," to put it in Goffman's terms.[9] From every new position we enter into a dialogue with the three components while re-assessing our experiences in a new light. As Goffman writes:

> Behind these realizations about oneself and illusions about others is one of the important dynamics and disappointments of social mobility, be it mobility upward, downward, or sideways. In attempting to escape from a two-faced world of front region and back region behavior, individuals may feel that in the new position they are attempting to acquire they will be the character projected by individuals in that position and not at the same time a performer. When they arrive, of course, they find their new situation has unanticipated similarities with their old one; both involve a presentation of front to an audience and both involve the presenter in the grubby, gossipy business of staging a show.[10]

Goffman's remark sums up the ironic aspect of behaviour, a kind of social anxiety, which is difficult to avoid when one is 'ignorantly' entering not only social fields, but research ones as well. And ignorance here does not imply the absence of any theoretical presumptions. Rather, it implies the absence of any presumptions about exactly what form our interactions will take with those new 'others' with whom we seek to communicate in the name of doing research. Clifford gives an insight into

7 Melucci 1996b, 44–45.
8 Bourdieu 2006.
9 Goffman 1959.
10 Goffman 1959, 132–33.

our "childlike status" within any new culture.[11] In each new situation we enter, however, we realise that all the aspects of the self that were previously annoying or confusing have not been necessarily replaced by a better, more structured, more sensitive, or more disciplined self. What does dramatically change is the way in which one perceives oneself in each different context, as well as the overall evaluation of the process, and the relation we acquire both to others and to the new 'polished' self.

It is this 'processual perspective' that I want to highlight in this chapter.[12] This kind of self-reflective report may well trigger questions as to whether such a "dramaturgy of revelation"[13] is really necessary and why I am focusing on myself and not on the group who are supposed to be the subject of my investigation. Such questions call to mind Lasch's scepticism regarding the author's internal dialogue with themselves. As he mentions, when absorbed in those internal experiences, the writer does not give an objective account of reality, but strenuously works on acquiring attention, approval, or empathy as a palliative to her/his own vulnerability.[14] This is, I think, a good place to start in problematising the element of narcissism that (it could be argued) is inherent in any research practice that foregrounds reflexivity. For such narcissistic elements may obscure the real issues of power relations between the writer and those s/he documents, and also obscure the question of whether the research product is as unique and excellent as the researcher her/himself claims it to be. These considerations reveal just some of the difficulties of what the job of a social scientist actually is, as opposed to what it ideally should be, and forces us to constantly re-assess the hows and whys of doing research.[15]

As we re-write the stories of others, we inevitably develop a certain layer of narcissistic and power-laden beliefs which comfort and strengthen us in order to accomplish our task. However, in taking the experience of someone else and re-inventing it in the context of a certain truth[16] that we want to present, we also acquire a certain level of sympathy with and recognition of someone else's experience. When borrowing someone's experiences in order to give life to a text, we cannot neglect to

11 Clifford 1983, 132.

12 Rosaldo 1993, 93–96; 106–107. Rosaldo discusses the idea of processual analysis, as a process that takes into consideration multiple aspects when examining culture rather than insisting on rigid epistemological frameworks.

13 Atkinson and Silverman 1997, 313.

14 Lasch 1979, 32–33. Lasch 1991, 37–38.

15 There is a lot of useful literature on this topic. I offer here a brief indication of those texts that helped me position myself: Weber 1949; Clifford and Marcus 2010; Gordon 1980; Seidman 1994; Andriakaina 2009; Denzin 1991; Coffey 1999; Trouillot 2003; Hastrup 2005/1992; Lincoln and Denzin 1998; Mills 1999; Geertz 1973; Berger 1983/1963; Dermentzopoulos and Spyridakis 2004; Haraway 1988.

16 Fassin's work is revelatory in this direction. See Fassin 2012. See also Clifford 2010, 8–10; Denzin 1997, 265–68. Plummer 2001.

take into account the aspects of our own experience that have affected how we do this; the different motives, the different locations, choices and positions that defined who we were and who we may have become.[17] But again, merely *stating* these aspects does not necessarily mean that we do not still neglect them. Thus, the present chapter can be read as an invitation to present some of the broader problems that trouble researchers in the production of the texts themselves and not in a subsequent discussion surrounding them. Simultaneously, it is an invitation to free ourselves from the various masks (the mask of integrity, or the mask of rigidity) that for better or worse have long characterised the ideal figure of the researcher. However, I will not pretend that it is possible to end up with a text that is entirely 'honest.' However reflective we may be, the finished project will always retain some elements of self-deception. To paraphrase Berger, honesty could be very well considered as the consciousness of a person who lets himself be deceived "by his own act."[18]

If this constant negotiation of the power of the writer and the legitimacy of speaking on behalf of others could be considered as a second stage of reflexivity, then a third stage would be the re-assessment and delivery of an end product which reveals a more authentic or meaningful relation to the field of research. It is through this third stage that one can relate to the field of research in a more adequate manner.

In what follows, I will distinguish those aspects of the above-mentioned stages which reveal my own constant reflection on the subject of my research, something of which I inevitably became a part as a participant observer. I will look at my motives when I started this research, at certain issues surrounding my conducting of the first interviews, and at the process of my participating as an observer and gradually as a member of the group. I will look at this last issue, of being an insider/outsider within the frame of social movements research, by referring to emotionality and vulnerability, and to the notion of friendship as a method.

If becoming an insider, a friend and a trusted member was one side of the process of participating in the group, then remaining an outsider and maintaining a certain distance from it was the other. The distance between the two, then, was to be bridged by different approaches and methods, self-reflexive questions, and emotional investments that make the research field an open source of constant reconsideration.

17 Coffey 1999, 115–27; Bourdieu 2006, 47–49.

18 Berger 1983/1963, 130. As Berger writes: "Sincerity is the consciousness of the man who is taken in by bis own act." Berger 2011, 148.

Motives

My initial observations started in 2009 when a friend of mine introduced me to some people who were already active in the group. I realised very quickly that observing from a distance was not the right approach if I was to really understand how the group worked. There were various daily tasks to be accomplished and those who were hesitant to initiate something on their own were excluded. In other words, an insider had to be a *doer*. My role could not be that of someone who would follow people around with a recorder and a notebook taking down everything I observed. Thus, very soon I started participating in the activities and the assemblies of AuRA. However, since I knew that without the writing process, the process of understanding would itself remain incomplete, from the start I recorded my experiences and thoughts about the group. It was through this act of writing that I started hesitantly realising that the course of my research would also reveal a lot about myself.

I spent a long time contemplating my motives: What was I looking for? What was it that made me pursue this kind of research? What was I doing among these people, who are relentlessly committed to their cause and spend every day fighting for what they believe in? There is a wide range of answers to these questions. The appeal of the process of research itself, the challenge of finding an insightful way to approach and analyse the field, the curiosity for answers – to a greater or lesser extent, all these factors contributed to my decision to engage with this project. Setting aside the emotions underlying these relatively grandiose answers, there was also the challenge of how to adopt an approach that expresses my own objectives without losing sight of the importance of consistent and coherent argumentation, as well as on the need for a complete account and an accurate representation of the object of study.

Primary Methodological Tools

Ruth Behar formulated the task of the ethnographer in the following eloquent way: "As ethnographers we are expected to travel somewhere, even if that somewhere is a return trip to a lost home, but always with the commitment to bring back a story,"[19] a story we "didn't know we were looking for in the first place."[20] But whose stories are they, that we bring back? The story of those being observed, or of the observer herself? This ambiguity makes it necessary to consider and problematise one's own practice. Interpreting my own biases and struggles, negotiating power issues, and embracing moments of strong emotionality were the main tools of this revelatory

19 Behar 2003, 21.
20 Behar 2003, 16.

methodological journey. I soon realised, that in terms of attitude, both as a participant and as a researcher I had to become more open to the new experiences and environments that I encountered.

Confessions

One of the most important issues that arose early on concerned the process of collecting data through relatively informal interviews. The members of the group had some difficulty giving interviews because it is not easy to agree on what should be regarded as an opinion shared by the entire group and what should be seen as a personal experience. It is important to understand that the members of the group have a hard time talking *on behalf of* the group or being openly critical of it. In a sense, an activist's 'natural environment' *is* the group, since the process through which they make sense of the world, achieve goals, and act requires the contribution of more than one person. In other words, they construct shared definitions of the world in a collective process that tends to marginalise individual actions and behaviours.

Interviews that tend to reveal what the members think or feel, or how they conceptualise meanings, ideas and everyday vocabulary, have a confessional character.[21] Foucault spoke about the power of confession in terms of its dual dynamics: on the one hand, confessing equated to a healing process in which the whole troubled, disentangled issue is shared and one feels relieved from the coercive chains of exhaustive internal dialogues that do not otherwise find their way outwards. At the same time the confessor becomes the one who holds the key to the soul, whether they be a psychotherapist, an expert, or some other "authority" figure.[22] Confession is a "ritual of discourse" that "unfolds within a power relationship," revealing a truth that is "corroborated by obstacles and resistances" that it has to surpass, and is "finally, a ritual in which the expression alone, independently of its external consequences, produces intrinsic modifications in the person who articulates it."[23]

The members of the group often seemed to want to free themselves by revealing, while constantly struggling with issues of morality, politics, and the self, and trying to find a balance as to what should be narrated. As the one who holds the power, the interviewer can either assume an equal position to the interviewees, a rigorous objective stance, or simply a more sympathetic or 'humanistic' one. The latter enables us to focus on the symbolic and the intersubjective elements of the exchange, pays

21 Atkinson and Silverman 1997, 313.

22 Foucault 1990, 62.

23 Foucault 1990, 61–62.

attention to the embeddedness, engages our "whole being," and has both moral and political characteristics.[24]

It wasn't long before I started to feel like there was something almost immoral about the process of interviewing, as if the interview were a laboratory and I, as the interviewer, were forcing these people out of what we might call their 'natural communicational setting' and into one that jeopardised the validity or authenticity of what they said. Above all, it seemed like the process of interviewing would undermine the relationships and trust that had been built up between myself and the members of the group. As a result, we all ended up dreading the prospect of going through this process. The personal relationships I had established during my first years of interacting with the members of AuRA, as well as the fact that they had often confided in me, put me off the idea of interviewing them at all and made me very wary of bringing up the subject. For this reason, I would sometimes attempt a different approach, such as a conversation involving more than two people, which felt more similar to our typical way of interacting with each other within the frame of the group.

This choice was validated by a group interview with three young female members. I asked Alkyone, whose house served as the setting for this conversation, to email me her thoughts on it:

> Where the interview is concerned... Personally, I feel that starting – let alone creating – a conversation and leading it in a discreet way are much more demanding tasks than preparing and conducting an "interview" in the strict sense of the word. As a result, I have to admit that as a participant in this process (we can agree to call it a "conversation" from now on), I felt completely free to share my thoughts. So, I became convinced that this type of approach is very effective in that it sets a tone that encourages the other party to share experiences and opinions they would neither be willing nor have the opportunity to share under different, more rigid conditions. Another thing that should be said about this type of approach (apart from the fact that you quickly forget that you are being recorded – which is another testament to how relaxed the atmosphere created is) is that it entails the physical presence of more than one "interviewee" and that the "interviewees" are also friends. The close bonds we have formed with each other would often determine the very course of the conversation. We even shared things we had never shared with each other before. It was extremely pleasant, if not particularly productive. I have no way of knowing whether or not you had decided beforehand to refuse to take on the role of coordinator (you probably had), but the fact that you did further confirms everything I said earlier about the relaxed tone of the conversation.

24 Plummer 2001, 262–63. Plummer discusses the idea of a critical humanism in the social sciences.

> This choice led you to pose very broad, flexible questions, the kind of questions that interviews usually do not allow for. This, in turn, required us to give shape to the questions before answering them and provided us with the space and time to talk about the things we feel comfortable talking about. You didn't expect every question to be answered by all three of us, which probably worked in your favour, as most questions did eventually elicit comments from all of us. Looking for the right words can be fun, subversive and unpredictable. It's fascinating to see how much inner turmoil a word you use on a daily basis – almost mechanically, without putting much thought into it – can put you through in a matter of seconds. As the "interviewee," you say what's on your mind (because otherwise you would be telling lies), and the "interviewer" gets what s/he wants. Which is a reflex reaction, an already internalised perspective on the word you have been asked to comment on, which is bound to be met with a million different reactions – a number of reactions equal to the number of the people living around you. [...] In all honesty, I'm not sure if I'm actually helping; judging by the questions I'm proposing. If I were in your shoes my approach would probably be inappropriately sentimental. In any case, I have to admit that I'm equally intrigued by this process of discussing the interview with you. That' s all... Although I think I would have even more to say if you asked me something more specific.[25]

I met Alkyone at the first annual festival in which I participated in summer 2010. We started talking to each other during the job delegations in the preparation-week of the festival and very soon we chose to work together. Before long a friendly relationship started to develop outside of the context of the Sanctuary and my research, although it was always somehow remained inside it as well. She was the one that brought me into contact with the other two young women, and she also offered her house as the setting for the interview so that we would have a relaxed, friendly atmosphere for our conversation. All three women who engaged in the discussion that night were reluctant to talk about the group, despite my assurances that this was not the aim, but were happy to talk about themselves in relation to the group. At the end of our discussion, I came back to their initial concern and asked them what we had ultimately discussed, the group or ourselves? The question provoked laughs on all sides, since one realises very quickly that one rarely escapes identification with the group, forming as it does a great part of their daily reality.

The conversation at Alkyone's house was unique in many respects, largely due to the more friendly context in which everyone was willing to share with others and recognised the importance of the bonds and the feelings this sharing created. Nevertheless, when rereading her comments, I felt that my approach was perhaps still

25 Alkyone Email, pers. comm. March 2011.

too formal despite its intended informality, something which greatly shaped my understanding of the methods I was trying to adopt.

Alkyone was not the only one with whom I was involved in this quasi-confessional process. Endless conversations, piles of notes, countless emails: they were all meant to help me sort out the conflicting feelings that my interactions with all these new people inspired in me, to keep sight of my most critical questions, and to articulate my own fears and hesitations. Interviews seemed to me to be an underhanded tool. They would abruptly turn a relaxed interaction with the members of the group into an artificial one, and I would have to look for the most effective way of asking the same questions I would ask quite naturally during off-the-record conversations.

I also soon came to realise that there were differences in the way my potential interlocutors viewed the idea of being interviewed; some of them unequivocally refused to be interviewed at all, some did not want to assume the responsibility of speaking on behalf of the whole group, some did not want to take credit for their participation in what they saw as an essentially altruistic practice, and some wished to avoid drawing attention to themselves in any way that could prove harmful to the group. Eventually I did manage to work out a balance, though.[26] I would interview those members whom I was, more or less, already acquainted with over a coffee or a drink, with the intention of recreating the atmosphere of the space that had brought us together. During the data processing phase, this kind of informal, relaxed interaction sometimes had to be translated into a relatively tight interpretation, with all the power-issues that this translation entailed.[27]

It is impossible to exhaust the topic of the responsibility that comes with the power to set the agenda (the power to decide what is discussion-worthy), but there are a few observations that are worth noting. Some of the things that were noteworthy to me were indifferent to the members of the group, and some things that were indifferent to me were of great interest to the group. In that respect, many of the questions we discussed helped me to both satisfy my curiosity and make decisions as to how to approach certain issues.

One thing I had to navigate was my involvement in the daily gossip that served as a cohesive force within the group.[28] Along with the mythology woven around the members' past exploits and accomplishments, gossiping also functioned as a unifying thread that holds the group together by substantiating its existence and allowing the members to create shared experiences, histories and memories. How much was I as the interviewer inclined to reveal about myself to the members of the group? There was a constant danger that being caught up in the gossip that is often prevalent

26 On the researcher/researched relationship, see Labaree 2002; Lincoln 1995; Fine 1998; Denzin 1997; Lincoln and Denzin 1998; Ellis 1995; Coffey 1999; Hastrup 2005/1992; Ladkin 2005.

27 Plummer 2001, 204–30; Rabinow 2010; Clifford 1983.

28 Goffman 1989; Fine 2003.

within such environments could not only undermine my position as a researcher, but also upset relations within the group itself. In this sense, avoiding this kind of gossip and focusing on positive rather than negative values during all conversations (not just interviews) was important to my approach.

My primary objective was for the interviews to feel as natural as the participants' everyday interactions with each other. Despite their busy schedules, most of the activists were generally quite willing to make some time for a coffee or a drink. And this was important not only because it provided a platform for discussing feelings, values and personal goals, but also because it often led my interlocutors to realise that there was nothing self-evident about their actions. It was as if talking about their engagement with these alternative spaces allowed them to put their thoughts on concepts like solidarity in order. Without the shield provided by the group, each interviewee would attempt to talk about her/his place in the movement and make sense of the group's existence and goals in her/his own individual terms. In this sense there is a dialogical validity that builds more on interviews' conversational characteristics[29] and allows members to bring to the fore elements of what they experienced as togetherness or fortify feelings of 'we-ness' within the group. Together, we were engaged, then, in a constant effort of negotiation between what was said, what was heard, and what was interpreted as we all tried to conceptualise the shared meanings and culture of the world that surrounded us.[30]

Encountering the Group/Engaging in Field Research

Summer 2011. The annual festival that AuRA organised every year was over, and it was time for my return to Berlin, but I decided to postpone it for a few days. Some members of the group had invited me to join them at an eco-festival. I was hesitant, torn between my need to steer clear of intense, overstimulating situations and a sense of obligation to accept their invitation. I had grown close to quite a few of them, and spending some time with them in a different, more relaxed environment would make for a more cordial farewell than vanishing into thin air, as I used to do when I was under pressure. I eventually decided to join them for three days. However, I kept wondering whether being there would really be beneficial to me, my research and the people that had confided in me and honoured me with their friendship. It was not my political or ideological convictions that had led me there; I had not chosen to belong to the group because I agreed with its founding principles or decision-making processes. Of course, I agreed with its principles, but I have always been wary of belonging to a group.

29 Denzin 2016, 24.

30 Hastrup 2005/1992, 116.

Up until then, I had had a hard time understanding what it is that motivates people to participate in a group, what it is about being fully committed to a group's goals that appeals to them, how conflicts are resolved, how it is possible to get into a heated argument with a comrade only to forget all about it a few hours later and, above all, how someone can let a group have complete control over their personal life, manage information that is personal to them, change their schedule to accommodate its own needs, and eventually also change them as a person.

On the one hand, there is something authentically human about this whole process. On the other hand, though, the 'initiated individual' is an individual who is dependent on other people, an individual whose identity is inextricably tied to a particular situation, an individual bound by the obligation to care about the others, to live side by side with the others, and to have the group's interests at heart. In this context, I found myself going through a transformative process of my own, as all anthropologists would do, I supposed. However, I still had to consider the moral dimension of my presence there and, more specifically, the group's interpretation(s) of it. I felt like I was a source of constant confusion: Was I a comrade? A researcher? A friend? All of these things? No-one knew what I was because I didn't myself; I was trapped in the gap between what I wanted to do and what I was actually doing, between how I wanted to present myself and how I was actually presenting myself, between what I wanted to say and what I was actually saying.[31]

These thoughts could be better described in terms of what I would call a 'deviant' faith[32] – the kind of faith that comes with the marginalised position of the researcher as someone who keeps going back and forth and yet ultimately remains an outsider, only occasionally sharing in the life of the group. My own outsider status was something I would constantly be reminded of – even if indirectly or unintentionally. It would often take the form of group members referring to me as "Maria from Berlin" or making well-intentioned jokes about my frequent absences. Apart from all this, I have to admit that it was also my own need to belong, as well as the fact that I was intrigued by the prospect of dealing with the challenges arising from interacting with a group, that led me to choose this particular subject matter.

Two days after we arrived at the camp on the mountain where the eco-festival was taking place, we decided to attend a concert by the Greek music band Chainides, which was being held at the festival's concert site. Chainides, whose name means "rebels" or revolutionaries but also something like mountain roamers, are quite popular in Greece.[33] They are an alternative band whose sound is thought to contrast with the 'easily digestible' music produced by other artists. They are part of what has

31 Kyriakakis 2004. Relevant accounts always relieve this uneasy feeling.

32 Inspired by the work of Howard Becker, See Becker 1997.

33 Kranioti, August 27, 2014. Commenting on the possible interpretations of the name 'Chainides.'

come to be called the 'quality Greek music scene,' a music scene whose origins can be traced back to the early 1990s and which aspired to express values that had allegedly taken a backseat to the pursuit of wealth, extravagance and superficial pleasures that characterised that era. Drawing inspiration from the Greek tradition and, in particular, traditional Cretan music, the Chainides' lyrics narrate their heroes' adventures in a way that marries an overview of the past and present with the constant pursuit of the future.[34] Their songs centre on existential and social themes (love, angst, self and other, mutuality and alienation), and their lyrics express an appeal for a return to the collective, which is not presented as a lost paradise, but as a liberating possibility, a promising (as opposed to a promised) land, and a testament to our very humanity.

I was unfamiliar with some of the band's songs and when the concert started I found myself desperately trying to keep track of all the lyrics I was listening to for the first time. These songs meant a lot to the people surrounding me, my comrades, and being unable to profess my agreement with them by singing along was nothing short of a nightmare for me. And then it happened. After an extended orchestral introduction, the band's lead vocalist started to sing: *I want to take my tribe and leave* (*"θέλω να πάρω τη φυλή μου και να φύγω"*)...[35] A frenzy ensued. Suddenly, it all seemed to come together – in the form of a contradiction that really made sense to me. The song's lyrics centred on the individual/group dynamic – on the oscillation between, on the one hand, the individual's subjective will and, on the other, the demands of reality and the expectations of the group. For a moment I thought I was trapped in this group, obliged to remain part of a 'tribe' I did not belong to.

This was one of the many instances when I was overcome with doubt. On the one hand, my friendship and bonds with these people felt superficial, like I was sacrificing pieces of my life for the sake of research. On the other hand, a part of me really wanted to be there with them, and I had a hard time figuring out the source of my discomfort. It did not help that I had recently gotten into a quarrel with a participant, who had aggressively questioned the legitimacy of my presence in the group during an interview. The group seemed to leave no room for what I perceived at the time as 'meaningful relatedness.' What troubled me was the feeling that, within the group, all uniqueness was stripped away; no-one's traits could be recognised and appreciated as singular. Indeed, it seemed at times as if there were no individuals. Within the group, everyone is the same, and everyone 'falls in love' with everyone else; demand is constant, and so is supply; everything is offered and reoffered continually, and everything is 'conquered' and 're-conquered' continually.

34 Kranioti, August 27, 2014. Dimitris Apostolakis, the band's frontman, once said that the utopias contained in names are distant buoys you hope to reach one day.

35 Chainides & Apostolakis 2000.

In the last part of the song the protagonist confesses his fear that there is no other road available, but realises that this is only the case because all roads are made by the act of walking. There were a lot of moments when I had to conquer my own fears and move forward. Besides, I was there, *with* these people, proving my allegiance to them by singing along and even though I was not part of their tribe, most of them would still readily extend gestures of affection and support to me.

It felt like the song had brought time to a halt. It was an ecstatic moment, filled with passion, meaningful looks, embraces and determination. It was like everyone was floating above the ground, jointly singing, "I want to take my tribe and leave."

Nostalgia, sorrow, catharsis, love, friendship, a purpose that was both shared and personal – but also an eternal repetition of the same. Everyone was looking at each other meaningfully, touching each other affectionately, and embracing each other, each affirming the other's very existence. Within the group, the other is a companion and a comrade. There is a well-intentioned, perfectly human aspect to all this, but there is also a darker undercurrent beneath it: an expectation that the other will never leave the group, an implicit appeal that verges on emotional blackmail. The other is there, and that is where s/he has to remain, because that is what constitutes the group, its existence and its identity. There is no room for the personal let alone the private. Everyone's personal history can become common property; everyone is transparent, fully exposed to the gaze of everyone else, and subjected to an endless reproduction of (often questionable) information about their circle of friends, their personal choices, their family and their love life. Otherwise, they may become a threat and an enemy.

That night, I felt like I was surrounded by people who were 'like me' as much as they were 'others.' I wanted to "take my tribe" and run away from them, but at the same time, my nostalgia for the life I had left behind – for my home country, for the places I had loved, for the relationships that had perished – made me feel like there were also many things that united us.

This incident epitomises my experience of engaging in this research study – a research study that was initiated in 2009 and plunged me into many years of complications and conflicting thoughts and feelings, as well as into a life torn between Thessaloniki and Berlin. My journey as a participant researcher oscillating between enthusiasm and discouragement was full of self-reflection and emotion. As I contemplate the feelings of stress and anxiety that accompanied me throughout this project, I realise that the fear of 'losing my identity,' along with my overall confusion and dilemmas, was 'simply' the result of my encounter with an environment where, like every other non-initiated person, I had to "un-learn"[36] as much as I had to learn, a fact that will be shown in detail throughout the book. After all, to recall Geertz:

36 Taylor 2011, 16.

> Doing ethnography is like trying to read (in the sense of "construct a reading of") a manuscript – foreign, faded, full of ellipses, incoherencies, suspicious emendations, and tendentious commentaries, but written not in conventionalized graphs of sound but in transient examples of shaped behavior.[37]

Eventually, I managed to take a more balanced look at the collective life of the group. While the spectre of collectivity still daunted me, I gradually came to the realisation that while it integrates and narrows the existing gaps between people it also creates a space where everyone can express themselves, a space that is shaped by the individuals inhabiting it as much as it shapes them. In this context, disagreements, conflicts, and losses are not only expected, but also necessary: they are evidence of pluralism and part of a process that continuously produces something new and unique.

The Emotional Dimension

Having looked at the major components of doing research (that is to say, conducting interviews and observing while participating in a group), I would now like to briefly look at some of the emotional processes that accompany the actual doing of research. It often seemed that one has to develop some tools of her/his own if emotionality – which after all cannot be put in brackets – was to serve the purposes of the research and not hinder it. Hence, friendship as a tool, issues of trust, mechanisms of dealing with emotions (such as fear, distress or hesitancy) as well as a compass of how all these things were to be confronted in the research field are all worth discussing.

Friendship and Trust

The role of friendship as an integral part of the research process has been discussed a lot by social scientists.[38] It provides an "ideal situation" within which the researcher can untangle the difficulties and meanings inherent in the research process.[39] "Friendship as method"[40] establishes the appropriate conditions for the participants and the researcher to gain better insights into the researched area while avoiding some of the risks related to more formal scientific approaches. But friendship cannot be part of a pre-agreed contract. It is a voluntary relationship that

37 Geertz 1973, 10.

38 Lather 1993; Taylor 2011; Tillmann-Healy 2003; Ellis 1995; Dreher 2009; Labaree 2002; Coffey 1999.

39 My understanding of friendship was greatly informed also by the following literature: Pahl 2000; Allan 1989; Bell and Coleman 1999; Desai and Killick 2010.

40 Tillmann-Healy 2003, 734.

varies in intensity and density, and is situated in and based upon shared aspects, sentiments and lived experiences. Levels of trust, reciprocity, acceptance, respect, generosity, and mutuality all greatly shape it and transform it. And yet, as Simmel once wrote, the complexity of the characteristics of various kinds of friendship leaves open the question of "discretion, of reciprocal revelation and concealment."[41]

However, as Dreher has pointed out, friends are "a fundamental part of the everyday reality in which we act" and "their togetherness–*symbolizes* the idea of friendship for the respective other, i.e. typifies the special, unique relationship between the friends."[42] In his view, friendship is "symbolically constructed" and relies on "a collectively shared symbolism with a repertoire of culturally defined categories."[43]

In this sense, becoming part of the group's symbolic universe as a participant observer presupposes that one is willing to create affirmative ties within the group. While growing closer to people and delving deeper into my own personal concerns, I – almost reflexively – started to create an environment in which I myself could meaningfully relate and which would simultaneously be accepted by the members of the group. One of the main characteristics of my initial interactions with the group was a friendly, open-minded, discreetly curious attitude towards those situations that were new to me. I had to become part of this shared experience, and my initial doubts, hesitation, and even embarrassment, did not help. Any absence from common activities or standard group obligations gradually became a source of great anxiety. Every time I had to abstain from the activities of the group, I would end up lamenting the missed opportunity to be part of the new stories that were being created and witness the new incidents that would later go on to become part of the group's narrative and memory. But somewhere in-between what I initially thought I had to do and what I later wanted to do, relationships were formed.

During the first phase of my time with the group, when I was still what we might call uninitiated, I remember that my mental images of the Sanctuary were somewhat distorted, as if I had been looking at a distant place through a looking glass. The place seemed much bigger than it was in reality, the walls seemed higher, and the distances between the rooms seemed greater. As time passed, and my memory started to be filled with familiar faces, and I started to ignore the pictures on the walls and to focus on the feelings of joy and familiarity that accompanied our meetings. Feelings of completeness and safety started to replace my distorted mental view of the place.

On the other hand, it quickly became clear that, in a sense, I was afraid to undertake the risk of not being unanimously accepted. I had a feeling that any kind of frustration on my part would threaten the research project or my presence there.

---

41 Wolff, Kurt, H. 2012, 326.

42 Dreher 2009, 412. Emphasis in original.

43 Dreher 2009, 408.

It is quite difficult to be part of a group and find a way to like and connect with everyone. Moreover, by forging friendly relations one risks more.[44] In this sense, the process of disclosure involves not only the participants but also the researcher, who finds her/himself subjected to the same procedures, pressures, and challenges as the participants themselves.[45] Being part of the group means becoming involved, sharing, confessing, being trusted and being able to trust, becoming more flexible, more accessible, and, in the end, more vulnerable.[46] The boundaries become unavoidably blurred not only for the researched, but also for the researcher. As has often been noted, one must proceed somewhat 'intuitively' in order not to hurt, betray, or offend.[47]

According to Taylor, when adopting a friendly approach to the field, one has to constantly search for, ensure and preserve an ideal balance between different roles and settings, and different demands; emotional, academic and those based on friendships.[48] While this prerequisite seemed, after the first year of research, to be largely fulfilled during the interviews, I often wondered about the shifts in position on the part of some participants with whom I had had the chance to exchange ideas or discuss certain issues in more depth. There were a few times when my jokes or some of my gestures rubbed off on the group or were turned into slogans. There were also times when I kept wondering whether my behaviour, my presence there, or my friendly ties with some members of the group could in any way influence them. There were other times when I had to explain the group's words and actions to a third party – but how was I qualified to serve as an adequate representative of the group? No matter how carefully I conducted myself, I could not but worry about the "*daimon*" of self-disclosure, the creature that "accompanies each man throughout his life, always looking over his shoulder from behind and thus visible only to those he encounters."[49] To recall Arendt's passage:

> This disclosure of "who" in contradistinction to "what" somebody is –his qualities, gifts, talents and shortcomings, which he may display or hide – is implicit in everything somebody says and does. It can be hidden only in complete silence and perfect passivity, but its disclosure can almost never be achieved as a wilful pur-

---

44 Goffman 1989, 128: Goffman warned of the effects of "going too friendly."

45 Taylor 2011, 15; Tillmann-Healy 2003, 743.

46 Tillmann-Healy 2003; Taylor 2011; Ellis 1995. For a revelatory account of "vulnerability" see Behar 2012.

47 Taylor 2011, 14: Taylor refers to "grey areas" of observation and the intuition required when it comes to off-the-record issues.

48 Taylor 2011, 14.

49 Arendt 1998/1958, 179–80; Arendt 1986, 247.

pose, as though one possessed and could dispose of this "who" in the same manner he has and can dispose of his qualities.[50]

Withdrawal and Betrayal

When one becomes engaged in the daily activities of the group, and as such in the group's life where friendly ties and relationships matter, one cannot but also be confronted with the danger of failure.[51] Indeed, feelings of betrayal or disappointment were not uncommon in the group. In the most unpleasant cases, frustrations over a chosen course of action, a practice that failed to earn the group wider support, or a decision that was made without everyone's consent could even lead to people leaving.

In many cases, the problem could be described in terms of a conflict between ethics and reality. The 'right way' to do things is dictated by the group's principles, but in practice there was not always room for idealism. A similar thing could be said about my own dilemmas. Although, for example, I should ideally have kept some distance from the group's decision-making processes, in practice I ended up having to discuss any issues that arose. At first, I considered initiating an open meeting and informing everyone of the reasons behind my presence there, my questions, and my goals. Realising, however, that this could itself lead to disagreements, quarrels, or at best endless discussions that would evoke an inquisition-like atmosphere, I eventually chose to discuss it all in more personal, face-to-face settings.

Carolyn Ellis has made some enlightening comments in relation to what it means for the researcher's fears to be confirmed. After the publication of her research, she had to deal with feelings of disappointment and frustration on the part of many of the members of the community she had studied. When she realised how painful her research turned out to be for some community members and was forced to recognise that in the name of research, she had neglected people's feelings, she experienced feelings of regret and shame. After her initial shock, and after re-entering the field, and dealing with people's frustration and anger about what she had written, Ellis felt like it was the first time she could consider herself a true part of the community. As she writes, she felt like an "authentic part" of the community for the first time as a result of "being herself" and being able to confront people's frustrations.[52]

This authenticity and its consequences, which also make the research process more meaningful, has served as a great source of relief in relation to my own anxieties. In this sense, relationships are tested not only at the level of friendship, trust,

50 Arendt 1998/1958, 179.

51 Taylor 2011, 15.

52 Ellis 1995, 81. For the idea of authenticity, see ibid, 94.

joy, and creativity, but also when they are faced with disputes, quarrels, and conflict. However, the issue of authenticity is not unproblematic, especially when what is considered to be authentic in fact has its own history and distinct cultural context.[53] Authentic, however, should not be read as a romantic idea of a universal, orderly authenticity. Rather, it acknowledges the fragmentary character of the complex relations formed within the field, the ambiguity that imbues them and the self-consciousness that accompanies them.[54]

The Ethical Dimension

Three of the most fundamental difficulties involved in conducting research are guilt, fear, and the spectre of ethics. I will treat all three of them as dual, as they affect both me (as the researcher) and the members of the group (as the researched). They are essentially related to the way in which the lines become blurred when an 'outsider' becomes an 'insider.' All the concerns that troubled me (Am I good enough? Do they mind me being here? Am I an intruder? Do I really understand the things they say and do? Am I doing things the way they are supposed to be done?) often turned out to also weigh on the group, and I often encountered this mix of guilt and fear in many informal conversations with friends and members. As far as I myself was concerned, the fear and guilt were amplified by the particular place I occupied in the group: I was not a mere participant asking for nothing in return. My presence there was not driven by the benevolent motives that drove their participation, and my interest in researching the group could be interpreted by members as a self-absorbed or egoistic stance. In other words, my presence there displayed features which many of the members would not hesitate to criticise.

At first, I thought I could do my research without my presence interfering with the group's way of being and functioning. I tried to act as if I were – as if it were possible to be – a perfectly unbiased individual observing a situation that she is perfectly indifferent to. However, that is not the way things work in the real world. My interest in the group was far greater than I thought or was willing to admit. And the truth was that personally, I did care about the group and its workings – I cared almost as much as its members did. I was mentally present, pondering the issues it was faced with and being defined by it, even when I was physically absent. Once I had become involved, I could never really keep a distance from it; I never had the option or the luxury of detachment.

Contemplating the feelings of anxiety and guilt induced by these concerns, I eventually began to realise that most of the obstacles I was confronted with could, in fact, be overcome. One of the main issues was finding a way to protect the members

---

53 Atkinson and Silverman 1997, 313.

54 Ellis 1995, 94.

of the group from having their identity discovered. Thus, I decided to start referring not only to its members but also to the group itself by alternative names. There is no point in exposing the members of the group to the danger of being identified; what I am interested in discussing is not who this group is or who its members are, but how certain people feel when they find themselves in a particular set of circumstances.

I also spent a long time acting as an advocate on the group's behalf, accusing myself of every wrongdoing I could think of, feeling ashamed or even trying to defend certain positions. Essentially, taking the role of a member rather than a researcher. As a result of having to reflect on the research process and to develop an awareness of my dual role in the group, I reached a point where I was able to feel like "myself," to recall Ellis.[55]

But this self was largely shaped by the things I saw, heard, read, and learned over the years of my engagement with the group and through the everyday struggles and activities of the people composing it. There were some things I never stopped regarding with suspicion, and some things I eventually saw merit in. Writing about them, however, should be more than an exercise in self-castigation; it should also be a pleasant journey in questioning, discovering and reminiscing. In essence, this journey turned out to be an ongoing consideration of the constitutive elements of relationships: feelings of friendship and trust, self-disclosure, betrayal, withdrawal, guilt, and moral reflections. As a result, this study often veers away from the socio-political toward the psychological or even the existential. This was a conscious decision on my part, as this study centres on people, relationships, questions and dilemmas whose political nature is not their only, or even their defining characteristic.

In order to communicate the materiality of these 'human affairs,' I have chosen not to place emphasis on their political dimension. I have always found the question of human relationships and affairs important in its own right. I wanted to avoid analysing an endeavour that is no more political than it is personal in a way that would entail the risk of emphasising the political at the expense *of* the personal. As a result, issues of power and politics are often only briefly addressed, in favour of an approach that is centred instead on emotion, interrelationships and people's feelings of belonging and togetherness. However, it would be wrong to reduce the political to politics alone, or even to issues of power. Instead, my approach aspires to follow the group's own conceptualisation of the personal and the political in the way members experience them.

While conducting my research, I often found myself wondering whether my almost existential concerns were legitimate or whether objectivity was impossible only because I was uncritically imposing my own analytical categories on the

55 As she characteristically writes: "My compartmentalization of roles finally has broken down and I am 'myself' in this community, simultaneously experiencing self and relationships in all the complexity and ambiguity that authenticity is supposed to entail." Ellis 1995, 81.

phenomenon I was studying.[56] This fear was never fully silenced. Anthropological research requires the researcher to become a channel for the phenomenon they study, and I feared that, by passing through the channel that is my subjectivity, the object of my study might become infected with all the 'viruses' that inhabited my head.[57]

I did wonder how many members would agree with this kind of approach, let alone with the parallels I was drawing between their own devotion to the group and a kind of religious devotion. On my part, however, I never misrepresented myself in order to gain access to the group. In fact, I would openly express my views and share my personal perspective on things at every chance I got. My discourse and the mentality underlying it have been inevitably shaped by my family history, the environment I was raised in, the school I attended, the relationships I have formed, the social and work environments I have encountered, and all the other influences I have been exposed to. And I can only agree with Novick's idea that the question of objectivity does not so much relate "to the (methodological) issue of *how* we do our work" but to the (existential) issue of "*who* we are, *what* we're doing and what we've done when we've done it"[58] – a point that highlights the ontological underpinnings of any research.

Doing Research/A Manual of Doing the Right Thing

After getting to grips with emotionality and reflexivity, a few clarifications about the research process itself are still needed. Interviews had to fit in with the schedule and the availability of the members, and were often postponed or cancelled, while the real conversations arose spontaneously at unexpected moments. Very often the interviews, (or conversations, as I preferred to call them) were long, friendly discussions, which went beyond the time limits appropriate for an interview, and in which both parties engaged in a deliberate conversation about the important issues. When listening to the interviews later, I could recall the atmosphere in which they took place and made notes on any thoughts that came up during my reviewing of the interviews. This process produced the first drafts of the thematic areas brought

56 Casas-Cortés, Osterweil, and Powell 2008, 25; Rudolf 2005, 12: Rudolf refers to the "imperialism of categories," when categories from a certain dominant environment are uncritically applied to other cultures and populations. Taking into consideration the knowledge production on the part of the group, it is interesting to see how those theoretical categories found practical answers in everyday life, see Rudolf 2005, 6.

57 For further debates on objectivity, relativism, and the researcher's standpoints, see also Andriakaina 2009; Mohanty 2001.

58 Novick 1991, 700. Emphasis in original.

out by the group's members.[59] Throughout the book there are rather long passages taken from interviews, which are crucial for a certain atmosphere to be recaptured. To this end, I have preserved spoken inconsistencies where they indicate something valuable in terms of the thinking process of my interlocutors.

While interview notes and a sort of diary I kept about my questions, images, and impressions of the group were valuable in terms of reassessing my material, when it comes to field notes I cannot claim a similar consistency. The daily reality of participation in the group did not allow for the systematic writing of field notes. After a strenuous day, with a lot of practical tasks to be accomplished, the extensive writing of notes was not a realistic aim. As such my field notes took a form that made sense to me. I was more keen to narrate what happened and share my thoughts via email with a good friend of mine who was informed about my research and very supportive to my approach. All those emails functioned later as my own narrative about my field research. These emails, which were quite comprehensive, served as another source of reflexivity, forming a constant dialogue between my own emotions and the issues that pertained to the group. Where revised versions of these notes appear in the text, they are cited as 'personal notes.'

As Schiffauer suggests, three important principles accompany research: the principle of agnosticism, the principle of symmetry and the principle of relativism.[60] As I understand it, this means that remaining ignorant, equal and flexible would be three of the most important qualities, that the researcher can cultivate when conducting their research. What this demonstrates is (1) the necessity of dispensing with the illusion of the validity of our own truth (if we accept and affirm the partial and particular character of our findings), (2) the need to recognise the validity of our interlocutors' own interpretations (allowing them an equal status to our own) and (3) the need to remain flexible and respectful when it comes to the researched's own capacities and claims to truth, while ensuring that our findings and language remain equally applicable to the researched's own definitions.[61]

This is especially the case when doing research into social movements, where the researcher also has to navigate the movement's own understanding of itself.[62] Casas-Cortes, Osterweil and Powel have drawn attention to the "centrality of knowledge-practices in movements and how these enactments destabilize the boundary between activist and academic (or other expert) knowledges."[63] Indeed, processes of learning and unlearning are evident throughout the book, indicating those aspects and experiences of transformation that do not refer solely to the researched group

59 On thematic analysis, see Riessman 2008, 53–76. See also Smith, Larkin, and Flowers 2009.

60 Schiffauer 2000, 318.

61 Schiffauer 2000, 318.

62 Casas-Cortés, Osterweil, and Powell 2008; Hirai 2015; Zavos and Biglia 2009.

63 Casas-Cortés, Osterweil, and Powell 2008, 23.

but also to the destabilisation of the researcher's own convictions, prejudices, and ways of being. As Fine puts it, "ethnography is ultimately about transformation" and transformation is "about hiding, about magic, about change."[64] For Fine "this is the task that we face and is the reality that we must embrace."[65] Where necessary, I have returned with more detailed reflections to certain issues.

One last challenge that taught me a lot was the bi-linguality of the texts. When it comes to people telling their stories, or engaging in moments of reflection and emotionality, being able to speak in their mother tongue relieves some of the tension. However, a degree of interpretation inevitably crept in to the process of translating these texts from Greek into English and a constant balance had to be achieved between translation and interpretation.[66]

Comment: Heretical Identifications

> And, in the end, there were thousands of questions that translated into ambitious reflections, guilty nights, narcissistic retreats, tentative interviews, endless conversations, unreasonable reactions, solitary investigations, circles of socio-poetic processes, withdrawal, and self-satisfied narratives. And, in the end, there were thousands of answers that were inspired by people, cantankerous behaviours, spoilt attitudes, stagnant mentalities, dead-end politics and social illusions. And, in the end, it is all these reasons that let the words be written, and make history unfold the way it was perceived by one of the heretics – a heretic confused and hidden among the faithful, living in guilt and fear that someone, somewhere, someday might reveal her/him for who she/he is.[67]

Starting from a contemplation on this extract from my personal notes, I want to summarise my thoughts about the actual act of doing research in terms of myself as a 'heretic' in the group. While reflecting on the group from a spiritual angle had initially been suggested by the members' own words, the act of interpreting them by using religious metaphors and vocabulary still seemed to clash with their own perception of themselves. Additionally, it seems rather narcissistic of me to present myself as a heretic, for this carries the implication that the others (my co-partners in the research, the members of the group) are 'believers' who interpret their situation in naïve, simplistic terms, that they perceive their actions strictly through the narrow prism of their ideology, or, even worse, that I presume to have gained real insight into the group's practices, mentality and culture by simply conducting some

64 Fine 1993, 290.

65 Fine 1993, 290.

66 On the issue of translation see also Riessman 2008, 42–50.

67 Personal Notes: *Confessions*, 2013.

interviews and witnessing some of their activities. Such a claim would be presumptuous on my part, as my participation in the group was intermittent, and the group was continually assuming new forms. Kaufmann has provided the following useful observations on the word heretic:

> In theology, any "opinion that is contrary to the fundamental doctrine or creed of any particular church" is heretical. From the point of view of the churches to which we do not belong – and none of us can belong to the lot – we are all heretics. But more narrowly speaking, a heretic is one who deviates from the fundamental doctrine of his own church, or of the church with which he was previously connected. So understood, not everybody is a heretic.[68]

Rather, my use of the term is closer to one of the old uses of the word 'heresy' in Greek, which signifies the individual's ability and freedom to choose (noun: *αίρεση*, verb passive voice *αιρέομαι*), although the word is mostly used in a religious context to mean the deviation from a religious dogma or belief. A heretic in this sense is not necessarily a non-believer, but rather the one who deviates from the norm and can easily become a 'traitor' to his own church. This reflected my own biases: when it came to the universe of activism, I used to have the impression that individuals either belonged entirely to a group or were faced with the accusation of being a heretic.

The notion of the heretic however, revealed another element that was more closely related to my methodological considerations and the actuality of doing research. It demonstrated my awareness of the limited scope and the partial character of the knowledge I acquired within the group.[69] In this sense, by being partly an outsider I was condemned to be a heretic. That is to say, I could never be a fully trustworthy member of the group. Likewise, being partly an insider, I have often been 'unfaithful' to my research in the way I have employed my methodological equipment. As insiders/outsiders, we cannot shed light on all aspects of the phenomenon we study; we can only capture moments of it, and we inevitably do so through our own analytical categories, or at best through those categories and elements of our investigated subject that capture our attention. And even though these categories are constantly transformed through our participation in the group, they never cease to be reflections of our own identities and various positions – a product of our own personal emotional, cognitive, and empirical journey.[70] Moreover, the characterisation of my approach as heretic is meant to indicate my attempt to address the issues pertaining to the group from a sympathetic and supportive standpoint. A heretic is, after all, still a believer, even if at times a more sceptical one.

---

68 Kaufmann 2015, 1.

69 Clifford 2010.

70 Ellis 1995, 87–89; Zavos and Biglia 2009.

3. The Origins of AuRA

Activist Responses in the Metapolitefsi Era

AuRA was initially founded as a small group of people back in 1998 and continued to grow until the moment of its 'rebirth' with the creation of the Sanctuary. The aim of this chapter is to outline the political climate in the era preceding the creation of the Sanctuary and to illustrate the conditions under which AuRA came into existence. The chapter begins with the histories of two of the main participants in AuRA, whose political involvement dates back to the mid-1980s. By looking at their initial decisions to engage in political action and at some of their first activities we can gain a sense of the political and social atmosphere that prevailed in Greece during the Metapolitefsi. They describe the conditions in which the Left in Greece found itself during the period of political and social changes that took place from the restoration of democracy in 1974 to the beginning of the 1990s; namely, the intense nationalism, the racism and the claustrophobic atmosphere that were the prevailing characteristics of the era. Against this background, they position themselves and their decision to take action against racism and introduce a new paradigm of engagement with political questions.

"The Left in a State of Peculiar Vigilance?"

I had arranged an appointment for my interview with Iakovos at about 2pm. After talking together during a long assembly at the Sanctuary some days earlier, we had decided to continue our discussion under different circumstances. The assembly had turned out to be rather volatile. The members of AuRA were discussing the prospect of accepting various groups to join that year's festival. There was intense disagreement over who should be accepted to participate and what impact certain choices might have on the festival's profile. After hours of discussion, many uncomfortable moments, and a prolonged failure to reach a conclusion, Alkyone, David, Iakovos and I decided to go out for a drink. It was the first time that I had spent time with some of the older members of AuRA outside the Sanctuary, and I was delighted to discuss various matters at a more relaxed pace. However, since I was exhausted after the long assembly, I asked Iakovos to have a more formal conversation sometime soon.

Our next meeting was at a small tavern run by a comrade who ensured we had everything we needed to make ourselves comfortable. The discussion with Iakovos lasted a couple of hours. It was a friendly talk which ranged beyond the limits of an interview. Iakovos was not only willing to answer all my questions in detail, but even provoked more of them with the way his extensive narratives evoked the feeling of another era. Iakovos was one of the first members of AuRA – he was in his thirties when the group was formed in 1998 – and he gave me a detailed account of the impetus behind his own decisions to engage in political action, the social and political landscape of the 1980s and 1990s, and the atmosphere within the Left at the time.

Iakovos' involvement in political activism dated back to the second half of the 1980s. Before that he had not even attended any of the annual commemorations of the 1973 Polytechnic School Uprising,[1] a fact that emphasised his previous lack of socio-political engagement. He had moved to Thessaloniki to study in 1985, and he became familiar with the youth political formations that operated at the university at that time. Although he did not feel especially close to any of them, he followed the meetings of some groups of what used to be called the extra parliamentary Left (a term which will be discussed further at the end of this chapter). The first time he went on a demonstration was during the Kaltezas case. In 1985 Michalis Kaltezas, a young pupil in Athens was murdered by a police officer during the polytechnic commemoration on 17th November.[2] However, the incident that really affected him was the Jet Oil accident in Thessaloniki.

In February 1986, a fire broke out in one of the oil tanks of Jet Oil, some kilometres outside the city. Eventually seven more tanks caught fire and there was a great fear that the fire would spread to the city. The fire lasted for seven days, and considerable amounts of mazut, diesel, oil and other fuels were released into the atmosphere. Iakovos seemed more than willing to give me a vivid description of this shocking event. A short time afterwards the accident at Chernobyl happened. As he laughingly told me, it was as if he had heard God's voice saying: *"you will get destroyed, you will get burned, do something about it!"* Both of these incidents functioned as catalysts for his engagement in the ecological movement. He recalled how all those whose political stance lay to the left of PASOK (Panhellenic Socialist Movement) and except for

1 The revolt of the polytechnic school in November 1973 lasted for three days and became the last organised resistance against the dictatorship. It started to be commemorated and celebrated as a national day in 1981 with the election of the Socialist Panhellenic Movement (PASOK). For an account of the events at the polytechnic school, see Kornetis 2015b; Panourgia 2009, 140–49.

2 Arvanitis 2014.

the Communist Party were present at the demonstrations about Chernobyl, a comment that provided a vivid picture of how broad the concern about this issue was. Very soon afterwards, a variety of independent ecological movements formed the Federation of Ecological and Alternative Organisations (in short Alternative Ecologists) and participated in the election of the European Parliament in 1989. They also participated in the national elections of November 1989 and April 1990. Iakovos was part of this initiative:

> Iakovos: You probably don't remember, but as you are obliged to know, in 1989 we had elections every three months [...]. However, things were simple back then, PASOK, New Democracy and United Synaspismos were the only three parties that had the majority of the electorate. We [the Alternative Ecologists] had one seat with 0.75 percent of the vote. In the next elections, we also had one seat [...]. Soon afterwards however, we split. A lack of maturity, intense controversies... We could not handle the situation. [...] In 1991 when the Macedonian issue started, this was impossible. 1991 is a deplorable moment in Greek history, only scarcely studied... this incredible national unanimity [...].[3]

The ecological movement differed from the majority of political groups and organisations of the time (communist, reformist, socialist, or anarchist among others) in that it foregrounded a new danger that societies faced, and one that greatly surpassed those that had provided the focus of previous political engagements. At the same time, however, its appeal was restricted as there was but small potential for a radicalised turn or mass participation. As Iakovos put it, it entailed an element of "self-evident consensus."

Through the ecological movement he acquired his first contacts with the conscientious objectors. The demands for the democratisation of the army, the restriction of national service to one year and the defence of soldiers' rights (especially their right to form their own unions) were already part of the political repertoire of the extra parliamentary and reformist Left in the 1970s.[4] The first organised attempts to radicalise the "movement for the army" had been made in the early 1980s with the formation of groups and committees within the army, a movement that was sup-

3 Iakovos Interview Extract: Elections, 2011.

4 Agelopoulos and Rotzokos 2010, 350. Following the Turkish invasion of Cyprus in 1974, and the occupation of the northern part of the island, the duration of the service in the army was extended to more than 24 months of military service. For the events in Cyprus and the involvement of Greece, see Svolopoulos, Konstantinos, D. 2004, 190–203. For the transition to democracy after the fall of the dictatorial regime in Greece in 1974, and the relationships between Greece and Turkey see Clogg 1995, 180–209. For the movement in the army at the beginning of the 1980s see also Agelopoulos, Pantazis, and Rotzokos 2014 and Panagiotopoulos and Pantazis 2010.

ported by various groups (students, unions).[5] However, the phenomenon of conscientious objection for ideological and not religious reasons did not appear until the mid-1980s. Iakovos, though still young, was actively engaged in what he referred to as "these spaces" (conscientious objection and ecology). These initiatives both responded to a demand for democratisation that was vivid during the period following the dictatorship and revealed the necessity of approaching broader social issues from an emancipative perspective.[6] As we will see, these initiatives provided a first ground for a gradual move away from the rigid organisational structures that had prevailed within left-wing groups over the past years, foregrounding instead ideas of autonomy and a more emancipative way of engaging in politics.

At this point, it may be helpful to take a brief look at some moments in the rather complicated history of the Greek Left and the context within which it evolved, since these are the ideological precursors of its various current tendencies. The Communist Party of Greece (KKE) boasted a rigid organisational structure, as well as a concrete ideological agenda.[7] In 1968 the party suffered a schism, which led to the formation of a second communist party, the Communist Party of the Interior (KKE es.).[8] The split was the result of a conflict between the orthodox communist leadership who were in exile in Bucharest and the United Democratic Left (EDA), whose members advanced their own political agenda in Greece (and who maintained a close relationship to the members of the Communist Party before the split).[9] The founders of the new party, which was of a reformist orientation, called themselves KKE Interior to emphasise that their party belonged to Greece, and in this way highlighted their opposition to the close ties with Moscow that in their view compromised the orthodox Greek Communist Party.[10]

In 1974 came the restoration of Democracy, and after seven years of military junta the country was caught up in the challenge of figuring out its socio-political orientation.[11] The KKE was legalised and secured itself a solid electoral base, while the more reformist KKE Interior managed to attract the support of the young urban

5 Agelopoulos and Rotzokos 2010; see also Panagiotopoulos and Pantazis 2010.

6 As Panagiotopoulos and Pantazis stress, at the beginning of 1980s the rise in suicides in the army explicitly linked the situation in the army with rising social problems which urged for reforms in the army. Panagiotopoulos and Pantazis 2010, 371.

7 Tsakatika and Eleftheriou 2013, 86–87.

8 Voulgaris 2002, 98–99.

9 For more on the EDA see Papadogiannis 2015a, 42–47.

10 Kapetanyannis 2014, 83–84. See also Kornetis 2015a, 491. Kalyvas and Marantzidis 2002, 667–68.

11 Voulgaris 2002.

progressives, who had first begun to act collectively against the dictatorship.[12] Even though it never enjoyed the same electoral appeal as the Communist Party, the KKE Interior exerted an important ideological influence on Greek society, as a party that both preserved traditional elements and yet was also forward looking.[13] Within the communist/socialist spectrum, the Euro-communist KKE es. offered a third way, beyond the dogmatism of the old communist ideals, and against the populist mentality that PASOK would bring in with its election in 1981.[14]

At the same time, within the student movement there were already various left-wing tendencies that distanced themselves from the political stances adopted by the two communist parties, or at least had different degrees of approximation to them. The history of these organisations in Greece is rather complicated.[15] It is characterised by continual coalitions, splits and shifts, with the formation of new organisations and also continuous re-positionings according to the official positions of other communist parties and various organisations. For this reason, the story presented here cannot but be an oversimplification of the emergence, development of, and interactions between, the different groups that make up the political Left in Greece.

Although the Left has a common opposition to the right wing, it is also differentiated along a number of lines.[16] Before the dictatorship, two main tendencies were to be observed, which remained in opposition to the communist parties. There was a Maoist tendency dating from 1964 (known as the M-L tradition, as its members aspired to uphold the traditional Marxist-Leninist values) which was comprised of two large organisations and various affiliated groups.[17] There was also a Trotskyist tradition dating from the interwar period.[18] During and after the dictatorship two further tendencies became prevalent in what used to be referred to as the extra-parliamentary Left: organisations connected to the New Left that were drawing on the ideas of May '68, and groups that were inspired by the Italian Autonomia movement

12 Voulgaris 2002, 110. On the youth organisations that were close to KKE Interior, see Kornetis 2015b, 268–73; on the ideological influence of KKE Interior on Greek society after the regime change, see Voulgaris 2002, 115–21.

13 Voulgaris 2002, 118–19. For a brief history of KKE and KKE Interior, see Voulgaris 2002, 103–121; 249–257.

14 Voulgaris 2002, 119. On populism among others, see Mavrogordatos 2014.

15 For an account of leftist organisations during the '70s and '80s see Kornetis 2015b; Papadogiannis 2015b; Karamanolakis, Papathanasiou, and Olympitou 2010; Kassimeris 2005; Papadogiannis 2015a.

16 This, however, has a long history among various political formations and identifications. For a comprehensive account of the topics regarding the right/anti-right dichotomy in post authoritarian Greece, see Moshonas 1995; Clogg 1995, 2014.

17 For an overview of the period 1974–1980 and a list of Maoist organisations, see Kassimeris 2005, 752–55.

18 Kornetis 2015b, 276–79; Avgeridis and Glistras Dimitris 2017; Kassimeris 2005, 755–57.

and similar movements in Germany.[19] Additionally, there was a rather small core of proponents of urban guerrilla tactics.[20]

However, despite (or rather because of) their differences, what all these tendencies taken together provided was an open space within which ideas could be contested, and from which the communist orthodoxy could be challenged. There was a constant exchange about the form of the class struggle, the levels of autonomy from official bodies, the nature of revolution and so on, but during the dictatorship this was mainly focused against the military regime. At the same time, they were engaged in a broader discussion about the form that the restoration should take after the fall of the dictatorship. Despite their fragmentation, then, these groups remain notable for their constant negotiation of new organisational repertoires, new demands, and new priorities both in political and gradually also in cultural terms.[21] From the mid-1970s the organisation of political demands escaped the strictly political setting and a series of practices were introduced (such as youth festivals, and the initiation of cultural associations within youth organisations) that brought two main issues to the fore: the relationship between the political and the personal, and the necessity of a fresh relation between the individuals and the collectives to which they belong.[22]

Iakovos and I spent a considerable amount of time discussing the conditions under which the Left found itself in the post-dictatorial period (the Metapolitefsi), the characteristics that defined the Left in Greece at that time, and its legacy for the next generations of leftist adherents.

> In Greece there was a hyper-politicisation during the Metapolitefsi, and an extensive turn to the Left. Although the New Democracy party had the parliamentary majority (1974–1981), it could not do many things, because at the same time there was a strong social movement from below that New Democracy could not neglect. After PASOK's election came the change. This created a completely different situation.[23]

---

19 Vaiou-Hadjimichali and Hadjimichalis 2012, 70–77.

20 Kassimeris 2005, 758–61; Papadogiannis 2015a, 91–92; Avgeridis and Glistras Dimitris 2017.

21 Karamanolakis, Papathanasiou, and Olympitou 2010; Papadogiannis 2015b; Papadogiannis 2010.

22 Papadogiannis 2015b, 139; 148; Papadogiannis 2015a, 27. Papadogiannis' work shows the richness of the ideas, debates and initiatives that revolve around cultural issues among competing ideological milieus and their positions towards a variety of social issues during the 1970s. The youth organisations stemming from Eurocommunist, Maoist, and several autonomous groups were combining broader cultural engagement (cinema, theatre, music, literature) issues of sexual emancipation, and leisure activities with their more traditional militancy.

23 Iakovos Interview Extract: Metapolitefsi and Change, 2011.

The restoration of democracy in 1974 did not result in the political changes that supporters of the Left had hoped for but was rather marked by the election of the right-wing New Democracy party under the leadership of Karamanlis.[24] For many of them, Karamanlis' return to the prime ministership evoked memories of the oppressive pre-dictatorship days. There was a pressing need for the state and its institutions to be democratised, and for the imprint of the dictatorial regime on the country to be removed.[25] Yet the later ascent to power of the Panhellenic Socialist Movement under the leadership of Papandreou in 1981 only temporarily fulfilled the demands for 'a different Greece' and in this sense only temporarily lived up to its main slogan of 'change.'

When PASOK rose to power in 1981, broad social strata who had long been socially excluded and ideologically marginalised throughout the post-war period were given new hope for social justice and the reconciliation of past inequities that PASOK had declared to be its main policies.[26] However, although PASOK did introduce some changes in family law, education and health, initiate reforms to the civil code which advanced women's rights, and tried to promote a general atmosphere of democratisation and progress, very soon it turned out that poor financial management and extensive foreign borrowing had virtually brought the economy to its knees.[27] At the same time, PASOK adopted an anti-European stance, that has subsequently come to be known as 'the third-worldesque nationalism' of PASOK[28] – a characterisation

24 For relevant accounts by people who participated in the anti-dictatorship struggle, see Kornetis 2015b, 576–97.

25 This was supposed to happen through the democratisation of the public sector, the modernisation of social and political life, the 'cleansing' of the military and the police of junta supporters. Clogg 1995, 185–86; Voulgaris 2008, 68–79.

26 Diamandouros 2014, 10. As Diamandouros puts it, PASOK's radical anti-imperialist, anti-establishment and populist rhetoric that was especially focused on the cultivation of anti-rightist sentiments, was an effective combination of two major elements: It was a systematic effort through "privilege rhetoric" to convince people of its intentions to reform and modernise the country, and "compensatory justice"– policies that would introduce the "era of change" and would "make up" for all past inequities. See ibid, 15; see also Mavrogordatos 2014, 48.

27 See Diamandouros 2014, 15; Kapetanyannis 2014, 80.

28 Botsiou 2015, 214–15: At the time, there was an ambivalent atmosphere in Greece towards the idea of joining what was then called the European Economic Community (EEC). From the fall of the military regime onwards, there were two tendencies when it came to the prospect of the country entering the EEC. On the one hand, there was the European vision of Konstantinos Karamanlis the Elder. Karamanlis strove to steer Greece in a European direction, as he believed that that was the safest way to ensure its prosperity, security and political stability. On the other hand, there was the Euroscepticism of Karamanlis' main political rival, Andreas Papandreou. For Papandreou, Greece's entry into the EEC would lead to greater social inequality and perpetuate its position as a dependent, subordinate state, thus not bringing about greater democratisation.

based on a narrative that portrayed Greece as a 'colony of foreign powers.'[29] PASOK drew away a significant amount of support from both the communist and Eurocommunist parties. However, the Euro-communists would criticise PASOK for its contradictory political discourses, particularly on the issues of European integration.[30]

The utterance of the word 'change' was accompanied by a grimace of disapproval by Iakovos. "To a great extent," Iakovos continued, "many comrades ensconced themselves" (*βολεύτηκαν*) within the new situation that PASOK brought about. By "ensconced themselves," what Iakovos was referring to was the way that many excluded and marginalised people, having spent years being isolated and stigmatised because of their political beliefs, were gradually re-integrated into society during the period of democratisation initiated by the election of PASOK. This had a double meaning for him. On the one hand, it showed how former comrades from the time of dictatorship, after the Metapolitefsi, lost some of the impetus for further action in this new situation. On the other hand, it revealed the legacy of the old political struggles for the new generations of left-wing adherents, their point of departure and their difference from the older generations.

> The division of society into left-wings and right-wings still existed. In 1981 people who previously could not find work [because of their political beliefs] gradually started to get jobs in the public sector. Previously they could not find a place to work, definitely they could not work in the public sector. Many of them were people who had probably spent a long time in exile [...] they continued to be pariahs in society. All these things initiated a hyper-politicisation which gradually, of course, faded.[31]

Iakovos is referring to the vocational rehabilitation of Greek citizens who had been labelled as communists, a tactic that was intended to keep society 'safe' and 'clean' from the communist threat. The main way that this took place was through the issuing of 'certificates of probity,'[32] which was initiated in 1936, and was finally abolished under the governance of PASOK. Until then, failure to possess such a certificate made it impossible to acquire a passport, enter higher education, get employment in certain work sectors and most importantly could lead to a range of punish-

---

29 Gazi 2015, 249; Clogg 1995, 191. For more on the idea of thirdworldism/tiermondisme, see also Kornetis 2015a. On PASOK, see Pantazopoulos 2001; Pantazopoulos 2011.

30 Voulgaris 2002, 256; Kapetanyannis 2014.

31 Iakovos Interview Extract: The Division of Society, 2011.

32 Or "certificates of social reliability" as Davies and Katsikas called them. The certificates guaranteed that someone was not a communist and after 1948, with the introduction of law 516/1948, were expanded to all public sectors, bringing a division of society into those who were "nationally minded" and those who could become a potential danger to the country. See Siani-Davies and Katsikas 2009, 564.

ments if it was alleged that someone posed an internal danger as an enemy of the state and the country.[33]

But why was Iakovos referring to all these details that pertained to another era, and what did this have to do with the groups we were about to discuss? There seemed to be two main reasons for this long backstory, and both had to do with an evaluation of the leftist movements in Greece and the efforts of Iakovos' generation to find their own place in them. The 1980s and the rise of PASOK seemed to have played an important part in the development of political struggles from this time onwards. Iakovos' sarcastic utterance of the word "change" was meant to convey the confusion that led to broad social strata, (including many of the left-leaning portion of the electorate) falling under the spell of PASOK. Many members of society saw their expectations for change get squashed under the weight of the national-populist political culture cultivated by PASOK.[34] Additionally, the Greek Left found itself in an awkward limbo between the past and a new era that had yet to come. Having implemented a series of leftist demands, PASOK seemed to strip both the traditional and the reformist Left of its vitality by attracting more and more voters from the centre-left parts of the electorate.[35] Moreover, to a great extent, PASOK appropriated the traditional priorities of the Left by incorporating the anti-Nazi resistance struggle of the National Liberation Front, the civil war and the Polytechnic revolt into its own political identity, and built a heavily left-leaning self-narrative that it did not hesitate to readjust whenever it saw fit.[36]

During this time, Papandreou introduced a reconciliatory set of policies that had mainly symbolic and moral weight. Some of these policies, for example, were the abolition of the gandarmerie because of its history of violent conduct, the repatriation of people who found shelter in Communist countries, the introduction of a pension policy for fighters in the Resistance, and the abolition of citizens'security files[37] – all of which indicated the official acknowledgement of the contribution of the communist struggle during the resistance period.[38] However, as Panourgia has

33 As Panougia notes, following the Foucauldian analysis, it is a question of "how the subject of the state is re-produced as alien, as a radical *other* impregnated with the certainty of danger." Panourgia 2009, 114. Emphasis in original.

34 On the connection between PASOK, populism and the reactions of leftist intellectuals see Lyrintzis and Spourdalakis 2017/1993, 139–40.

35 Voulgaris 2002, 256–57.

36 Fitili 2015, 33–36; Tsakatika and Eleftheriou 2013, 83. After 1981, PASOK gradually abandoned the fiercely anti-American, anti-European, anti-NATO rhetoric it had espoused in the past. It adopted a watered-down discourse in order to expand its appeal to centrist and conservative voters. See Botsiou 2015, 222; Moshonas 1995.

37 Clogg 1995, 200–202.

38 For the 'restorative' character of the 'national reconciliation'- policies in Greece, see Siani-Davies and Katsikas 2009, 561. They stress that pensions, memorials and street renaming were policies which tried to counterbalance the absence of courts in processes of restoring justice.

noted, these practices not only allowed “a (re)turn to normalcy” for many members of society but also “secured the past in the furnace of the steel mill.”[39] As she characteristically puts it, “the Left was made, at once, both legal and forgotten. Enforced amnesia.”[40]

I asked Iakovos if he had any gripes with the Left:

> Eh, well, yeah, I do, but my gripes are the gripes of a friend. The Greek Left has some special characteristics; it is more nationalistic than the Left in the rest of Europe. [...] Greece has never been an imperialist power, because it never managed to become one, as I explain in my latest article (laughs); it tried to but failed. They are not [...] the ones in charge; they are not [...] the slaves; they are the in-betweeners. That's what Greece – the Greek social formation, not Greece in some abstract sense – continues to be, which results in the development of all [possible] tendencies – dependence, imperialism etc – and [thus] it becomes easy to develop conspiracy theories [...]. The [Greek] Left has these characteristics. Nationalism is not restricted to national issues; it extends to the patriarchy, to masculine virtues, [and] is tied to all the things we're discussing, [such as, attitudes towards] homosexuality – all these [characteristics] can be found in the Greek Left to a great degree.[41]

During this period, the Left's dominant ideas and slogans centred on demands for freedom, democracy and liberation from domestic autocrats and foreign exploitative powers[42] – that is, demands that revolved around national issues. The nationalism of the Greek Left would often extend beyond national issues to other aspects of social life, such as family law and personal relationships,[43] and also harboured some conservative tendencies. Even though the Greek Left was heavily influenced by international movements in terms of the forms of action it adopted during the dictatorship (building occupations, extensive revolts), its struggle differed dramatically from that of the Left in other Western countries in terms of the discourse framing

As Papadogiannis notes, the objections raised by youth organisations regarding the 'culture of commemoration' were sound. Papadogiannis 2015a, 216.

39 Panourgia 2009, 151.

40 Panourgia 2009, 153.

41 Iakovos Interview Extract: The Greek Social Formation and the Left, 2011.

42 The main slogan used by the students who participated in the greatest revolt that took place during the dictatorship – the revolt at the Polytechnic School of Athens (1973) – was “Bread, Education and Liberty.” For the atmosphere during the Polytechnic revolt see Kornetis 2015b, 535–53; Kassimeris 2005, 746.

43 The Greek leftists' stance towards the first feminist groups that appeared in Greece is characteristic in this regard. Kornetis 2015b, 411–28.

it.[44] It revolved around a heavily anti-imperialist discourse and it consistently centred on the freedom and independence of the Greek nation,[45] while simultaneously making frequent references to the historical Left's struggles (for example, during the resistance against the Nazi occupation of Greece and the civil war). In the leftists' collective consciousness, their anti-dictatorship struggle was a continuation of their ideological ancestors' struggles for the protection of Greek national interests.[46]

> Of course, this resulted from a historical disadvantage, from the hyper-politicised atmosphere of post-authoritarian Greece. There may have been a junta that ruled until 1974, but essentially the country spent the years between the end of the [civil] war and 1974 in a state of emergency. That is to say, the civil war ended in 1963 – with the 1963 decree[47] – but it took Papandreou rising to power for the last political prisoners to be released. So, this has kept the Left in a state of peculiar vigilance.[48]

This active aspect of the Greek Left was to be attributed to the political situation that prevailed until 1974, and to a great extent defined its ideological development. As Iakovos emphasised "this is a Left that still takes to the streets – even if it's only [left-wing party] cadres who do so. Where have you seen this in Europe?" It seemed to me that Iakovos' discussion of this long period highlighted a kind of break between the old struggles of the Left and the situation that young activists now found themselves in. On the one hand, there was an affiliation with the broader leftist space and its history. On the other, the new generations had yet to adjust to the new demands of the era and find their own way in terms of political participation and action. However, the political developments of 1989–1991 brought further scepticism into the circles of the Left, as we will examine below. This period is the next key moment in Iakovos' discussion of the history of the Left.

In 1989, spurred into action by a financial scandal that revealed PASOK to be not only unreliable but also corrupt, various parties of the Left – including the KKE and EAR (one of the successors to KKE Interior) – formed the "Coalition of the Left and

44 For an overview of the similarities and differences between the Greek anti-dictatorship student movement and the international movements of the '60s and '70s, see Kornetis 2015b, 624–34.

45 Kornetis 2015b, 547.

46 Kornetis 2015b, 545–47.

47 The civil war ended in 1949. The Decree 4234/62 – the decree Iakovos refers to – actually proclaimed the end of the "communist insurgency." The end of the Greek civil war found Greece deeply divided at a political and ideological level. For the post-civil-war politico-ideological landscape of the country, see Voulgaris 2008, 25–42.

48 Iakovos Interview Extract: The Left in a State of Peculiar Vigilance, 2011.

Progress" (Synaspismos)[49] and went into both elections that took place during that year as a united front. The decision by a large part of the Left to unite itself in this way had a great symbolical value. In the light of international events, this striving for a common ground revealed the tendency to overcome all fragmentation and disputes and play a decisive role in the political scene. However, the Coalition engaged in a movement that provoked discussions in the circles of the Left for a long time. The Coalition came in third in the 1989 elections (with 13.1 percent of the vote in June and 10.97 percent of the vote in November). Both times, they agreed to participate in a coalition government: first with New Democracy, and then with both New Democracy and PASOK.[50] However, with New Democracy being viewed by numerous left-wing people as a symbol of oppression, exclusion and rampant anti-communism, and with PASOK being viewed as a symbol of corruption, the Coalition's decision to cooperate with them turned out to be a massively miscalculated move.[51]

From Iakovos' point of view, this was exactly the period when the political formations in Greece started to reveal their real character. It was a time when things started to become more clear on the political scene, or as he characteristically puts it, a time that "unblurred a variety of issues" that had remained entangled under the power of PASOK and the political developments of the previous decade. The Coalition of the Left, of Movements and Ecology that emerged in 1991 was, then, a party that aspired to bring a new perspective to the left-leaning spectrum.[52]

Offering a brief review of the political action of the Left in Greece, Iakovos essentially emphasised its dynamic presence within the history of political protest. He called attention to the movement's *resolve* – a resolve that seemed to pay tribute to the Left's historical struggles and functioned as a cohesive, driving force that kept leftists rallied and politically active. The marginalisation of many groups in the absence of new ideas and guidance, the consolidation of right-wing nationalism and the double language of the socialist, but national-patriotic PASOK – all contributed to the gradual erosion of political projects that marked the period from the restoration of democracy to the end of the 1980s. The smaller-scale projects that came to the fore in the late 1980s revolved around the newly emerging ecological issues and the conscientious objectors' movement among other smaller scale initiatives (feminists, human rights, etc) that did not resemble the intense politicisation of previous years.

49 After the split of the Coalition in 1991 the so-called SYN emerged, "The Coalition of the Left, of Movements and Ecology," which in 2004 would form a subsequent coalition with the "The Coalition of the Radical Left" (SYRIZA). In 2012 SYRIZA became a political party and in 2015 formed a government together with ANEL (Party of Independent Greeks) which lasted until 2019. For SYN see Tsakatika and Eleftheriou 2013; SYN 1992.

50 Kapetanyannis 2014, 89–90.

51 Clogg 1995, 214–18.

52 Tsakatika and Eleftheriou 2013, 89–96.

The new endeavours were beginning to assert themselves, communicating with broader international organisations and bringing to the fore global (ecology), and local (ideological objectors) issues. At the same time, the new projects were partly responding to two main concerns: first was the necessity to overcome a strictly national setting, and second was a broader concern, usually not admitted, about establishing a common ground within which the variety of broader leftist spaces could interact. They remained, however, *minority-oriented,* a phrase that came up several times in our discussion, indicating the restricted appeal of those projects and the small core of people that were addressing them. While emphasising how minority-oriented these endeavours were, Iakovos laughingly contrasted them with the situation of the popular Indignant Movement that was taking place in Thessaloniki during the time of our interview.[53] As he told me: "Passing by with a colleague the other day from the square I told her: "Damn, it is the first time we are with the majority!" It really felt strange!"[54]

"What Can One Do in a Time of Socialism?"

I met Ezekiel shortly after I had made my first contacts at the Sanctuary. As he was one of the more experienced members of the group, I was urged to go to him for any information I may have needed. I let some time pass before I eventually asked him to meet and have a discussion in person. My hesitancy was probably linked to the first time that we met, in summer 2010. It was one of the first days of my fieldwork in the Sanctuary, and I politely asked him if we could talk for a while. Ignorant and reserved as I was, I referred to him in the second-person plural, as I used to do with strangers at the time. Initially these verbal slips frequently happened on occasions when I felt overwhelmed, and people would correct me, usually teasingly, as they expressed their preference for the more informal second-person singular form. From Ezekiel the reaction was a bit more complicated. He was sitting at a table at the Sanctuary, rolling a cigarette, and he refused to look at me for quite a long time. When he eventually replied, also in the second-person plural form, with "of course Miss Maria," he immediately challenged my "Anglo-Saxon habit," as he later called it. I realised that the polite plural form was indeed very impolite in this context. It was perceived as distant and unfamiliar, or even as pretentious and arrogant. What is more, it could have been perceived as an effort on my part to differentiate myself from the other participants – all of which made for a very bad start. I laughingly

53 The Indignant Citizens' Movement was a broad mobilisation of citizens in Athens, Thessaloniki and other cities following European movements that took place against the austerity and the crisis in spring and summer 2011. See also Chapter Six.

54 Iakovos Interview Extract: Being with The Majority, 2011.

apologised and we switched to a more relaxed way of talking, but I still let a year pass before I even suggested having a conversation with him.

It was a hot summer day. We chose a rather crowded place to sit down and talk about "my work," as he called it smiling. He was extraordinarily polite, although from time to time his humour turned unexpectedly into a rough sarcasm. He told me about a lot of incidents that happened to him over the years (during demonstrations and during his overall participation in various movements) focusing on every little detail, complemented by theoretical views on collective action and political struggle, as well as their practical day to day dimension. However, at the beginning he presented himself as someone who would be rather reluctant to speak about "the movement or about other collectives." During the first hour of our conversation he repeatedly used the phrases "as far as I can say" and "as far as my head and my choices are concerned." Although the latter phrase is not entirely clear in Greek any more than it is in English, what Ezekiel wanted to stress was that he took sole responsibility for everything he said during our conversation. This gave me the impression that he would not like to 'represent' the collectives he belonged to and preferred to focus instead on his own political choices. When touching on different theoretical issues, such as the meaning of negotiation, or the role of the movement and the state, I had the impression that it was important for him that I keep in mind the difference between his own viewpoint, and that of the movement. Maintaining this distinction between his own history and the collective past to which he belonged made him feel comfortable during our discussion, once it was clear that he was not speaking on behalf of anybody else. To this end, I would occasionally reiterate that what I was interested in was his own history, and whatever topics he considered it important to narrate.

Ezekiel started taking part in political activities when he was just 16 years old. He told me that he chose the "most leftist" youth organisation that existed in the town where he grew up. It was a Marxist-Leninist group and had a large presence at the universities, especially during the long squatting period in 1979 when students opposed the new legislation that the government had introduced, and which they considered to be too authoritarian.[55] Ezekiel supported those endeavours and started similar activities at his school. At the same time, he also had a strong religious interest that was combined with both his religious activism and his "reading of Marx,"

55 Law 815 stipulated a limit to the years of study, reduced exam periods from three to two, and stipulated that assistants at the university exclusively followed the needs of the professors. After a long period of revolting and squatting, the law was abolished early in 1980, a fact that was received with great enthusiasm by the student movement that engaged in squatting. Tsakiris, December 02, 2019. See also Papadogiannis 2015a, 214–16; Giovanopoulos and Dalakoglou 2011, 93–95.

something that he acknowledged to be somewhat of a paradox. These concerns affected his behaviour and his conduct at school:

> I spent another year in trouble at school. I could not become president of the class, as I had a record of bad conduct and was forbidden, so I had to sit at the very front desk in class. Apparently, I also did not get my prize that year. The last year they called me to get my prize I climbed up half of the stairs, spat and came back down. It was a peculiarity of mine. I wanted to be the top pupil and at the same time I did not want this to be publicly recognised. I did not want this fact [of being a good pupil] to create any privileges [...]. So, it was with great sadness that I then heard Papandreou's speech in '81, that he would abolish the riot police. What would I do? Why would I go to the university? What could anyone do at the university in a time of socialism?[56]

Ezekiel described his time at school humorously, providing me with a real glimpse of the atmosphere in which he grew up and the rebellious elements in his character that led him to disregard any "privileges." Papandreou's announcements for the forthcoming 'change' produced the mixed feelings that Ezekiel expressed in his humorous statement about socialism. When he moved to Thessaloniki to study, he started to become acquainted with new political spaces and to form his own identity within them:

> In any case, I have always operated within the frame of autonomy, obviously influenced by the Italian Autonomia, but in Greece autonomy is not directly correlated with that [...]. In reality it has to do... it is a mix of anarchy which, through libertarian communism, meets Marxist theory and vice versa, Marxist theory and libertarian communism meet organisations modelled on anarchy. [It retains] assembly-like elements, based on local intervention and not on a general future vision, not that that is absent. This means that it continuously feeds into a constant experimental thing. It is not a single model.[57]

The 'experimental character' of the endeavours that Ezekiel drew attention to were largely a response to the demands that were articulated by the new social movements and were related to initiatives that had been formed in many countries already in the late 1960s. During this time, the work of Antonio Gramsci and Henry Lefevre among others functioned as a source of inspiration for many of the new social movements that had started to emerge in Europe and America in response to the new conditions of political and social participation.[58] A different understanding of the 'public

---

56 Ezekiel Interview Extract: What Can One Do in Time of Socialism, 2011.

57 Ezekiel Interview Extract: Ideological Influences, 2011.

58 Vaiou-Hadjimichali and Hadjimichalis 2012, 70.

space' started to emerge in conjunction with the changing everyday experience.[59] One of the main issues was how citizens' rights could be restored within the public space, and how they could make use of the cultural space that the cities provided as a free space of mobilisation, a ground for both political and cultural fermentation. What these critiques stressed was how the *city* (aside from working places or the unions that one belonged to) could become an inclusive space through the creation of places that would function as political and cultural meeting points.[60] In Italy and Spain especially, after the regime-changes, such spaces and initiatives drew heavily on the Gramscian aspiration regarding the creation of "neighbourhood councils."[61] Those councils or associations implied a double recruitment of their members. People would both take part in their party or union, and also in the neighbourhood assemblies that promoted other issues related to the city and to people's daily life.[62]

Having an assembly as the main body of decision making, striving to advance emancipative demands, gaining as much support from society as they could and looking for a potential dynamic of the movement were all elements that Ezekiel considered important to his own political engagement. However, not all the initiatives he participated in during his youth had what he called a "majority-driven potentiality." That is to say, they had a restricted appeal:

> Yes, this is a paradox. Most part of my life I have spent in minority-oriented things. My first involvement [in the movement] was with the initiative for prisoners in 1985–1986. Yedi Kule was still functioning at that time and was a real hellhole; the prison in Kerkyra was the same. Of course, you will tell me now how majority-oriented this [endeavour] was. I always used to marry those things. On the one hand, I participated in the mass student movement but at the same time I belonged to collectivities whose overarching purpose was the element of human rights, the element of the universality of human rights.[63]

Ezekiel's first involvement in a political movement was in an initiative for the rights of prisoners. Yedi Kule was a central prison in Thessaloniki which shut down in 1989. This and Kerkyra (the prison in Corfu), were both notorious for cruelty and torments against prisoners. In 1985 a movement was started to raise awareness about the poor living conditions in prisons and the urgent need for reforms. These demands for a modernisation in the way prisons functioned after the dictatorial regime took their place alongside a number of similar demands that would lead to the overall modernisation of a number of aspects of social and political life (for example, there were

59 Vaiou-Hadjimichali and Hadjimichalis 2012, 56; See also Lefebvre 2005/1991.

60 Vaiou-Hadjimichali and Hadjimichalis 2012, 70; See also Castells 1983.

61 Hadjimichalis 2020, 145–46. Hoare and Smith 1986b.

62 Hadjimichalis 2018, 240–43.

63 Ezekiel Interview: Extract Minority-Oriented, 2011.

demands for a democratisation of the functioning of the public sector, and for the cleansing of the military and all affiliated sectors in the army and the police). Recalling his own standpoint regarding the demands that were formed at the time, Ezekiel positioned himself as follows:

> To have self-organised prisons, that's extreme humour, maybe even bad humour [...]. And evidently a part of it is better living conditions, and the most fundamental part is less prison sentences. So, I will negotiate in the direction of more probations. The main goal is less prison sentences. What you can easily get out of negotiations, which is better living conditions, you will turn down.[64]

Closely related to the issue of the prisoners' rights were certain thoughts Ezekiel had on the negotiation process when there is an inevitable inequality between the movement and the state. As he told me, he is "pro-negotiation, but not pro-dialogue":

> You do not engage in dialogue with the dominants, with the state. You do negotiate, however, with your opponents as [you negotiate] in every field of confrontation. [...] But obviously you do not engage in dialogue, since dialogue demands equality, and this is not to be found [in this setting].[65]

Ezekiel was also involved in the ecological movement, which had many of the same characteristics that he appreciated in the movement in general: its mass appeal, its direct-democratic organisational structure and a fresh view that strongly contrasted to the traditional far Left during the same period of time. As he pointed out with some hesitancy, it was a time in which the far Left showed some signs of an "introverted attitude":

> I remember the increase in the DAP's [the student youth group of New Democracy] membership at the university. It was overwhelming! And [I remember] this autistic, insular attitude of the far left, which could not see what was happening outside their own group, because the comrades and their interactions remained the same for years. It was amazing, especially when the Rangers, the armed divisions of the far-right extremists of Averof [the leader of the New Democracy party in 1981] clashed with the PASP [the student youth group of PASOK] and the KNE [the youth organisation of the Communist Party]. The rest (of the far-left organisations) still assumed that they [the Rangers] did not constitute a danger! You see this statement, that "someone or something does not constitute a danger" very often in the history of the Left from the interwar period onwards. Later on, when the ecological movement fragmented or degenerated into NGO directions, we kept in

64 Ezekiel Interview Extract: Prisons, 2011.

65 Ezekiel Interview Extract: Pro-Dialogue, 2011.

> friendly contact, and we broke [with them] (laughs). This, however, does not mean that we did not get influenced by it to a great extent.[66]

The polarisation of the youth organisations at the university reflected the prevailing social, political and ideological atmosphere.[67] It was not, however, only a matter of selective engagement in debates about what is worth taking action against. Primarily, the situation at the university reflected the great hostility that did not only exist among "bourgeois" organisations and those on the left-wing spectrum. It equally affected the relationships between members of the competing left-wing organisations. Charges and accusations from all sides, as well as violence between the various groups at the university was a common phenomenon.[68] The unbending attachment of people to their own particular groups and the identification of the members of other groups as 'enemies' (bourgeois, reformists, traitors, revisionists, anarchists, anarcho-autonomists and individualists, to use some of the vocabulary of the time) soon led Ezekiel to seek out alternative spaces.

The prisons movement and the ecological movement were two such spaces that attracted Ezekiel's interest. However, like Iakovos, Ezekiel emphasised the difficulty that those movements had in attracting a broader social majority at the time of their appearance, partly because of the political climate during the Metapolitefsi and partly because of PASOK's rise to power, but also because of a need in the left-wing organisations to re-orient themselves and adjust to the new demands of the time. It would take more than a decade for the character of these as well other endeavours to come to light. However, at the time, it seemed as if some parts of the leftist space had been decimated by the prospect of the domestic 'socialist change' and the large majority of leftist adherents felt that they had reached an impasse regarding the future direction of their political activism.

---

66 Ezekiel Interview Extract: The Left at the University, 2011.

67 On the political parties' discourses in the '80s and the civil-war-like atmosphere of the time, see Moshonas 1995, 173. See also Fitili 2015, 29–39; Clogg 2014. For an overview of the atmosphere amongst student groups and youth organisations at this time see Papadogiannis 2015a.

68 The night in the chemistry department in Athens where various groups had a violent confrontation with each other is still discussed now. For a description of the events of the time see the Journal of the youth student group commenting on the events in 1979, Progressive All-Student Unionist Camp 1980. For Photos and comments from the time, showing the violent climate among defenders of squatting and dissidents in 1979 see Kanali 2010. See also Papadogiannis 2015a, 214–15.

The Emergence of AuRA

A key factor in AuRA's emergence was the intensive nationalism and racism of the 1990s. The illusion of "national homogeneity"[69] meant that a context for the implementation of migration policies was lacking and a series of factors made it clear that action was necessary, in terms of both the legal frame within which the migration issue was approached, and of the representation of otherness within Greek society.

A Long-Forgotten Slogan

From the end of World War II until the beginning of the 1990s, Greece was essentially thought to be a monocultural country. It was believed to have achieved a remarkably high degree of "national homogeneity" and, moreover, it did not perceive itself as a host country for migrants.[70] The last decade of the twentieth century found the country consolidating its presence in the European Union, implementing significant modernising reforms, adopting Western values, and establishing a strong social welfare system.[71] At the same time though, there was a complicating factor: the unravelling of the Balkan communist regimes. On the one hand, there was a sense of national confidence and optimism over the country's potential for modernisation and financial growth, while on the other, the political instability following the collapse of communism in the Balkans and the breakup of Yugoslavia, along with the immigration issue, gave rise to feelings of national insecurity.[72] During this period, Greek nationalism assumed an intense form that led to an absolute refusal to acknowledge other populations within its national borders.[73]

One of the most important national issues of the period was a dispute over the use of the name Macedonia. After Yugoslavia's breakup, a federal region within the former Socialist Federal Republic of Yugoslavia, announced its independence under the name of the "Republic of Macedonia." The Greek state, fearing potential territorial claims, refused to recognise it.[74] On 14th February 1992, one million people gathered in Aristotle Square in Thessaloniki for one of the biggest demonstrations the city had seen. The speech given by the Mayor of Thessaloniki was characteristic of the period's nationalistic discourses, claiming that the 'rulers' of Skopje [The Republic of Macedonia] have tried to subjugate the Greek spirit, the continuity of the Greek nation and the great civilisation and traditions that had remained intact

69 Christopoulos 2001; Venturas 2009; Fragoudaki and Dragona 1997.

70 Venturas 2009; Christopoulos 2001; Petrinioti 1993; Triandafyllidou and Veikou 2002.

71 Voulgaris 2002; Voulgaris 2008; Avgeridis, Gazi, and Kornetis 2015b; Gazi 2015.

72 Voulgaris 2008, 337–39. For the Balkan states, see Veremis 2004; Koppa 1997.

73 Venturas 2004, 1994; Lipovats 1995; Triandafyllidou and Veikou 2002; Trumpeta 2000.

74 On the Macedonian issue see Walldén 2004; Veremis 2004, 147–64.

throughout the centuries, inviting the people gathered to say loud and proud that "Macedonia is us." He announced that Thessaloniki is the eternal capital of Macedonia and that it presented on that very day its own strength by the multitudinous gathering sending out the message that "Macedonia is one and it is Greek," another famous slogan of the period.[75]

The Mayor's speech was delivered in an already heavily emotionally charged climate. The idea of the sacredness, unity and timelessness of the Greek past, and the virtues of the Greek people, evoked an alleged 'cultural superiority' and 'historical stature' of the nation that contrasted strongly with the instability of the neighbouring Balkan states and provoked a passionate response from the gathered crowd. The emphasis on the "true Macedonians" and their strength ("δύναμη") reflected the "willingness of the nation" to protect its cultural heritage and verify its political power, as well as to consolidate a coherent and unified national identity.[76]

From a psychoanalytical point of view, we might say that the Macedonian issue evolved into a locus of what Lipovats has called "mythological thinking," a process that results in unresolved social problems being translated into national issues,[77] with the consequence that other nations appear to function as reminders of the nation's perceived deficiencies and are even held responsible for them. The Macedonian issue becomes the national problem par excellence, bringing to the surface the "fetishes" meant to make up for these deficiencies: the Greeks' superiority, the uniqueness of their ancient past, and the purity of the race.[78] The symbolic battle between the real deficiencies and the promotion of national virtues results in a 'divided identity' ("διχασμένη ταυτότητα") that engages in a painful effort to avoid confronting itself.[79] In this confrontation, a kind of knowledge about the self and the other is produced that cannot be other than stigmatised and elliptic, and is imbued with a constructed consciousness of national/racial origins and purity.[80] This results in the grandiose fantasies of the continuity of Greek culture, and the conception of the Greek past as 'a unified whole' certified by the underlying ideas of Hellenism and Greekness.[81] This view of the nation as a homogenised aggregate of 'relatives' who

---

75 For relevant material, videos, photos and commentaries on the day see Michani tou Xronou, n.d.; Psaras, 28/01/18.

76 Lekkas 1996, 146–47. On the issue of nationalism and national identity, see ibid, 139–62.

77 Lipovats 1995, 129. Lipovats also refers to the perpetuation of the mythological mentality ("η διαιώνιση της μυθολογικής νοοτροπίας"). Ibid, 128.

78 Lipovats 1995, 130.

79 Lipovats 1995, 130; see also Lipovats 1996, 185–99.

80 Bhabha 2012, 137–139. Bhabha explains this interplay of fetishism and the cultivation of stereotypes.

81 On the construction of a "cultural continuity" see Herzfeld 2020. See also Fragoudaki's contribution on the topic Fragoudaki 2013, 166–71 and Gazi's comment on it. Gazi 2015, 258. Further on the topic Christopoulos 2001, 57–80; Venturas 2009.

love their country allows for the introduction of defensive mechanisms to protect its interests.[82]

During this time, stereotypical representations of the Balkan states became more and more common in Greece.[83] The Balkan states were widely regarded as a single entity, and the fact that each of them constituted a separate historical reality was largely disregarded. As Todorava sees it, this "Balkanism" seemed to absolve the "West" of its "racism, colonialism and eurocentrism" in a process where the 'Balkan Other' served to contrast with the self-proclaimed 'civilised West.'[84] With reference to Greece, it is interesting to note that even though it shares a history with other Balkan states, it was skilfully exempted from the Balkan area, and there was a genuine effort from internal and external elites (since the time of independence) for the country to be included in the western sphere of influence and to disengage from everything it considered to be 'eastern,' 'uncivilised' or 'barbaric.'[85] This, of course, had certain implications for the political and ideological course of the country. As many scholars put it, the Greek nation has always wavered between feelings of national grandeur ("εθνικού μεγαλείου") and a sense of cultural inferiority ("πολιτισμικής κατωτερότητας") towards Europe[86] that perpetuated the vacillation between eastern and western ideals.[87] During this period, the Balkan states were considered to be a highly destabilising factor, condemning the region to constant political unrest, and this very fact strengthened the belief that Greek nationalism was more 'refined' than that of other nations.[88]

---

82 Fragoudaki 1997, 145–46.

83 Venturas 2004, 194–96; Trumpeta 2000, 149–153; 161–164.

84 Todorova 2009, 188; Todorova 1996, 62.

85 Todorova 1996, 105–6; Fragoudaki 1997. On the construction of Greek national identity and competing discourses on the topic see Herzfeld 2002a; Herzfeld refers to the idea of crypto-colonialism, which explains how the 'cultural superiority' that has been attributed to Greece in western representations was instrumentalised as the locus for the construction of financial dependencies. In the case of Greece this whole argument was based on the idea of antiquity, and the continuity of the modern Greek nation state from ancient times. Herzfeld 2002b.

86 Gazi 2015, 258. See also Fragoudaki 2013, 166–71; Herzfeld 2020, 27–28. See also Giakovaki 2006.

87 Voulgaris 2008, 347. See also Fragoudaki and Dragona 1997. This is an interesting study on how conceptions of the nation are presented in educational course books, and the way in which national identity, other identities and racism are approached through them. One interesting finding is the atypical system of hierarchy that seems arbitrary among those who are perceived as "superior" (central European industrial countries), and others who are "inferior" (for example the Ottoman Empire). Fragoudaki 1997, 168–70. See also Askouni 1997; Avdela 1997.

88 Trumpeta 2000, 166. Trumpeta refers to the positive representations of Greek migrants in contradistinction to other populations.

Thus, when Iakovos referred to "the deplorable year of 1991" and to the "national unanimity" it was these rallies concerning the Macedonian issue that he was thinking of. For Ezekiel, Iakovos and a small number of their comrades who found themselves at one of the Macedonian Name demonstrations, those moments were experienced as a great shock. Confronted with the huge crowd in one of the city's biggest squares, the "dissident," as Ezekiel called himself, experienced what he called "the violence of being an absolute minority":

> At least one and a half million people protested in Thessaloniki against the state of Macedonia, in one of the most horrifying events ever experienced by a dissident, who may not have experienced the violence of weapons but has experienced the violence of being an absolute minority – a trivial minority, so to speak. [...] it was one of the most horrifying moments, and you could hardly address society, [because] society would lynch you.[89]

The "violence of being an absolute minority" is meant to express a feeling. It expresses the feeling of absolute isolation. It is not physical but is rather an immaterial form of violence, a figurative punch in the stomach. To the group's eyes, the rally signified an absolute invalidation of reality. It demonstrated the power (or better, the irrational force) of a massive crowd chanting nationalist and isolationist slogans. Ezekiel speaks of the violence of marginalisation in an attempt to make sense of the situation they found themselves in – a situation in which they were a small minority subjected to the violence of being treated as a threat to the nation's interests and cohesion. Iakovos:

> There were schools participating in the demonstrations. They were organised, and the children were enjoying it. It was not only to miss the class. No, they felt it was for good. They participated, going around to hang posters [calling for the demonstration], in stores and in the entrances to buildings.[90]

The political discourse in Greece during the 1980s and early 1990s was shaped by nationalism, intense xenophobia and racism, in the form of a belief in their historical and cultural superiority, ethnic purity, historical significance and timeless existence. The main slogan from the Mayor's speech "there is only one Macedonia and it is Greek," applied not only to the national borders, but also to the national consciousness, and consequently to the self-determination of the populations residing within these borders. Over the course of the 1990s, the myth of "national homogeneity"[91] would start gradually falling apart. As Greece gradually received more and more mi-

89 Ezekiel Interview Extract: The Violence of Being a Trivial Minority, 2011.

90 Iakovos Interview Extract: Demonstrations 1991, 2011.

91 Christopoulos 2001, 58–66.

grants the majority of whom the state was reluctant to integrate or accept,[92] the conditions emerged for a conceptualisation of the issue of racism.

Racism

> In 1998, the annual festival in Athens was in its second year. The problems with migrants became too obvious, the racism especially against Albanians was really obvious. "Albanians are thieves," "murders" and that kind of thing. So, we discussed it and we decided we had to do something, a campaign, a concert. We could not organise a demonstration, but a concert we should be able to organise.[93]

During the years 1991 to 1997 Iakovos was to a large extent dedicated to the ecological and the conscientious objectors' movements. Having been engaged in the heated nationalist debates at the beginning of the 1990s and being faced with the marginalisation and isolation the anti-nationalists faced, the next few years would find him travelling abroad, engaging in coalitions and discussions with broader groups and initiatives. During this period, he spent a lot of time writing for journals and newspapers. Together with a small circle of comrades, he initiated the publication of a journal about conscientious objection. Their meetings took place in the office of the ecological movement he belonged to, a space that was also shared with other initiatives. By about 1998, the issue of racism had found its way into the discussions of all these groups as the one issue that now demanded some form of action. Let us now take a look at the rise of racism during this period, which provided the conditions and the impetus for anti-discriminatory and anti-racist campaigns in the second half of the decade.

Greece first became a host country for migrants at the end of the 1970s, but it was during the second half of the 1980s that immigration into the country intensified.[94] Yet during this time there was a widespread lack of public acknowledgement of the existence of migrants at all and by extension, this meant there was also a lack of acknowledgement of the rising existence of racism, xenophobia, and discriminating practices towards them. Furthermore, there was no implementation of proper policies to deal with the situation.[95] The prevailing impression was that there weren't

---

92 Triandafyllidou and Veikou 2002.

93 Iakovos Interview Extract: Racism, 2011.

94 Petrinioti 1993. During the same period, and more specifically in 1981, Greece becomes a full member of the European Economic Community (EEC), and research conducted on a European level produces the first data on racism and xenophobia in Europe. Trumpeta 2000, 156–57.

95 Kountouri 2016; Pavlou 2009; Pavlou and Christopoulos 2004; Pavlou and Skoulariki 2009; Trumpeta 2000; Petrinioti 1993; Marvakis, Parsanoglou, and Pavlou 2001; Triandafyllidou and Veikou 2002, 192–94.

that many migrants in the country,[96] allowing a belief in national homogeneity and unity to continue in a rapidly changing political and social landscape.[97] In terms of political practice and legislation, this translated into laws that completely ignored migrants in an effort to further enhance national cohesion. Indeed, there was no coherent immigration policy until 2001, while there were laws that actively encouraged people of Greek descent (especially Pontic Greeks and Albanian Greeks) to relocate to Greece, something that involved a redefinition of who is considered to be Greek as Triandafyllidou and Veikou put it.[98]

The myth of national homogeneity, the belief in cultural unity in Greece, the insistence that there were no migrants in the country and the resulting denial that there was a problem with rising racism were all prevalent in the 1980s and 1990s.[99] In media representations, the focus on 'security issues' and the perception of migration as a threat to the country's coherence and the citizens' well-being prevailed, both in political and religious discourses,[100] a situation that facilitated the absence of coherent policies or legal frameworks that would deal not only with ongoing migration itself, but also with the increasing number of migrant people who already resided in the country.

This legislative failure to adequately deal with migration further reinforced xenophobic attitudes and reproduced racism.[101] The political unwillingness to properly address the issue both perpetuated simplistic conceptions of national identity and failed to recognise the growing problem of racism.[102] Anna Fragoudaki describes the way in which many Greek citizens would understand racism and anti-racism. Racism seems to be the acknowledgement of an inferiority *which is objectively given* ("αντικειμενικά δεδομένη κατωτερότητα"), while anti-racism is rather an altruistic stance or a charitable sympathy ("φιλανθρωπική συμπάθεια") for those who are recognised as inferiors.[103] The power of Fragoudaki's definition lies in the ironic simplicity of the terms she uses.

---

96 Trumpeta 2000, 158.

97 Venturas 2004, 192–94.

98 Triandafyllidou and Veikou 2002, 191.

99 Christopoulos 2001.

100 Pavlou 2001. For a current discussion on this issue: Karyotis and Patrikios 2010.

101 Fragoudaki 2013, 85–114. Fragoudaki highlights some of the reasons why racism was a long-neglected issue. A characteristic example is that the first law granting Greek citizenship to the children of migrants was not introduced until 2010. Previously the children, many of whose parents had lived in the country for a long time, remained undocumented. In 2010, children who were born in Greece and whose parents had been living in Greece for five years were allowed citizenship. However, the implementation of law 2838/2010 turned out to be sporadic, as bureaucratic processes and enormous delays further hindered its implementation. See also Fragoudaki 2013, 86–90.

102 Fragoudaki 2013, 171–76.

103 Fragoudaki 2013, 171.

The 'objectively given inferiority' is actually made up of a wide range of *subjective evaluations* of the reasons behind what could be perceived as 'inferiority.' These evaluations may draw on biological or cultural assumptions or indicate institutional inequalities and structural asymmetries.[104] As Tsiakalos notes, in post-regime-change Greece, racism and xenophobia were regarded as two vastly different concepts. Racism was thought by most Greeks to be non-existent in the country because people widely associated it with past and faraway regimes (e.g. Nazism, Apartheid etc), as well as with violent acts.[105] Xenophobia by contrast, was seen as a legitimate feeling towards the foreign and the unknown.[106] Consequently, most people were not inclined to acknowledge racist discourses and forms of discrimination for what they were, and their belief in "their own inherent hospitality" and the nobility of Greek culture further reinforced the alleged incompatibility.[107]

During this time, the media played a decisive role in encouraging the propagation of false perceptions and stereotypes about migrants. Several studies conducted during this period highlighted the methodical way in which 'the Albanian' is represented as a threat to the security of the 'native' population.[108] In most news reports of the time, Albanians were consistently presented as criminals and blamed for an upsurge in crime,[109] while simultaneously being demonised as the main cause of allegedly rising rates of unemployment.[110] Nationality is treated as an indicator of moral integrity or lack thereof and it is taken to be a valid criterion for determining whether or not an individual has a proclivity to criminal behaviour.[111] In this way, migrant populations were consistently represented in terms of a dichotomy between the good self and the dangerous other,[112] mirroring the broader political dichotomy of Europe/Balkans (as civilised/savage),[113] when in fact the reality of the newly incoming migrants as well as the consolidation of the country's status as an EU member state highlighted the pressing need for modernised immigration policies.

---

104 On racism and anti-racism see the following literature Balibar and Wallerstein 1991; Gilroy 1999, 2002; Lentin 2004; Macedo and Gounari 2008; Miles 1999; Taquieff 1999; Weiss 2008; Modood 2015; Bonnett 1993; Bonnett 2015; Bulmer and Solomos 1999.

105 Tsiakalos 2006, 87–91; Trumpeta 2000, 161.

106 Tsiakalos 2006, 87–91; 97.

107 Trumpeta 2000, 161; Tsiakalos 2006, 89. On hospitality see Papataxiarchis 2014. Papataxiarchis refers to a hierarchical structure ("ιεραρχική δομή") which results in advantages for the one who offers hospitality and obligations for the one who receives it. Papataxiarchis 2015, xxi.

108 On media and constructed news see Pavlou 2001, 127–59; Kountouri 2016; Pavlou 2009.

109 Pavlou 2001, 127–162; Pavlou 2004, 39–87.

110 Kountouri 2016, 52.

111 Pavlou 2001, 135.

112 Trumpeta 2000, 166.

113 Todorova 1996, 113.

At the same time, NGOs, migrant communities, and a focus on human rights were starting to gradually reshape the discourses on anti-discrimination in civil society. Following the example of Athens, where initiatives had started to take action against racism in 1996, a small group in Thessaloniki started preparing to organise their own anti-racist campaign:

> Ezekiel: Yes, and we decided to do a public appearance immediately. We approached the Filipino association, there were some people from Bulgaria who were already some years in Greece and integrated, some political refugees and people from Albania, and we held the concert in Aristotle square. Shortly after, we decided to form AuRA. AuRA emerged as an assembly.[114]
>
> Iakovos: In June 1998 we organised the concert in Aristotle Square in Thessaloniki. This concert was later called 'the first AuRA festival'. You see, it's a matter of regulation, how you write history, it is ours to do with as we wish (laugh).
>
> Q: And what about the money?
>
> Iakovos: There was no money! We had some coupons.
>
> Q: Where did you meet?
>
> Iakovos: We met at the offices of the ecological group [we belonged to].[115]

During this time, it was usual for many groups and organisations to rent a place, or to use the office of an affiliated party or organisation, which would often serve as a meeting space for other initiatives as well. Being based at the office of particular groups restricted attendance at the meetings and discussions to a few comrades. This meant that recruitment had to take place outside of the offices, often at the university. AuRA called for a meeting between leftist organisations in Thessaloniki, in order to see if they were willing to support the initiative of the anti-racist concert. This idea of a concert that would exclusively address the issue of racism met with acceptance from broader leftist groups in the town. Iakovos:

> It was supported by a lot of organisations, other people joined it as well, there were people who supported the endeavour because they realised that it was an essential initiative. All this leftist, anarchist space, a lot of people embraced it [the initiative]. And they all managed to leave the stupidities aside, all those people who would fight over where to put a comma, they came and participated in the AuRA

114 Ezekiel Interview Extract: The Emergence of Assembly, 2011.

115 Iakovos Interview Extract: The Festival, 2011.

> festival, the AuRA concert [at this time]. It met with success and thus we decided to start meeting regularly. [...] In 1999 we decided to have a two-day festival, with all the elements of a festival.[116]

We can see here the variety of political backgrounds that came together on this occasion, and the firm political positions that had to be abandoned in favour of a new common objective. The decision to put on a similar event the next year was made after the murder of two migrants and the injury of another seven people. The perpetrator insisted on the patriotic motive behind his actions. The attacks came as a great shock to the majority of people, and the newly formed AuRA started to attract more members. Iakovos:

> Gradually more people joined, for various reasons. Times change, things change, some had kids. [...] Many people have come and gone from AuRA. And that's when it started, and it proved very important. Of course, we could not have known this from the start. David joined us while he was still at school, he got engaged in [the group]. After that we had a constant influx of new people that would undertake various tasks.[117]

Over the course of the next few years, the group would organise regular concerts at the university in Thessaloniki. It seemed that these first concerts partly realised the founding members' aspiration to create a platform that would unite broader political spaces. The agreement that those first concerts brought about between different political spaces created an optimism in the group regarding its future potentiality. What was considered to be important was the fact that the various groups that agreed to support the anti-racist campaigns that AuRA initiated also agreed to a certain extent that they would not enlarge upon other politically significant issues that remained in the exclusive scope of the distinct groups/organisations. In this way, a large number of left-leaning groups were united under the umbrella of anti-discriminatory, anti-racist action. Individuals, groups, organisations, migrant communities, and even political parties or their youth organisations would gradually start to support the endeavour.

What is The Movement?

As we have already seen, for quite a long time the activities that Ezekiel and Iakovos along with other comrades were initiating did not gain much attention from the broader society. This important issue had been expressed through their repeated

116 Iakovos Interview Extract: First Initiatives, 2011.

117 Iakovos Interview Extract New People, 2011.

statements about how minority or majority-oriented the endeavours they were devoting themselves to were. However, another mass mobilisation that would make a real difference to the way in which activists saw and organised themselves came at the beginning of 2000 with the anti-globalisation movement. Seattle, Porto Alegre, Genoa and Florence became landmarks in the re-emergence of collective endeavours, as activists, organisations, syndicates and movements became united in their opposition to war, neo-liberalism, imperialism, as well as in their vision of "a planetary society."[118] The initiatives born out of the massive demonstrations in Seattle aspired to challenge the neo-liberal aspects of globalisation from below, by joining forces against world capital. Using slogans such as "Another world is possible" and "People above profit" they created an open space for those who wished to fight for peace, equality and justice – a space built on the principles of diversity and pluralism.[119]

When the European Social Forum made its appearance in Florence, this provided the impetus for similar organisations in other European countries. The Initiative for the Greek Social Forum was established, and in 2003 the Greek movement welcomed international forums and groups in Thessaloniki on the occasion of the EU Summit meeting in Chalkidiki. This is held to be the beginning of a new period in which activists in Greece connected to other European groups and Forums to face the global issues of war, injustice and exploitation.

For the Greek participants especially, these endeavours seemed to open up new fields of action, serving as an antidote to the lack of purpose the Greek Left had inherited from the 1990s. Iakovos found people's eagerness to join the Greek Social Forum very promising:

> Well, after that, I became engaged in the Forum. The Forum is promising, really promising. What we're witnessing in Athens, with the Indignants, resembles the Forum in many ways [...]. There was a great gamut of people, from people who were socially aware but not left-wing and wanted to protest the war – in 2003, the most prominent issue was the war in Iraq – to SEK [Socialist Workers Party] members, the guy selling the newspaper ("Buy Labour Solidarity," "I will if I feel like it" (laughs), the Jehovah's witnesses of the movement...). We did very well for some time; I mean, in '03, the Forum's demonstrations were bigger than Communist Party's demonstrations [the KKE] – they far surpassed the KKE's in size.[120]

He notes that at the time, the Forum boasted a wide appeal; it was a dynamic initiative that brought together people from the entire political spectrum who wanted

118 WSF Document 2001, para.1.

119 WSF Document 2001. For an overview of the movement, see Seoane and Taddei 2002; Portaliou 2007; Teivainen 2002; Vaiou-Hadjimichali and Hadjimichalis 2012, 224–28.

120 Iakovos Interview Extract: The Forum, 2011.

to declare their opposition to the war in Iraq, as well as their support for anti-globalisation endeavours. Fedonas was a younger participant who became involved in activism while still at school, in the squatting scene of the late 1990s. The demonstrations in Genoa (2001) and Florence (2002) were two of the most memorable experiences of his life:

> I also went to Genoa with the same people. With the same people – I mean, we were all on one bus [mentions everyone's name]. It was very intense, Genoa; I mean, it was all quite simply very intense! I was young, too young to be able to grasp what was happening, to understand things. Now I see it differently. Those were the biggest marches I've ever been on. No, wait, that wasn't in Genoa; the biggest march I've ever been on was in Florence – one million people. Genoa was something unprecedented for everyone. Essentially, it was after Genoa that the Forum was created. [...] And Florence was... if we set aside all the procedures we had to go through, the march [in Florence] was eight, ten, fifteen kilometres long – I mean, it covered a very long distance. We were meant to march to a stadium, where there would be a concert. Even after the head of the march had entered the stadium, there were still trains coming [into the city], full of people who wanted to join the rally. The organisers said there was one million people; the authorities said there were 500,000 people minimum – basically 700,000 – 800,000. What a feeling [to be there with so many people]![121]

For Fedonas, who had been very active in the city where he had studied, and who with a few comrades had initiated their own anti-racist group, the mass appeal of the movement on an international scale and the know-how of foreign organisations were the two things that struck him the most. The Greek participants seemed to gain a renewed sense of purpose from these international movements. The Greek movement now had the chance to reclaim its relevance. During this period there was a shift towards a new, broader movement-oriented type of co-ordination, involving extensive networking and engaging with all sorts of people but still with an emphasis on local intervention. At the same time a different relationship to the idea of the "city as an object of contestation"[122] was being formed. As Portaliou pointed out, both the European and the Greek initiatives of the time expressed the possibility of "another perception of unity and inclusion among cities and within every city in particular" by restoring "grassroots communication."[123]

Ezekiel treats the founding of the Forum as a great moment in AuRA's history, as it allowed its members to reshape their priorities. AuRA had a leading role in the demonstration to raise awareness about migrants' rights, which took place on the

121 Fedonas Interview Extract: Genoa, Florence, 2011.
122 Portaliou 2007, 165.
123 Portaliou 2007, 171.

second day of protests against the EU Summit in Thessaloniki in 2003. However, the protesters' main goal was to cancel, or at least interrupt, the EU-Summit meeting in Marmaras, Chalkidiki. With a kind of frustration, Ezekiel recalled the different assessments of the movement's success in June 2003. Although the protests were considered to be successful, at a certain point the "symbolic dimension" was emphasised by the organisers, as a way of compensating for the fact that the movement had fallen short of expectations regarding its ultimate goal, namely the cancellation of the EU Summit:

> This was a shift [from the true demand] to the field of the symbolic. And the truth [the true demand] was to go and cancel this [EU-Summit] meeting in the 'ironclad' Marmaras, some kilometres away from here [Thessaloniki]. So, the over-emphasis placed on the symbolic field came mainly in order to veil this weakness, or lack of will-power to face reality.[124]

Ezekiel refers here to the fact that protesters did not in the end interrupt the meeting and that the protests did not exhibit a more agonistic stance. In these terms, although there were a great number of participants in the demonstrations, the ultimate goal was not achieved.

It is necessary at this point to clarify some of the group's vocabulary. The main focus of this research is the evolution and functioning of AuRA, which was initiated at the end of the nineties and achieved a new level of appeal and success with the opening of its new centre, the Sanctuary, which we will discuss in detail in the following chapters. One of the main issues that I would like to briefly look at is the use and the meaning of the term 'movement' in the group's vocabulary and how it is related to the different groups that may be said to be a part of it. Even a seemingly straightforward question such as which groups are part of the movement and which are not, cannot be provided with a simple answer, since this was a shifting situation, and any answer would be very soon outdated. In the context of the meeting in Thessaloniki in 2003 the 'movement' refers to all the organisations and groups that were participating in the international, anti-war and anti-globalisation protests.

Sometimes these self-evident questions were not welcomed by the participants of the group. Self-evident questions provoked hesitancy. On my part, I had the impression that out of these spontaneous definitions that were used on a daily basis, one could better grasp how the world of their action was conceptualised by the members. These spontaneous responses revealed a lot about the common-sensical categories that activists use in their daily reality without really paying attention to them. For this reason, I often left the question "what is the movement for you?" (among other "what is" questions) until towards the end of my conversations with my interlocutors.

124 Ezekiel Interview Extract: The Field of the Symbolic, 2011.

Fedonas: [After a prolonged silence] Many things; something peculiar; something that rises above you, and something you rise above; something that demands justice.[125]

Evdokia: Ha! What is the movement? What is it to me? It's the need to take your life into your own hands – that's what it is. Without any of it coming from above. [...] And I think that, right now, it's the most active part of society. I mean, if there's any hope for change, or for something different, it lies with the movements and the people participating in them.[126]

Stefanos: Action.[127]

Generally, the term 'movement' seemed to evoke a sense of belonging to the members of the group, although its exact meaning, in terms of the subjectivities it refers to, varies depending on the socio-political context of each group's activities. Thus, in the case of AuRA, the 'movement' is usually regarded by its participants as the sum total of various left-wing organisations; it is open, diverse, internationalised, anti-nationalist, anti-war, and anti-racist, and aspires to include as many people as possible. Thus, 'movement' is a condensed form, used when individuals want to refer to all those abstract principles that inform their activism, and it usually goes beyond any member's particular affiliation with smaller groups. As such, one could say "the movement demands justice." It constructs a collective 'we'. The movement lies in the power of people, it mobilises, it resists, comes from below, and it is insubordinate.

The movement is a "frame" as Collins put it.[128] The idea of the movement is to be found as far back as the 1960s in the emerging new social movements. Being unable to draw clear cut distinctions between the various tendencies of the civil rights movement, the hippies, and the anti-war movement, since all these practices and ideas were overlapping, participants tended to refer to all of them collectively as the "movement" or the "space."[129] I will use the term 'space' in a similar way throughout this book as more or less interchangeable with 'movement.'[130] But I will try to avoid

125 Fedonas Interview Extract: What is the Movement, 2011.

126 Evdokia Interview Extract: What is the Movement, 2013.

127 Stefanos Interview Extract: What is the Movement, 2013.

128 Collins 2001, 39.

129 Collins 2001, 38. For the idea of "space," see also Vaiou-Hadjimichali and Hadjimichalis 2012.

130 The "movement" and the "movement-oriented things" came up very often in my discussions with the participants and my comments here serve only as a preliminary note on the vocabulary used by the group. The "what is the movement" question will recur in Chapter Six to give us an idea of how the concept further frames strategies, action and ideology. For the time being, however, I would like to focus on the translation of the terms that frame the movement in the Greek usage. I will keep referring to "*κινηματικά πράγματα*" (kinimatika pragmata, movement-oriented issues) and to "*κινηματικός*" (kinimatikos, people who belong to

any further categorisation,[131] keeping instead to terms that my interlocutors themselves use, and through which they understand their daily interactions. Preserving, using and understanding the group's own terminology is important if we are to have any sense of the feeling people have of their own participation in the movement.

The European Social Forum, the participation of members of AuRA in the Greek Social Forum, the participation in the demonstrations of Genoa and Florence among other cities, and the preparation of the meetings in Thessaloniki in 2003 gave rise to a fresh sense of enthusiasm that spread throughout the collectives and gave them further impetus regarding future collective action. It was a time of the internationalisation of action. AuRA and the Greek movement generally both aspired to meet the goals of the broader European and global communities and to further radicalise their action in view of their common struggles. What one has to observe here is that despite the heterogeneous nature of those distinct endeavours, their major contribution is that they stress an interconnectedness and interdependence of the local movements with international demands. In this sense the anti-globalisation movement in its broad and heterogeneous synthesis presented a new form of opposition to global capitalism.[132]

During this period, a heated debate opened up within the movement regarding rights, their universality and the need to protect and defend the rights of marginalised populations within Greek society. The question of how rights were to be defended provoked a wide range of reactions, with the discourses of various left-wing organisations opposing the discourse of the NGOs.[133] While they were both

---

the movement) as adjectives that describe the kind of action and other qualities that my interlocutors refer to.

131 I would like to briefly clarify the all-inclusive terms "parliamentary Left" and "non-parliamentary" or "extra-parliamentary Left." As we have seen, there was a long tradition of leftist organisations in Greece, each with their own history, tradition and evolution (Trotskyists, Maoists, anarchists, socialists among others). The "parliamentary Left" describes the main parties that had a parliamentary presence, although this did not remain unchanged throughout the years we are investigating. For the description of these broader left-wing collectives there are several terms in use: "extra-parliamentary Left," "non-parliamentary Left," "anti-establishment Left," "ultra-Left," "far Left," "revolutionary Left" and so on. However, the groups and collectives these terms refer to occupy a wide ideological spectrum and cannot be subsumed under one and the same category, considering their organisational complexity, their distinctive courses, their past heritage, their decision-making processes, and their stance towards resistance. At the same time, the various groups' respective levels of proximity to or distance from the traditional ideals of the Left are subjects of constant negotiation and even conflict among their members.

132 Vaiou-Hadjimichali and Hadjimichalis 2012, 227–28.

133 Vasilaki's research goes in depth into the different stances adopted by a variety of organisations and the different understandings developed with reference to rights and their protection during the said period. Vasilaki 2017, 10–11.

oriented towards supporting the same groups of people (migrants, refugees, ethnic minorities), they did so from a range of different perspectives and sometimes even opposite standpoints. The NGOs foregrounded identity politics and focused their efforts on ensuring that cultural differences were respected, and every minority group (be it ethnic or cultural) was protected.[134] Even though this approach had often proved useful in helping defend difference (it has led the state to acknowledge minorities, ensure their rights and help them integrate), it ultimately failed to address the underlying problems. For example, it often seemed to avoid the issue of 'race' by speaking instead in terms of 'culture,' thus allowing 'cultural differences' to serve as an alibi for covert racist tendencies. As some scholars have noted, the separation between racial and cultural arguments is not only dangerous, but also artificial:

> A language of culture and values has almost completely supplanted one of race, but the effects of such a language, couched though it often is in relativist terms, produces racial dividends: division, hierarchy, exclusion.[135]

This approach caters to the dominant culture, legitimises neo-conservative, neo-racist attitudes, and serves to keep minorities within the confines of their own communities – even if only inadvertently.[136] The discussion about the replacement of the category of race with that of culture has been theorised in terms of a universalist ("Universalismus") versus a culturalist position ("Kulturalismus").[137] As Schiffauer notes, this debate often obscures possible solutions to the problems of repression and power, as well as blurring the boundaries when it comes to the position of various communities within a dominant culture. At the same time both positions take the term culture to be the main problem. As Schiffauer suggests, a conceptualisation of culture that would respond effectively to this problem should always bear in mind two things: on the one hand we should think of culture *as if* it was a "closed system of standards and rules," and on the other hand, we should think of it *as if* it was always "in a state of flux/in progress."[138]

---

134 Vasilaki 2017, 14–15. On the uses of the notion of multiculturalism in connection to these issues, see Agelopoulos 2015.

135 Lentin and Titley 2011, 62.

136 For more literature on these debates see Taylor 1997; Walzer 2001; Delanty 2003, 78–79; Bauman 1993, 39–53; Bhambra and Margree 2006; Yioka 2006; Kyriakakis and Michailidou 2006.

137 Schiffauer 1997, 144–56.

138 Schiffauer 1997, 149. My translation. In Schiffauer's words: "Kultur [...] muß einmal betrachtet werden, *als ob* sie ein vergleichsweise geschlossenes System von Standards und Regeln darstellte, und zum anderen, *als ob* sie ständig im Fluß wäre. In gewissem Sinn muß die Kulturanalyse deshalb verfahren wie die Physik, die einmal die Teilchen – und ein andermal die Wellennatur des Lichtes ins Auge faßt." Schiffauer 1997, 149. Emphasis in original.

In lieu of any legal framework for migrants' integration (the first law that addressed this need only came in 2005), both NGOs and movements stressed the urgent need for action to be undertaken with reference to migrants communities and minority issues.[139] Many of the organisations of the Left were highly critical of the state and its mechanisms, a fact that contrasted them with what was often considered to be the 'depoliticising stance' of NGOs who often overemphasised 'cultural identity' and failed to recognise the real issues of class and inequality.[140] Ezekiel expresses his view on the subject:

> Rights come into the class struggle as an autonomous element. They do not constitute a complete theory, but they create the appropriate conditions for a better constitution of the subject and for the betterment of the subject's position within the class struggle, and it is only in this way that the struggle for rights is legitimised. Otherwise in the case of NGOs [the struggle for rights] exhausts itself in an occasional participation, which means [it exhausts itself] in privileges. [In the NGOs] there is a monolithically institutional orientation and not a social one.[141]

Ezekiel was very sceptical about "defending rights" in the way the NGOs do, although as he admitted during our discussion, it took him some time until he formulated any concrete ideas on the topic. The "struggle for rights," in his opinion, is an autonomous field of action, which leads to an enhancement of people's position in the class struggle. Otherwise, the struggle for rights lacks legitimisation and tends to advance a positive discriminatory policy (it "exhausts itself in privileges"), while underneath this ground of social and political awareness, participation and equality remains uncultivated.

The debate on human rights centred on educational and health issues, especially due to the lack of a legal framework that would be delivered for the first time in 2005.[142] Members of AuRA attempted to address some of the problems that arose from the limitations of the preventative migration policy that was in place until 2005 by offering volunteer language courses in the small hangout where they were housed at the time. The intention was to provide migrants with an alternative way to become familiarised with the Greek language, and to cultivate a feeling of belonging within an inclusive place, a feeling that would gradually start to be communicated to others, thus having a broader positive effect.

The institutional framework followed a year later, in 2005. Law 3386/2005 was the first coherent attempt to regulate issues of entry, residency and work permits

139 Chryssochoou 2009. Chryssochoou eloquently analyses different understandings of integration.

140 Vasilaki 2017, 25.

141 Ezekiel Interview Extract: Rights, 2011.

142 LAW NO. 3386 2005.

for non-Greek residents, and stressed the necessity for migrants to become an integral part of Greek society. The law highlighted the importance of language for this aim to be achieved, and the need for migrants to familiarise themselves with Greek history and culture as well as with the contemporary Greek lifestyle – all of which were considered to be basic parameters defining social integration.[143]

During this period groups that focussed on social and political rights, or with the rights of prisoners were the most common in the small hangout where AuRA was based. Over the next few years, many new members joined AuRA and in 2004 the idea for the language-lesson groups for migrants and their children emerged, following similar initiatives in Athens. The language courses provided migrants with the chance to meet new people, to come together with others, and to start feeling more like an integral part of society. At the same time, the idea started to develop that they should actively engage migrants in handling their own business, and support them in starting to assert their rights themselves in order to enable them to build the proper conditions for a better life.

Evdokia recalled the discussions in which people were urging that AuRA should find a larger space that could house all their activities, as the appeal of the group was steadily growing.

> I was looking for something more active and direct in comparison to the youth organisation [I belonged to] which was restricted in an office at the time. And I found this in my first assembly with AuRA and since then I have never actually left![144]

As we will see in Chapter Four, the decisive characteristics of the group was its anti-hierarchical structure, its openness, its horizontal networking, its great receptivity when it came to accepting external influences and its capacity to engage with a variety of actors in the city. At the same time, the broad anti-racist framework that the group maintained would raise its popularity in the town over the next few years. The small hangout was one of the first of its kind in the city that was actually legal rather than squatted,[145] and it would soon have a predominant role in Thessaloniki in working with migrants and their rights.

---

143 LAW NO. 3386 2005, Section 12, Article 66, p.56: "The actions and measures taken within the framework of the Integrated Plan aim at the successful integration of third country nationals into Hellenic society and mainly cover the following fields: certified knowledge of the Greek language, successful attendance of introductory courses about the history, culture and lifestyle of Hellenic society, integration in the Hellenic labor market and active social participation."

144 Evdokia Interview Extract: First Assembly, 2013.

145 Daliou 2015, 52–58. Squatting was quite popular in Athens, although less so in Thessaloniki which only had a total of five squats at the beginning of the 1990s.

A plethora of new social demands emerged during this period, demands that were not only synced with global developments, but also contributed to a politicisation of the debate on migration and human rights. This opened up a new chapter in the way Greek society would start to thematise and respond to issues of racism and xenophobia, and to reconsider the phenomenon of migration on a more fruitful ground. Various organisations engaged with the migration issue and challenged hegemonic discourses and practices by prompting a discussion on migrant rights, by undertaking initiatives and anti-racist campaigns and by gradually establishing spaces that would function as shelters from racism, xenophobia and exclusion, as well as promoting inclusion and integration in a meaningful way. Before focussing on one such place – the Sanctuary – in the next chapter, I would like to briefly mention one final moment that played a part in its emergence.

December 2009

My first visit to the Sanctuary coincided with the anniversary of the December Revolt.[146] The revolt was prompted by the death of a young schoolboy who was shot by a police officer on 6th December, 2008 in the quarter of Exarheia, in Athens. The reasons for the shooting were not properly investigated, and a riot broke out on the very same night with protests, occupations of public buildings and conflicts with the police carrying on until Christmas. Thousands of young people, students, unemployed people, workers and migrants in many cities participated in the demonstrations. The media interpreted the revolt as indicative of a deeper-rooted political crisis which in essence emanated from the economic difficulties facing the "generation of 700€" (a label indicative of the low salaries in Greece), widespread political corruption (many scandals had been brought to the fore over the year) and the Greek people's overall disappointment and anxiety over the future.[147] The remarkable thing about the December demonstrations was not only the large scale of people's participation in them, but also the fact that the participants were not of a specific national, political, or social background. In other words, it was not just the students, the leftists, the migrants or any other particular group that protested, but a considerably diverse crowd were urged to express a generalised discontent at the deplorable loss of the child. The December movement was massive and multifarious. Enriched with slogans ranging from the sharp to the provocatively humorous ("the state murders,"

146 Vradis and Dalakoglou 2011; Kallianos 2012; Douzinas 2011; Kallianos 2011; Hadjimichalis 2018.

147 Left Voice, December 21, 2008.

"your democracy stinks like your teargases," "Christmas is postponed, we lie under revolt") the riots went on for almost twenty days.[148]

The riots of December seemed to have paved the way for the emergence of new activist ventures. It was often argued that the December revolt stimulated "a diverse crowd" to flood the streets in protest;[149] it gave rise to new concerns and led to a subversion of established certainties and convictions. As Kallianos insightfully claimed, December equalled "the unexpected event."[150] On the one hand it involved a much broader demographic than would usually participate in such movements, including many people who didn't have any previous knowledge or experience of similar modes of resistance, and on the other hand, it was "a point of excess/surplus in time": it functioned "out of the domain of the past, the present, and the "forthcoming.""[151] December 2008 marked a new political landscape and a new condition in radical politics and collective action.[152]

My first visits to the Sanctuary in December 2009, some months before the official outset of my research there, coincided with the anniversary of the December Revolt. The members of AuRA together with other collectives and groups, participated in a commemoration march. It seemed, however, that in the city something had been changing over the last year. During this period an anarchist centre had made its appearance in Thessaloniki. On their internet page they directly related the creation of the centre to the events of December. For them, direct democracy, freedom, and an active participation in the co-shaping of the future were the main characteristics of the new endeavour they initiated. The Sanctuary, on the other hand, appeared to present a more reconciling face. They also took the decision to base all their actions at a spacious location, stating the need for broader spaces of inclusion to emerge within the city, where resistance and action would take the form of an everyday experience, and where everyone could participate in them.

148 Vulliamy and Smith, February 22, 2009.

149 Douzinas 2011, 187–220.

150 Kallianos 2011, 153.

151 Kallianos 2011, 159; 153.

152 Vradis and Dalakoglou 2011.

4. Solidarity is Us

> It was when the guys had moved into the new space and painted the walls! I was shocked, a huge space, very differently structured [from the previous one], and a great risk for us at the time. Well, the Sanctuary came very quickly to life; it was framed by a lot of people, a fact that we had never imagined in the past – and not only people but [it was framed] by activities as well, it was an orgasm of creativity at that time.[1]

This chapter introduces us to the Sanctuary, which was established in 2009. While AuRA had held its meetings in a place it shared with other collectives since 2004, the need for more space in which they could host different activities accompanied the group's intention "to become more extroverted," as Evdokia put it. After the founding of the Sanctuary, she observed a "massive movement of exodus" of centres, squats and places, attracting more and more "non-initiated people," showing their "effort to integrate in the real life of the city."[2]

What was so unique about the Sanctuary then, that it should become an example that other similar organisations would imitate? What was new about the new place? I will start this chapter by introducing the Sanctuary as the main hub for all the initiatives and actions of AuRA. I will also focus on the assemblies as the main sites of decision-making, and on the annual festival that was prepared throughout the year. Through the daily interactions within the Sanctuary, the collectives and individuals that were housed there restructured a familiar atmosphere for themselves, whether members, newcomers, or friends. The main impression one acquired when first visiting the Sanctuary was of people's effort to creatively restructure relationships and communications in such a way that everyone would feel welcomed. We will observe the processes through which feelings of belonging and a home-like atmosphere are consolidated for all the participants. In short, the new world of the community of the Sanctuary is analysed in terms of its alternative vision, that aspires to keep individual needs and the community's life in congruity.

1 Evdokia Interview Extract: Moving In, 2013.

2 Evdokia Interview Extract: Moving In, 2013.

Figure 1: The Sanctuary and the participant groups according to thematic areas.[3]

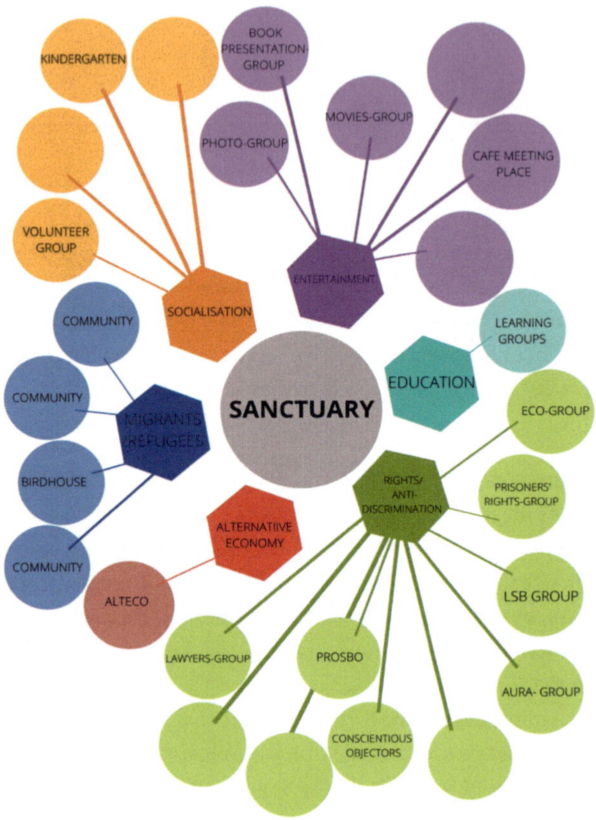

The Sanctuary

The Sanctuary was to be the space where all these aspirations would be actualised, and where solidarity would function as a cohesive force towards the realisation of the group's vision. A pamphlet of the Sanctuary elaborated on the group's function: a self-organised place, open to locals (*ντόπιους*), refugees and migrants, a place that

3 While this graphic cannot exhaust the participant groups as those were under constant change, it does show some of the basic groups and collectives that participated in the Sanctuary during 2010–2011. Most of the groups held weekly assemblies which offered a space of exchange, discussion, and decision-making, as well as taking part in the general assembly of the Sanctuary which also met on a weekly basis to discuss issues related to the overall functioning of the place. The empty circles indicate that new groups were always on the horizon.

is multicultural, pluralist and above all solidarious (αλληλέγγυο). It is described as a continual festival, hosting events, book presentations, music and cuisines from around the world, which expresses the group's aspiration *to fit many worlds into a single one*.[4]

The Sanctuary provided the overall structure within which various groups, including AuRA would coexist and function. My initial impression of the Sanctuary was of a place where people could hang out and come back to on a daily basis. It was a place where the neighbourhood could find shelter, where different people could become acquainted with each other, and where interaction could unfold at a slow relaxed pace, unaffected by the tense, alienating, neurotically fast-paced urban environment. The habitués are what we would call 'nonchalant' and their attention is hardly ever focused on who comes and who goes; people casually say "hi" and exchange a few words summarising the news of the day.

With a general greeting addressing everyone and no-one in particular, the people crossing the Sanctuary's threshold immediately dispensed with formalities and effectively paved the way for relations to form. There was no pressure to recognise who people were or to hastily ascribe identities to those present. The Sanctuary accommodated social relations of a different sort. There was nothing about the place or the looks of people that could spawn the usual reflexive reactions of curiosity or even scrutiny of any newcomers. The place itself did not have anything pretentious about it, or anything even remotely suggesting that materialistic concerns played any role in determining its identity. Apart from the colourful walls, a few posters and photos, and some information pamphlets, one could hardly spot anything sophisticated in the lighting, the chairs, the tables, the way things were arranged. Here, it was the people, not the objects, that filled the place with their uniqueness and constituted the scenery: small groups forming circles and talking, or solitary newcomers awkwardly trying to fit into the general cosy atmosphere.

People moved around the place freely, as if they were at home, and didn't seem to be concerned with observing or being observed by others. Whether sat around the tables, sat at the bar, or moving around the corridors of the Sanctuary, nobody seemed to take particular notice of anyone. People made their orders or even served themselves since a note on the tables told them that "the place is self-regulated." The volunteers in charge of the bar contributed by serving others, but only to the extent that it was necessary in order to help them understand how they should learn to fulfil their own needs. The same principles applied when it came to entertainment.

On AuRA's website, I read that the new Sanctuary is meant to be a space of active solidarity; against market exploitation, against racism, against sexism and any form of repressive power. Equal participation, volunteering and self-organisation are among the key words, contrasted with profit, dependency and sponsorship, to

4 Pamphlet of the Sanctuary, 2010b.

which the group expresses its strong opposition. They introduce themselves as a 'social centre' (and not as a political group or assembly) which houses groups and activities and remains open to all contributions and new ideas.[5]

The Sanctuary was an attempt to put into practice the appeal for a return to more personal and intimate conditions of interaction. The first impression when one entered the place was that it very much resembled a traditional coffeehouse. The traditional neighbourhood coffeehouses, usually found in the village square, were places where fellows came together, shared their table, and connected. The kind of companionship that people found in coffeehouses emphasised an equality in the relationships between them.[6] During the 'alcohol rituals,' as Papataxiarchis puts it, people (and in the case of traditional coffeeshops men) express a more "authentic" self, and their identities are not representative of social positions and disparities, but rather stress equality ("ισότητα") and commonality ("ομοιότητα").[7]

The "world of the coffeehouse" contrasts sharply with other modern urban meeting places. Commenting on the different qualities of interaction in modern Greece, one scholar observes, that in an environment characterised by constant changes on all levels, individuals tend to break their life into continually smaller pieces[8] and increasingly concentrate on their connection with the material world. At the same time, they find it impossible to manage their leisure time, since the pressures of everyday life and the pace of public life spawn a tension which cannot be decompressed through socialising.[9] On the contrary, modern social gatherings impose on individuals a compulsory conformity to endless roles, essentially hindering them from truly living their life.[10] Modern entertainment was perceived as a novelty in Greece, which further intensified the incapacity for a true participation in social life. According to Karapostolis' critique, modern entertainment in Greece remains a source of ceaseless pressure for impression management and a constant coercion into acting out social roles and meaninglessly projecting instrumentally constructed identities, which people promote in order to meet the requirements of modern gatherings.[11]

Karapostolis' work comes out of the same scholarly tradition that in the late 1980s opened up the discussion about the existence of a fluid 'objective world'

5 Page of the group, 14 April 2010.
6 Papataxiarchis 2006, 231–40.
7 Papataxiarchis 2006, 237.
8 Karapostolis 1987, 140. Karapostolis uses the term detail-ised "λεπτομεροποιήθηκε" to describe the fragmentation that characterises everyday life with uncertain institutional frames and a constant need to produce new knowledge in order to remain functional. See ibid, 28.
9 Karapostolis 1987, 147–148.
10 Ibid, 148.
11 Ibid, 80–85.

regarding the way individuals organise their lives in Greece;[12] a world that leads individuals to draw conclusions regarding the stances and behaviours they encounter based on the memory of a 'shared lineage' and common sensibilities.[13] According to this kind of popular critique, which called for processes of increased modernisation in Greece, the idea of the 'objective world' is largely founded on an emotional certainty of the homogeneity of a people, and manifests itself in every interaction with others and with institutions.[14] At the same time those characteristics constitute the only stable and certain sources of typical knowledge. This critique is particularly relevant to what came to be defined as the "culture of the Metapolitefsi."[15] As one theorist commented, the 1980s and 1990s were to a great extent characterised by fast growing individuation, a voracious pursuit of personal growth and well-being, a generalised atmosphere of disinterest in social affairs and a general feeling of abiding progress.[16] This critique revolved around the consumer culture that replaced the overarching politicisation that had prevailed for the last two decades. The culture of Metapolitefsi signified a period in which everything was going well, and people could live in the certainty of affluence and stability, despite the surrounding social and institutional uncertainties.[17] Within this frame, theorists often interpreted the 'weak modernisation' of Greece in terms both of a 'lack of law,' and a lack of willingness on the part of civilians to adjust to any rules that would regulate the fields of social and political organisation.[18]

The idea of the Sanctuary seemed to me to approach these concerns from a different perspective. The Sanctuary provided an opportunity for people to reset their modes of interaction to something more authentic and tackled the issues of social life by offering alternative modes of entertainment and consumption while simultaneously constructing a frame of political education. It established a ground on

---

12 Karapostolis 1987, 27–28. See also Tsoukalas 2017/1993; Diamandouros 2014. For an overview of the debates surrounding weak modernisation in Greece, see Kouki and Liakos 2015. See also Featherstone 2006.

13 Karapostolis 1987, 72–73.

14 See also Tsoukalas 2017/1993, 24.

15 For the idea of political culture see Demertzls 1995; For an overview of the Metapolitefsi time see Avgeridis, Gazi, and Kornetis 2015b. See also Voulgaris 2019.

16 Panagiotopoulos 2015, 352. See also Panagiotopoulos and Vamvakas 2014: These scholars suggest that the 'elliptic modernisation' argument does not suffice in order to understand the development of the country and its people, nor to explain the crisis. Their suggestion revolves around important aspects of people's daily experience. By looking closer at the development of certain institutions, such as the nuclear family, mass media and consumption, they argue that one can better observe both traditional and modern elements which in their interplay reveal the processes of social modernisation in Greece. Panagiotopoulos and Vamvakas 2014, 119–27.

17 For the schemata stability/instability and security/insecurity see Panagiotopoulos 2015.

18 Tsoukalas 2017/1993, 23.

which individuals and society itself could re-approach certainties they had taken for granted, such as commercialism and the idea of affluence. In contrast, then, to the old ideas and models of public gathering and entertainment that Karapostolis and others were criticising, the Sanctuary provided a space that fulfilled the demand for more authentic interrelationships and communication. The emergence of the Sanctuary demonstrated in practical terms that the political works through personal. In this sense, the aim to unite political concerns with personal needs was embodied in a very tangible way in the life of the Sanctuary. The members of the Sanctuary were exploring an alternative way of being that centred on self-organisation, responsibility, and togetherness in the construction of a world that would include many different cultures, individuals, and groups. These values were represented in the humbleness of the Sanctuary itself, and in the way that human interaction regained its meaning and importance in the context of solidarity. In this sense, the members' suggestion for active solidarity heavily contrasted with the mainstream presumptions about how individuals organise their lives and arrange their obligations. Conversation, dialogue, calmness, mutual understanding and responsibility were all affirmed on an everyday basis, as steps towards a future possible world, with the Sanctuary operating as the model within which all these alternative preparations for 'a society to come' took place.[19] The patterns of interaction in the Sanctuary provided an alternative to the general sense of confusion from out of which Greek society was said to reproduce its structures and certainties, its institutions, and the knowledge of and about its members. In opposition to the alienating social relations which prevailed in the modern urban world, solidarity could be seen as a kind of anti-ethics, in which tiny everyday transformations show the path to a more convincing and permanent transformation.

A minor, yet very illustrative detail in this respect is the fact that within the group the plural form ("the plural form of politeness," as it is called in Greek) was never used to address someone. All members were considered equal – on the basis of their humanity, their solidarity, their companionship, and their shared wish to transform the 'outside world.' The members would generally address each other as "comrade" or "fellow," a straightforward term, that connoted walking alongside each other on an alternative path. By highlighting the intimacy of communication, this formula allowed people to avoid the use of redundant more elaborate characterisations relating to the professional, the personal, or any other type of identity. This also reflected the movement's answer to the predominant sense of hypocrisy that would ascribe value and social status through the use of the 'correct' language in order to represent someone's identity. The constituent elements of the members' interactions consisted rather in the gradual cultivation of personal relations, based on trust and intimacy.

19 The society to come was a common expression in the Sanctuary.

The new Sanctuary was perfectly in tune with the grounding principles of AuRA. It was a place where locals, migrants, refugees and migrant communities could freely meet, exchange their views, and cooperate on concrete tasks. By creating an open space of exchange between various groups and individuals, it allowed all of the parties involved to come closer to each other and to have an equal share in decision making. People cooperated on campaigns that pertained to the issue of anti-racism, promoting anti-discriminatory policies, and the protection of fundamental rights. During the first years of its existence, considerable efforts were devoted to attracting individuals, groups and migrants' communities to join the Sanctuary. Gradually the place developed a great dynamic, adding groups that ran a variety of courses (on music, computers, photography, and literature).

The creation and maintenance of the Sanctuary added to the responsibilities assumed by AuRA, among which was the preservation of the refugees' shelter, the Birdhouse. The running of the Birdhouse was taken over by AuRA in 2010, after it had been abandoned by the non-governmental organisation that had supported it for no less than ten years. The Birdhouse sheltered more than seventy people from Somalia, Afghanistan, and Pakistan. The preservation of the Birdhouse by AuRA was an ambitious project that required significant volunteer support, but also generated financial and organisational problems that ultimately led to its closure two years later. However, the Birdhouse was an important point of reference in people's discussions and concerns over the first two years of the Sanctuary's existence, and the running of the Birdhouse was a central responsibility of AuRA during this time.

The Sanctuary was a rather new and complex phenomenon in the city, due to its horizontal organisation, wide-ranging networks, and its approach to building relationships and recruitment patterns. The project was "self-organised," "open," and beyond any specific political commitments. It was a project that aspired to host various activities, and foremost to create not only a safe zone for migrants, communities and individuals, but also a broader communication platform between them. It aspired to create a world that "encompassed various other worlds" as one of its pamphlets described it.[20]

The responsibility for running the Sanctuary rotated between various groups on a weekly basis. Each group took turns in welcoming its friends and visitors, and in hosting important one-off events: documentary shows, book presentations, open discussions – all held in parallel with the regular assemblies and the language courses. As there were no individual or group contributions, the costs for the rent and the various activities were mostly covered by the small café, and thus the proper functioning of this aspect of the Sanctuary was a high priority for all the participating groups.

20 Pamphlet of the Sanctuary 2011.

At the beginning of my research, as a newcomer to the place I mostly participated in the assembly of AuRA, and when necessary in other assemblies, or ad hoc meetings that I attended through my acquaintances in these first years. Let us now take a look at how these assemblies were organised.

Figure 2: Major Tasks during 2010–2011.

The Assembly

AuRA's weekly assembly was the official gathering of the group's members. It was the platform where all the weekly issues were discussed, where people's activities were prepared, and solutions to problems were elaborated. It provided an open space of dialogue, exchange, and inspiration. Participants used to gather in one of the rooms of the Sanctuary, usually forming a circle which allowed everyone to look into the eyes of their interlocutors. At the beginning of the assembly someone would announce their willingness to take the minutes, which were later distributed via email to the rest of the participants. The purpose of this unofficial role of writing and disseminating the minutes was to keep all the participants of the group informed about decisions, priorities, and unfinished tasks for the forthcoming week, and highlighted the open character of the gatherings. While attendance at the assemblies was not obligatory, all members of the group had to update themselves later and be able to express their opinions on the crucial issues. Each group had their own assembly, date of meeting and internal email list. At the same time, the Sanctuary had a general assembly which was responsible for the overall functioning of the place, and which involved all the groups that participated in the Sanctuary. Everyone could join this assembly as a friend or a participant of the Sanctuary. Thus, most of the people who participated in AuRA were members of the Sanctuary's assembly as well.

> Evdokia: What interested me the most was the hierarchy issue, and this was one of the reasons that I stayed in the Sanctuary and its groups [...] the way decisions were made and their implementation.[21]

> Anthi: What I really liked from the beginning was the open assembly.[22]

The nature of the assembly as the main body for collective decision making was characterised by what Ezekiel termed "an obsession with the anti-hierarchical structure of AuRA." Many participants spoke of how they had also been members of parties, groups and collectives that had much more rigid organisational structures, or followed certain (political) lines which discouraged them from participating further: "Yes, I did not like waiting for the texts to reach Thessaloniki from Athens, when all we had to do was approve them," said Evdokia when I asked how her participation in AuRA and the Sanctuary compared to her previous experiences. The open assembly provided an opportunity for all the members to equally take part in decision-making, and this had an immediate effect on their desire to join the group. Participation had a direct, obvious, and binding function for the members, and thus established a greater commitment towards the group. This commitment was what some members interpreted as "devotion."

Iakovos spoke of this devotion, as he told me about the younger generation's enthusiasm when participating in the assemblies. Alkyone's weekly "hyperactivity" seemed to mesmerise him, and he vividly described his confusion when it came to Alkyone's presence in the group. He had a sense that she had always been part of the group, which left him wondering what provoked such a thought and led him to consider the new generation as one that takes its role seriously:

> And I asked Alkyone, since I was rather confused: "Alkyone you have participated in the group for two years?" It is as if she has always been here. She knows she has not, we know that she has not, but a meeting of AuRA without her [seems impossible]. "Who is going to keep the minutes"? We miss Alkyone! This does not mean that previously we did not take minutes. Everybody has done this job, but her hyperactivity has really saved us. Nobody can do what she does, nobody from the people I know in AuRA can do it in the way she does [...]. She really seems to

21 Evdokia Interview Extract: Anti-Hierarchy, 2013.

22 Anthi Interview Extract: Assembly, 2011.

> enjoy this [writing of the minutes] and it is incredible, do you understand? It is much better![23]

Alkyone's job was not only to take minutes during the assemblies but also to type them and email them to everybody, a task that she did with clarity and efficiency and was greatly appreciated by the other members. Some years later, I had the chance to ask Alkyone why she believed her presence in the group was considered so necessary, and how she felt about hearing how much the members valued her contribution. With a smile of pleasure, she admitted that she had never attended a class at the university during the years of her participation in the Sanctuary, and her 'visits' to the university were restricted to each semester's exams. However, as she told me, "the university I actually attended was far greater," implying that her constant participation in the Sanctuary during the years of her studies greatly surpassed any academic studies in terms of her acquiring knowledge and experience. Despite her heavy daily schedule with numerous voluntary roles at the Sanctuary, she also volunteered at the Birdhouse, and participated regularly in the assemblies of various groups.

This was not at all unusual: many people used to participate in a lot of the assemblies. Apart from AuRA's assembly and the Sanctuary's assembly, many of my interlocutors also participated in the Birdhouse's assembly and the teachers' assembly, with most of them attending a total of at least two or three regular weekly assemblies. Laura:

> I am part of AuRA, but I also engage in the lesson-group that offers lessons to migrants. There are also the kids from the Birdhouse [that I have a relation to], and lessons for anyone who may need help at school. Then, I am also part of the prisoners' rights group. When we organise activities in the kindergarten, I also have to be there. Among my responsibilities is participating in certain groups in the Sanctuary and taking part in all the processes that I have to in order for the Sanctuary to exist. I also follow the assemblies of the objectors sometimes.[24]

This multiplicity of belongings was something that fascinated me at the beginning of my research. Gradually I started to realise how these belongings, and as such these multiple identifications that each individual maintained, simultaneously cultivated a sense of openness and flexibility as they provided members with the freedom to choose more than one field or area of affiliation, and thus created a more open sense of what 'devotion' was. This also resulted in the great difference that many members felt when they compared the Sanctuary and AuRA to their previous experiences of groups. Often these would be youth organisations affiliated to a particular party, in

23 Iakovos Interview Extract: Minutes, 2011.

24 Laura Interview Extract: Participations, 2013.

which one felt obliged to follow its rules and was always aware that they exclusively belonged to this monolithic organisation. In this sense, however fragmented or incoherent the multiple belongings at the Sanctuary may have felt at times, and however hard members found it to remain devoted to all these different groups with the same intensity, the 'multi-belongingness' that the Sanctuary cultivated nevertheless provided a valuable experience that the older groups did not: allowing a constant re-negotiation of members' identities (which were multiple, fragmented and flexible) and creating even stronger ties to each other and to the Sanctuary.

The assemblies would start late in the afternoon or in the evening on fixed days and were open to all who wanted to join them. In order for the schedules of the multiple assemblies to not clash with each other, an extensive plan of activities, dates and times was provided every September when the Sanctuary opened its doors to its friends and visitors. People announced which groups they were interested in attending and declared their availability for certain undertakings. The beginning of an assembly was initiated by an unofficial gesture, a "let's go!" (*πάμε!*) – and was accompanied by coffees, drinks, and many cigarettes. It seemed like after an exhaustive working day the assembly was more akin to the relaxing atmosphere of a family gathering than a meeting, a kind of home to which members returned, sharing the day's experiences, and exchanging their news. The weekly assembly was a time of contemplation and reflexion, as well as one of planning and scheduling upcoming activities. The assemblies cultivated a culture of dialogue. People learned to be patient, to express their opinions, and they experienced a sense of equality which strengthened the bonds between them. However, assemblies were not just a relaxing evening activity. They were also a time of dispute and disagreement, of conflict and argument. But overall, the frequent attendance of the assembly was one of the ways people became familiar with the group and gradually integrated into it.

The most frequently discussed issues related to the functioning of the group, its participation in internal and external initiatives and campaigns, and any current disputes and problems that the members needed to discuss and confront. Towards the spring the assemblies focused on the preparations for the summer festival, setting up the agenda for the festival's activities. Thematic groups were established and undertook the task of organising the various aspects of the festival: the cuisine group, the group responsible for events at the festival, the writing team, the banners group, the theatre group, and the group responsible for the music were just some of the many groups that were responsible for the festival's success. People announced their interest and availability to participate in one or several groups. There were people who were eager to engage in the construction of the stands and kiosks for the festival, others who were keen on writing the texts that would accompany the various activities, others who presented a more artistic disposition, and the teachers from the Sanctuary were ready to welcome the kids in the festival kindergarten.

Shortly before the creation of the festival's poster, the group invited various organisations and groups to participate in the festival by setting up their own space or activity. A general call of interest resulted in various meetings with groups in the city that wished to take part in the festival, either in public debates on topics of interest to them (migration, specific initiatives, issues related to work conditions, human rights, anti-racism, and so on), or in the workshops that would take place in the festival, or to simply help out. After the general call addressing all the groups that may have an interest in participating, several assemblies followed which finalised the festival's line-up. The groups, organisations, parties and other collectives who were interested, were invited to sign the poster of the group to confirm their participation, and to discuss their availability and plan of engagement in the activities of the festival. There were groups who wanted to present or suggest a particular discussion panel, others who wanted to engage in a workshop, and others who were simply present during the three days of the festival, so that visitors could have personal contact with them as representatives of their group.

The Festival

The festival is the group's public face, an open invitation to the broader society to familiarise themselves with the projects, activities and ideas of the group. According to a pamphlet advertising the festival, the main concerns that year were migrants' struggles for freedom, and a recognised legal status, and people's dignity (both for locals and migrants). At the same time, the group's main aspiration was to experiment in a creative way with how a world without exploitation, exclusion and repression could be. The pamphlet evoked a joyful atmosphere, offering vivid pictures of what a festival means: discussing and deciding together, playing music, setting up the site, participating in theatrical and musical performances, sharing beers and celebrating.[25] The open dialogue and the atmosphere of joy was what allowed anyone to have access to this project and were the reasons for many people joining AuRA and becoming part of its diverse initiatives.

The official launch was planned, as always, for one of the weekends at the end of June or the beginning of July. However, the festival began one week earlier for the members of the group, who engaged in the intense activity of preparation from Monday morning till the official opening on Friday afternoon. Volunteers and members of various groups worked enthusiastically to transform the chosen space into a festival venue.[26] A lot of effort and attention was put into every detail, since the mood and the satisfaction of the public would depend on the atmosphere they themselves

25 Pamphlet of the Sanctuary 2010a.

26 In the first years of my participation the festival took place in a park in the centre of the city, but later it moved to an old army camp, which was on the west site of the city, a fact that was

created. The preparatory week was a time of intensive activity for everyone who wished to participate, making sure that everything was ready for when the wider public arrived at the official opening of the festival.

During the preparations, the activities and jobs started early in the morning and for a lot of people did not end until the night. There was usually a lunch break that was offered to all volunteers. The days of the festival were a great celebration for everyone involved. It was an opportunity to socialise with acquaintances and friends, and to identify with people who have common interests and social aims. It also provided a great opportunity for the group to assess their strength in the city, to form new coalitions, and to gather together with other groups and set an annual agenda that would follow up the social and political issues they discussed. Some members described the festival as a "political irritation," since it breaks with the norms and the rules of a well-ordered social reality, poses questions, and allows alliances to be formed. The festival is the "event of the year" and, as one participant told me: "it is debated, expected, organised."

The selection of slogans and themes, the preparation of the press releases that accompanied the festival, and the distribution of crucial information about the festival were all strenuous jobs that intensively engaged people in the preparation of this "great feast" as they often called it. The slogans of the annual festival were painted on banners which decorated the spaces that hosted the festival every year. The groups that wished to participate signed the poster, declared their availability, and thereby placed themselves on the map of the festival.

All these groups contributed to create a space for interaction, offering visitors a lot of parallel activities that took place simultaneously. People could participate in a public discussion on subjects such as migration, civil or human rights, touching upon political and social issues. Others could join a workshop, follow a theatrical performance, enjoy a photography exhibition, or simply walk around the different kiosks of the festival, discussing with representatives of various organisations and groups what it was they were trying to achieve. At the same time various local cuisines were on offer from the two bars that were usually set up during the festival with the voluntary participation of various groups and individuals. As the festival is a 'co-organisation,' the participation of every single volunteer is considered highly important. From the very first day of the preparations, where people help in arranging the place and constructing the kiosks, the kitchen, the bar or the stages, right until the very last day when the space will be cleaned and everyone will have collected up every single bit of litter, the festival is a celebration of voluntary engagement.

The Sanctuary, the assemblies, the various groups' meetings and activities – all formed the broader space of daily activity, which the festival solemnised. These ac-

---

considered important as the festival could attract people from areas where the right-wing had a lot of support.

tivities inspired a constant change in the participants and in how they related to the spaces in which they took place: such places become cosy, familiar topoi (*τόποι*), while the members, through their daily interactions with the diverse groups and individuals involved, become flexible, open and even more extroverted. The festival, like the Sanctuary itself, allowed its members to no longer be restricted to their own specific, small group: their activities could now address wider audiences, seek to mobilise a greater majority, and encourage more people to become part of their alternative vision. Egalitarian relationships, horizontality, and self-organisation were all part of a new type of engagement which differed dramatically both from the older projects that we saw in Chapter Three and from the kind of organisations that newer participants were once members of. This was not a quest for political or ideological identity; it was a quest for an open space of dialogue and exchange in the heart of the city, where everyone could have free access, feel creative, engage in communal activities and practice 'active solidarity.' It offered an opportunity for the formation and consolidation of personal relationships of all kinds, and not only those that were interwoven with a political cause. It aspired to become a place where everyone could feel at ease with being visible and proud to be heard, a place where everyone could feel confident in their power to effect a positive change, to assume responsibility and take immediate action.

In the following pages, I will discuss this unique connection between individual needs and the group's overall objective, a connection that members often referred to as distinguishing AuRA and the Sanctuary from past and also current endeavours. Consideration will be given to the enthusiasm with which individuals adapted to the pace of the group and made sense of the way it functions, and to the way they evaluated both their contribution to it and the group's influence on them. How was the Sanctuary perceived by its participants? What distinguished AuRA from other enterprises? Was it the solidarity that appeared to be the driving force behind it? How were people integrated and socialised into the group? Let us look at what they themselves had to say on these questions.

"Solidarity is Us"

Let us now take a look at some of the ways in which the idea of solidarity came up during discussions with my interlocutors, especially in connection to the Sanctuary during the first period of my research (2010–2011). We will see how an image of the Sanctuary as people's new home emerges, with solidarity being the fundamental principle that guides their interactions in the group. For many members of AuRA, the Sanctuary succeeded in consolidating intimate, friendly, everyday relationships which imbued solidarity with meaning. It gave them a feeling of belonging, in many cases encouraging them to re-write their biography by placing emphasis on their participation in the movement and by re-assessing their identity in relation to the function of this alternative community. It is these aspects of the members' devotion and participation I now wish to examine, focussing on three main points: people's feelings of belonging to AuRA and the Sanctuary, their consolidation of the new world that the Sanctuary and the group offers them, and the aspirations that stem from the idea of solidarity.

A New Home

The old apartment-block in the city centre where the Sanctuary occupied the first floor gave visitors the impression that they were entering a household-like place from the moment they started up the first few stairs. Indeed, the Sanctuary presented a very homely environment; familiarity and friendship, quarrels and teasing, were all part of life at the Sanctuary, which created a welcoming atmosphere for all those who chose to spend time there, whether engaging in the organised activities, or simply hanging around. In our conversations, the members of the group often described the place and the people involved in it as their "home" or "family." Valia:

> It feels like home to me. And when I say home, I mean home; very, very intimate, that is, and intimate in that I can go there and, let's say, get some sleep, or hang out, or start screaming, or start laughing...[27]

Valia had already been engaged in AuRA for more than a year, and although she had never been part of a collective before, she had immediately felt at home with AuRA, the Sanctuary and the Birdhouse, all three being close to her interests at the time. Valia's family had themselves experienced racism, and after her studies she had decided that she wanted to work with migrants and was searching for organisations that provided such an opportunity. Soon, a friend of hers invited her to visit a new place that was offering language courses to migrants, and in this way she discovered the Sanctuary. Anthi, a very close friend of Valia expressed a similar feeling about the place:

> To me, it feels like a really big family, which has its pros and cons, because there are some relatives that you love, some that you love and appreciate, and then, there are some whom you care about, yet barely tolerate; so, this is a very big family, really...[28]

Anthi was one of the more prominent figures one would meet in the Sanctuary, as she had been engaged in AuRA since 2007, participating in the old hangout and especially in the group for prisoners' rights. She told me how it had taken her some

27 Valia Interview Extract: Home, 2011.

28 Anthi Interview Extract: Family, 2011.

time to find "the right group for her," one that would combine those elements that she considered important. For a long time, she had been looking for an anti-racist group that did not belong to any political party or youth organisation, since for her autonomy was an important criterion:

> AuRA could function as an umbrella group because it could cover other organisations as well [...]. As such you can be an autonomous member of AuRA without participating simultaneously in another organisation or having to tow a strict party line.[29]

Her account of her feelings about the Sanctuary and AuRA often struck a chord with her friends and comrades, as when she spoke about her participation in the new endeavour:

> And I always have this feeling, that out of my participation in all this, I get so much, which unfortunately one cannot describe, cannot... present to anyone who considers this whole situation arduous, who thinks it takes away from your life, from your time, from your personal life, while to you, this is your personal life, it really is... Your life without this part, without solidarity, is really empty. I mean, to all those people who usually criticise my involvement in these things, I honestly wish they could have this sense of solidarity and the sense of completeness it brings about whether the outcome is positive or not, even if they could only experience it for one moment.[30]

We can see here how Anthi's perspective changed as she became integrated into the group, resulting in a strong contrast between her perception of how people saw the Sanctuary from the outside, as something that drains its members of their time and energy and takes them away from their life, and how it is viewed by the members themselves, for whom the Sanctuary actually *was* their life, providing them with a sense of completeness and satisfaction that they couldn't find in the world outside. Rather than giving or sacrificing anything to AuRA, Anthi understands herself as gaining from it: participation in a solidarious frame like AuRA or the Sanctuary counterbalances emptiness and loneliness and leads to feelings of fulfilment. For Anthi, the idea of a "personal life" outside of the group's solidarity lacks meaning – and the outsiders who fail to recognise this when they imagine (from their perspective) how she must be feeling, are contrasted to the new friends and comrades she had found in the Sanctuary who share her perspective. Anthi:

> For example, when the power at the Birdhouse was cut off and we spent hours standing outside, there was nothing we could do – it was Peter who would restore

29 Anthi Interview Extract: AuRA and Autonomy, 2011.

30 Anthi Interview Extract: Solidarity, 2011.

> electricity; but we would all be there, we would all help so that electricity at the Birdhouse would be restored, and we would wash people's clothes at our house, because they do not have a washing machine, and [what mattered was] this whole feeling that we are becoming one and that there is neither personal time, nor personal space, because... because right now all this needs to be set aside and we need to work as a team.[31]

What we get from Anthi is an insider view of how solidarity is experienced in day-to-day interactions, with people participating enthusiastically in all the various issues that arise. Regardless of whether these issues concerned collective goals or minor everyday problems, the members felt the imperative need to be there, to be informed, and to be active. They did not experience their engagement as anything special, and they certainly did not see their participation in terms of personal loss or gain. Nor did they participate in order to establish contacts that might be useful in the future, or in order to put on their curriculum vitae an activity that, in the language of the market, would translate as 'participation in public affairs' (as was the case with some of the volunteers, as we will see in Chapter Five). Instead, many members felt 'privileged' to have seen 'the true light,' a solidarious way of life which they opposed to the individualistic and materialistic values of the outside world. The material world appears less important as a source of joy and fulfilment, when compared to the members' affirmation of the new values that they found in the Sanctuary.

One thing that Anthi's comment reminded me of was Paul Tillich's considerations about the peculiar balance or interdependence between the "courage to be as oneself" and "the courage to be as a part" of something broader.[32] Tillich argues that "individuation and participation" are correlated, in the same way that the self and the world are.[33] Taking part in something can take different forms: it may signal "sharing," or "having something in common," or "being part of something," but what all these forms have in common is the meaning of participation as "a partial identity and a partial non-identity."[34] For Tillich, who was interested in the implications of this double nature of participation in a theological context, the question it raised was how can one be part of a whole without losing oneself, as is often the case when it comes to adherents and followers? In the context of the Sanctuary, the partial 'loss' of self, involved in the participation in the group, was a positive response to what the members saw as the alienating nature of modern relationships and the modern way of life. In this sense, their participation in the Sanctuary acted as a corrective to this, by forming a more authentic relationship both with the group they belong to and with themselves.

31 Anthi Interview Extract: Personal Time, 2011.

32 Tillich 2000, 89–90.

33 Tillich 2000, 88.

34 Tillich 2000, 88.

Hence, the participation, the willingness to offer, the physical presence, and the everyday interest in the life of the group were not considered to be a sacrifice; on the contrary, they signified for those involved a form of liberation from the precarious conditions for self-actualisations of the world outside it.[35] The members processed their need to contribute to collective life within the frame of mutuality and a socially necessary reciprocity. From Ezekiel's perspective, it was precisely their being in the group that rendered life worth living:

> Well, that is, the movement [is] my life, my life [is] the movement, and this includes AuRA as well. To be honest I do not have a life outside the movement.[36]

I heard a lot of statements like this during my time at the Sanctuary. Anthi's comment that there is *"neither personal space, nor personal time"* was another one – and I gave this aspect of participation a lot of thought over a long period of time. Early on in my research, the members' stories often gave rise to a certain amount of scepticism due to what seemed at the time to be an overly utopian vision and a uniformity in their expectation for a better future to come. I was reminded of Kollakowski's comments on the kind of irrational appeal of many utopian projects which essentially mean the abolition of the individual's creativity, uniqueness, and freedom.[37] We might expect to encounter something like this in the case of fanatics, be they religious or political. What I later realised was that without having previous experience in the sort of feelings that stem from this kind of commitment, it was rather difficult for me to grasp the depth, the seriousness, and the existential weight that those feelings had in people's lives, not to mention the reality to which they corresponded. Some of my first attempts to sympathise with the concerns of the members about the group and its function were far from successful. One night, while I was waiting to meet some members who had to solve a problem that suddenly broke out in the Birdhouse, I took the following notes:

> The movement needs its participants at every moment, every moment something new arises, and everything that arises has the status of urgent. The first time I found myself in the group, every moment seemed the wrong moment to pose a question. It seemed rather indiscreet on my part to pose questions to simply fulfil the research requirement. It seemed arrogant on my part to have the kind of luxury to engage in research, while others engaged in real jobs. Moreover, it somehow undermined the stress that members experienced with reference to the tasks they had to accomplish or the pressure of responsibility they felt during this accomplishment. Questions had a meaning if they sprang out of your position as a

35 Ibid; see also Berger 1961.

36 Ezekiel Interview Extract: My life – The Movement, 2011.

37 Kolakowski 1997, 131–45.

> participant, if they were practical and short, and promoted collective aims. I had a similar feeling today. Anthi called me to inform me about the problem and the delay we would have. I asked her "how bad is the situation?" And Anthi replied: "Really bad! Anyhow, don't worry, we will have time for what we planned." I tried to express my concern about the situation they faced in the Birdhouse, but my question had already been perceived as concerned with how long I had to wait, probably because of my clumsiness.[38]

The passion and ardour with which the participants described their experience at the Sanctuary demonstrated the extent to which it took precedence over their past as if they should not only distance themselves from, but also forget their past life in order to be successfully re-socialised.[39] Their new life entailed a new home, a new family, and new people surrounding them and inspiring a sense of belonging, while also offering safety and protection similar to the primary structures of trust that are found within the more conventional setting of families.[40] The shared values and daily practices formed part of the new 'plausible world,' the new life which sustained its coherence through the Sanctuary, AuRA and all the affiliated initiatives to which one belonged, as well as through the new important people in one's life, who helped one to renounce the old world and to create solid foundations for the creation and the consolidation of the new one.

A New Life

When asking people to describe the key moments in their process of becoming part of the group, two types of incidents kept coming up. The first one, which we have already briefly discussed above, was comprised of everyday events which confirmed structures of trust between the members. The second was comprised of incidents that reinforced their convictions regarding the enterprise as a whole. Alkyone gives her own example of an everyday experience of the first kind:

> One incident I will never forget [took place] at the festival, when... it was when I stressed over... I had taken the bike with me, I think, and I feared... during the first two or three days, I feared that the kids would fight over the bike and that I'd lose it at some point –something like that, let's say. And I remember that on Tuesday, while we were organising the festival, in the afternoon, the kids had all come to me

38 Personal Notes: *Exercising Emotions*, 2011.

39 Berger and Luckmann write: "This involves a reinterpretation of past biography *in toto*, following the formula, 'Then I *thought*... now I *know*'." Berger and Luckmann 1991, 179. Emphasis in original. See also Berger 1961, 23–47.

40 Berger and Luckmann 1991, 174–78. See also Kleinman 1996. Kleinman's research is very telling in terms of the family bonds formed within communities.

> to announce that they had made a program and they would ride it in turns, that they wouldn't fight anymore. Because at the playground... when I worked at the playground, we had a problem like this – "I want the red pen," "I want it, too" – and I had to explain to them that "not all of us can take the red one" and "you will take the green one this time" and so on... Things like that... And when they came to me at the festival, I told them "kids, the bike... I'll give it to you, but I fear that you'll fight over it and everything, and you'll get yourselves hurt etc." And they came back on the third day – I remember it was the third day [of the festival], I'll never forget it – and they said: "Alkyone, can I tell you something?", it was Fikret who came to talk to me, and he said... um... "we'll ride it in turns," and all that, so I gave it to them. But there's more to it: at eight o'clock at night, when they left, I found it locked, and they had given the key to one of us, I don't remember whom, and they gave it to me, which... that was really impossible. I realised, at that moment, that we understand each other.[41]

Such cases, although seemingly insignificant in their scale, are highly illustrative in that they clearly demonstrate how trust among the participants was established, through little everyday interactions and experiences, confirming that the time and effort invested in the collective yields results. Stories about children's accomplishments were very popular among the teachers who were volunteering either at the Sanctuary or the Birdhouse at the time. What overwhelmed Alkyone when the children made sure her bike was safely locked up was not just the children's achievement in acting so responsibly, but more the affirmation this provided of the structures and principles on which she has founded her faith in the group and its values. It is this kind of affirmation that produces meaning for her and for the community. It is a "genuine understanding" – to use Schutz's terminology – that has definite influences on the way people decide to act further.[42]

The second kind of incidents that people often referred to as important to their becoming part of the group were those that reinforced their convictions regarding the enterprise as a whole. Valia's feeling of belonging arose especially when she encountered people whom the group sought to support. The group's visit to a detention centre, the group's support of the hunger strike of 300 migrants in Thessaloniki,[43] and other events functioned for her catalytically. Valia:

> What I meant to say was... that, essentially, it was three things that made me... how should I put it? One thing that made me feel part of this group that's called

41 Alkyone Interview Extract: Events, 2011.

42 Schutz 1972, 113–16. Schutz was assuming a ground of simultaneity where thoughts and actions seem to coincide, and which allows for an "interpersonal relationship" to be developed. See also Walsh 1972, xxv.

43 The hunger strike is also discussed in Chapter Six.

> AuRA... was the Birdhouse, [...] [it was] a catalyst. Then, in terms of action, I also felt a lot of things... okay, apart from the festival... I'm putting that aside... it was at Evros, when we went where Frontex is, where it was... The feeling was unbelievable, really unbelievable for me at least, I don't know. This thing... Seeing another person behind the bars, yelling. [...] To me it was really shocking, seeing the people inside shouting "Freedom" while we were outside. This solidarity, I mean, and the companionship of those moments, with the inside and the outside, but to such an extent and with such power, to me it was huge. Those moments. [...] It was... it was those moments, outside the detention centre, it was those moments, clearly. And then, it was the [hunger] strike... So, it was three incidents about which you feel that... that they make you think differently... I don't know how to express it... But, anyway, they were very intense, meaning they change your... no, not change; they bring order to your thoughts, they do not even change your... they bring... at least, to me... they brought order to my thoughts... I don't know, I'm rambling now...[44]

For Valia, experiences like AuRA's visit to the detention centre were defining moments in her decision to become part of the group. She recalled those moments as a transformative stage that altered her perception of companionship and gave real meaning to the idea of solidarity. The strong emotions people experienced in situations of this sort functioned as a transitory phase that allowed them to 'abandon' the old world in favour of a new more desirable one, perhaps more authentic, or perhaps one that simply made sense to them. In this case, people's decisive contribution manifested itself right in front of them: they see their aspirations intersecting with those of the group, thus solidifying their faith in both themselves and the group. The impact that experiences such as these have on members allowed them to make sense of their own participation in the group as a reflective, continuous process, which had a 'revelatory' character. The impact of such an event or a revelatory moment greatly surpassed the previous experiences of the individuals and revealed new unexpected or unthought of structures of plausibility.[45]

Similar experiences have been described in anthropological terms as *rites of passage*.[46] That is to say, rites that mark a transitory period in the lives of individuals leading to a new stage in their life course. This kind of experience can also be found in religious or spiritual communities and has often been described as "the call": the beginning of a long period of conversion that starts with an unexpected event and introduces a strong difference before and after this moment.[47] In the activist world, the call is perceived as a defining moment when members experience the overall goal

---

44 Valia Interview Extract: Events, 2011.

45 Berger and Luckmann 1991. See also Gómez 2019.

46 van Gennep 2019; Turner 1977/1969; Geertz 1973.

47 Gómez 2019, 5–6.

of the group as something they want to contribute to, as was the case with Valia listening to the word 'freedom' shouted out by people inside the detention centre. The enchantment Valia felt when she encountered the refugees in the detention centre was the stimuli for her to realise that AuRA, and each individual in it, had a *raison d'être.*

To sum up, in the first kind of response, as we saw with Alkyone, seemingly insignificant moments that arose during the accomplishment of everyday tasks could produce a surplus of meaning for future action and community building. They produced a feeling of "looking forward"[48] that encouraged the consolidation of a collective 'we' and generated collective action. Responsibility, mutual respect, and compliance with the rules not only fortify the group's functionality, but most importantly verify the meaningfulness of the enterprise. In the second kind, the emphasis was laid upon this meaningfulness itself and the conviction that the group (and hence the movement as well) has an overall purpose, the realisation of which was experienced as life-changing by the individuals concerned.

The members of the movement experience each day dynamically and the enthusiasm with which they describe their new life, having entrusted their whole being to the group, brings to mind a re-enchantment of the world.[49] In the organising of the annual festival, in the daily and weekly routines of the Sanctuary, in the rotation of the roles and the tasks the members would perform, and in the various events that the members of AuRA and the Sanctuary organised, the members' experience and imagination would merge together in order to express their unity under their common vision of change. Here Geertz's comment about rituals becomes highly relevant:

> In a ritual, the world as lived and the world as imagined, fused under the agency of a single set of symbolic forms, turn out to be the same world, producing thus that idiosyncratic transformation in one's sense of reality[...].[50]

The importance of the group was demonstrated not only in this re-construction of the subject's identity ("I am part of AuRA or the Sanctuary"), but also in the bonds and structures provided by the group for the solidification of one's faith in the certainty of this other world.[51] The conditions of participation enabled members to maintain their belief in the new reality that surrounded them and according

---

48 Schutz 1972, 97–138.

49 The "re-enchantment of the world" is opposed here to the "disenchantment of the world" by which Weber was referring to the loss of mysticism and of the element of magic brought about by the end of religious perception. The disenchantment of the world was accompanied by processes of rationalisation and intellectualisation. Weber 2004b, 12–13. See also Löwy 2002, 54.

50 Geertz 1973, 112.

51 Berger and Luckmann 1991, 178–80.

to which they interpreted the new situation, in which a better, truer world than the previous one was revealed. Experiences such as those that Alkyone and Valia singled out as particularly meaningful to them were essentially the cohesive threads within the group that allowed the individual to create her/his new biography under conditions of safety (family) and trust. Let us now examine how this is further accomplished through the idea of solidarity.

Solidarity

As we have seen so far, the idea of solidarity appeared in my conversations with members of the group as a quality that helped them to understand their life within AuRA. For Anthi, solidarity was a vital element in her life, and for Valia solidarity was a moment of realisation of her aim within AuRA. Before examining the idea of solidarity in depth, I think it is important to summarise some of the important characteristics of AuRA, as members presented them. First, it seemed that the group had succeeded in establishing the principles of anti-hierarchy and self-organisation. Ezekiel:

> There is nothing similar to the AuRA initiative that I know of. At this time there was not. This hybrid formation of a condition of parity between individuals and the collective, where there is an appeal to individuals to understand that the collective partakes [in the action] with more individuals and with solid principles, and [to understand] its own internal difficulties [...].[52]

Equal importance is placed on both individual autonomy and the unity of the collective. It is as if the members came to a realisation that the group is not something separate from themselves, a fact that is expressed by the emphasis on its anti-hierarchical function. It was neither the adherence to principles that made the endeavour distinct, nor the charismatic qualities that some members may have had. I was very interested in learning what Ezekiel considered to be the distinctive characteristics of AuRA that allowed for its success:

> The basic characteristics of AuRA are the devotion of its members, the tremendous nagging, and the tremendous self-depreciation. It can be that publicly we give our man-hours, and among us we claim "come on, what is AuRA! The last cog in the wheel!" Or even that there are always some others worthier than us, who initiated a collective or a group... Hmm, fifteen years later there will still be two persons [in this group]. This self-depreciation, [that] everyone is doing better than us![53]

52 Ezekiel Interview Extract: Parity, 2011.

53 Ezekiel Interview Extract: Self-Depreciation, 2011.

The qualities that Ezekiel stressed revolved around the humbleness and modesty that characterised the members' work and devotion in their engagement with the cause of solidarity. Without the acknowledgement of their own contribution, the members often struggled to offer more to the group. Their devotion, according to Ezekiel, was reminiscent of the communist parties of an older time:

> It is the man-hours [the time we invest] that distinguishes AuRA. I have to say it, I have to go way back to communist parties of the interwar period to find a similar level of dedication to a group and collective.[54]

What struck me the most in this comparison of AuRA to the communist parties of the interwar period was the combination of different characteristics that the comparison implied. On the one hand, there were the different qualities that AuRA presented: its open and self-organised character, beyond strict political lines, which allowed its members more autonomy; and on the other hand, it had the same kind of enormous dedication that was found in more disciplined ideological and organisational structures. How were ideas of fluidity, openness and anti-hierarchy combined with a level of personal commitment such as the members presented? Why did members return, remain, and seem to be particularly attached and devoted to it?

In order to answer these questions, one needs to go beyond their politico-ideological components, without at the same time disregarding the ideological aspects of the endeavour. The members often emphasised the transformative qualities that their participation in the Sanctuary and in AuRA had for them, and solidarity emerged in our discussions as a link to this transformation. As such, one question that helped me a lot in understanding the depth and seriousness of members' participation during my discussions with them was the playful "what is solidarity" that I often introduced in the last part of our conversations:

> Solidarity is the ability to put your I [self] aside, to make it one with a we that you may not be familiar with, to become part of a group you may not know at first, but which you can easily integrate into and offer your whole being to and perform true miracles with. And by miracles, I mean these little things in everyday life, which to me are small everyday revolutions. Without solidarity, these things cannot happen. They are a link; solidarity is like a chain.[55]

Here, solidarity is linked not only to the material but also to the immaterial world, it allows people to perform "miracles" together. The miracle seems here to be a metaphor clothed with the spiritual affirmation of the realisation of the members' vision. Solidarity often revealed a mystical atmosphere in people's stories. It served

---

54 Ezekiel Interview Extract: Man-Hours, 2011.

55 Anthi Interview Extract: Solidarity, 2011.

as an abstraction through which the world recaptured its vital meaning and through which people redefined their relations, their goals, and themselves. It seemed to announce a rupture with past attitudes, announcing a new constructive way to both individual and collective transformation, as if it provided a kind of spiritual fuel that imbued them with the capacity to mould the world into what they envisioned. This spiritual fuel consisted of the sum total of all the ethical values, assumptions, behaviours and rituals that were woven within and permeated all daily encounters, and all stressed the importance of reciprocity and collective action in the culture of the Sanctuary. Solidarity does not only function as a call for unity with reference to the outside world, but also provided an existential impetus for members' participation. To a certain extent, this is why it also replaced the old political vocabulary with spiritual affirmations.

Spirituality here does not imply some sort of metaphysical affirmation. It rather expresses strong relationality by emphasising the new in-between relations that the members were forming.[56] Solidarity is the link that allows us to take a look at what could be considered to be the more spiritual dimension of the way in which the members of the group organised their coexistence. Buber's locating of spirit in interrelatedness is relevant here:

> Spirit is not in the I but between I and You. [...]. Man lives in the spirit when he is able to respond to his You. He is able to do that when he enters into this relation with his whole being. It is solely by virtue of his power to relate that man is able to live in the spirit.[57]

Becoming part of a greater whole allows both "self-affirmation" and participation in a greater whole that constantly produces new insights for its members: in short, a "*transcendence of the self*"[58] that allows members to affirm the equality and fraternity inherent in their participation. Giving their "whole being" is a process of continually overcoming boundaries and becoming something new through their participation in the group and devotion to its cause. In AuRA, the impetus behind the process of surpassing one's own boundaries appears to be the idea of solidarity. Valia:

56 Kurtz and White 2015, 65–66. The authors discuss the link between spirituality and the prepositions of 'beyond' and 'between,' noting how spirituality leads to a transcendental experience that expresses connection, mutuality and between-ness. For an account of spirituality as juxtaposed to the materiality of the world see Huss 2014. See also Kourie 2007; van der Veer 2009.

57 Buber 1996/1970, 89.

58 Tillich 2000, 165. Kurtz and White 2015, 65–66.

> Solidarity is us... There is no I or you; there is not here and there, I am here and you do not belong here, you are an alien; there is not I am here and you are different. This is my opinion. It is all of us...[59]

In the world of solidarity there is no room for egoistic selves and self-absorbed desires. There is no place for discrimination and exclusion. The actualisation of individual selves is accomplished through contributing to the common good and through the active promotion of the group's vision. The group's objectives are achieved through the overall well-being of its members, and the members in their turn imbue the collectivity with their creative energy and perform, together with the others, "true miracles."

Some of the members' descriptions of their sense of belonging, their experience of togetherness, and the way they generated the idea of 'we-ness,' brought me to a better understanding of communal bonds and commitment. This strong sense of what we might call *communitas* helped me to conceptualise the existential gravity inherent in people's engagement, especially in the early stages of their involvement. *Communitas* emerges in the way people relate to each other; it is a relationship created within the experience of coming together. And it is this "generic bond between men" and the Buberian sentiment of "humankindness" (*Zwischenmenschlichkeit*), as Turner puts it, that allows them to engage in something with their "whole being."[60] Spontaneity, immediacy, interrelatedness and spirituality, are intrinsic elements of communitas,[61] which, as Turner also says, incites "men to action as well as to thought."[62]

What people describe as distinctive about AuRA and the Sanctuary is precisely that they allow for this kind of experience, for a high degree of individual and emotional transformation. Metaphorically, it could be said that through their collective life and action individuals in this way achieve immortality.[63] This is not to imply that the members aim at pursuing individual interests. Rather it is to acknowledge that the impetus for transformation works through the contribution of the individual members to the community of belonging. It could be seen as a kind of 'redemption,' achieved through flexibility, mutual understanding and recognition, spontaneity and creativity that both the individual self and the community as a whole experience. This community, then, differed dramatically from others in that it constantly strove to express both "similarity and difference" (as we will further explore in Chapter 5).[64]

---

59 Valia Interview Extract: Solidarity, 2011.

60 Turner 1977/1969, 128; Buber 1996/1970, ibid.

61 Turner 1977/1969, 127.

62 Turner 1977/1969, 129.

63 Tillich 2000, 100.

64 Cohen 2015/1985, 3.

Solidarity could also be seen as a symbol – in the sense of a "mental construct"[65] – of the way in which the community involves a whole new value system and way of life. It is a starting point for the expansion of an egalitarian worldview that will lead to equal relationships, to anti-hierarchical organisation, and to the recognition and embracing of differences.

What elevated AuRA above other similar groups in the eyes of its members was its dual effort to address inequalities in the world outside of the Sanctuary and to explore the creation of a new kind of community inside of it. This is why it appeared to challenge the common perception of a political group, particularly in terms of identity construction and boundaries.[66] Indeed, the very intention of the alternative community that formed within the space of the Sanctuary was the construction of a new world that is not limited by past ideas: their aim to create a "single world out of many" meant that their own world – and their own understanding of it – would necessarily constantly change as it included more and more others. This inclusive and egalitarian vision of change can be usefully understood through the personal and charismatic qualities that defined the group as an evolving whole. This aspect of the group was clearly evident in the annual festival. As Gadamer points out, what experiences of festivals have in common is:

> the fact that they allow no separation between one person and another. A festival is an experience of community and represents community in its most perfect form.[67]

For the members of the group, community was constructed through the imaginary contemplation of a society to come.[68] This is not to say that politics were less important to this group than it was to others. In their daily vocabulary their use of the term solidarity united the political with the existential element. It did not only lead the way to political transformation but more importantly it did so through the everyday exercise of transforming one's self and thus paving the way for the practical metamorphosis of both the individual and the collective. It is in this sense that the members would identify themselves as "solidarity itself," representing both themselves and the collective as part of "solidarity's chain." This pattern was verified on a daily basis, at every single moment that people were called to act together. Solidarity appeared then as a cohesive force keeping the group united; it gave rise to the uniqueness of the bonds created within the collective at each single moment and created sustainability for the whole endeavour. With this in mind, the "miracles" that

65 Ibid, 10.

66 Cohen 2015/1985.

67 Gadamer 1986, 39.

68 Delanty 2003, 124.

we have heard Anthi talking about can be understood as meaningful action; action that cannot be reduced to the anticipation of a better future, but rather signals an immediacy of participation[69] and acts as an open invitation to the broader society.

The group's aspiration to provide an open space for exchange which allows individuals to come together, share experiences, and learn about the anti-discriminatory, anti-racist attitude, reveals the broader content that the members associated with anti-racism. It is this openness that will allow for a "leap in consciousness"[70] to be realised and a new understanding of the world to be obtained. Thus, to affirm solidarity is to affirm the 'us,' the we-ness in its differentiation. This re-conceptualisation of the autonomous self in her/his engagement with others is what allows people to experience the new world they are becoming part of. Solidarity functions, then, as an overarching imperative in the Sanctuary's culture that accompanies all transformative processes: the new places one has to be familiarised with (the Sanctuary, the festival, the assemblies, the Birdhouse); the new people one encounters and will coexist with; the new guiding principles and moral codes. Solidarity becomes a call to transform ourselves by embracing the everyday task of transforming the world.

Some Self-Reflections

AuRA's egalitarian vision, the members' unconventional beliefs, and the prioritisation of the cause, seemed to me to often reveal a 'sacred' way in which people related to each other and to the group. This came through on certain occasions, and the way they spoke about solidarity in our conversations seemed to indicate that it was a significant way in which they made sense of their new world. This kind of faith, which was revealed in the members' devotion to the group, often made me wonder how you can analyse something that you may not ultimately understand? How can you do justice to all the elements that are important to other people's lives? How can you represent people's devotion and put their emotions into words without degrading them, without falling into the traps of stereotyping or re-producing caricatures?

Being a good member meant being a faithful, heartfelt and devoted one. And those qualities were not to be acquired outside of the daily struggle of the movement and its relationships. My motives, both as a researcher and a member did not feel good or adequate enough, something that was reflected in my long absences from both roles. Thus, constant struggling with conflicting feelings constituted the daily reality of my participation. On countless occasions and for prolonged periods

69 Passerini expresses this here and now utopian element in a very eloquent way: "In this sense it can be taken to indicate that what until yesterday was nowhere can come into existence here and now; it means not struggling for something to come, but starting right now to put it into practice." Passerini 2002, 17–18.

70 Melucci 1999, 423.

I was confronted with what it felt like to commit a 'double infidelity': I couldn't sacrifice the relationships I was invested in for the sake of the research, but how could I sacrifice the research for those relationships? In the end, out of the multiple negotiations of my position in relation to the group, the idea emerged that my place in relation to the group was that of the 'heretic.' And probably I have been a heretic with reference to both roles, as a researcher and as a member. From another point of view, however, I was, in a sense, enchanted. The enchantment I felt was not linked to the ideological elements of the endeavour, but to the strength and the willingness of those people who strove to accomplish them, and the intensity of their commitment to their goals. It is for this reason that this chapter has not just delineated the principles and the culture of the Sanctuary but has also presented all the diverse and idiosyncratic elements that were significant to my interlocutors, in order to recapture the particularity of the Sanctuary's overall atmosphere.

5. Solidarity's Faces

In this chapter I will look at the distinctive roles taken on by the members of the group. This will involve looking at their various responsibilities, modes of engagement, and emotional investment. Through the examination of these roles, various ethical considerations regarding the evolution of the group's project of solidarity emerge. Starting from the members' own perceptions of both their own roles and the roles of others in the group, I will identify certain issues that are relevant to an understanding of both the group as a whole and the individual experience of its members. In order to examine the various positions of the members of the group, I will make reference to five different types that will help to guide our examination of their function within the movement, as well as their interrelationships with each other. Thus, solidarity's various 'faces' will be depicted through the metaphorical types of the 'intellectuals,' the 'believers,' the 'others,' the 'good comrade,' and the 'non-believers.' First, however, I would like to elaborate further on the selection of these five categories, and the way in which they first emerged.

As I proceeded with my research, and as I gained a deeper understanding of the group, a picture of the various roles, responsibilities and duties of its different members started to emerge. This understanding was in part coloured by the way in which the different members of the group characterised the roles of themselves and each other. For example, those who did a lot of practical tasks and spent a considerable amount of time in the Sanctuary referred to themselves as the "water-carriers." The older members were called by some younger members the "gurus." Very often then, people referred to various "others," in their accounts of the overall objective of the group or the meaning of solidarity. Additionally, the word "comrade" was frequently used by the members when addressing each other, acknowledging the ideal of the activist who is entirely devoted to the movement. Most of the time, the use of these names was innocuous, serving as a compass during daily interactions to refer to the function and the distinct position each member held. However, since they unavoidably ascribed to individuals certain patterns of behaviour and implied certain characteristics, they were also sometimes used in a friendly, teasing way and occasionally as sarcastic comments. But whether used to tease or merely to refer to people, those names were still value-charged, and revealed an underlying ethical order which I wanted to explore further.

There were two ways in which the use of these types appeared to be of great importance. Firstly, the fact that they suggested an invisible hierarchy within the group raised several questions about how its members really perceived themselves and each other, although claiming to be equal. What kind of assumptions about the various roles within the group were people from different positions making? Were they aware of the hierarchical categorisation that they were implying by using those names? It would be revealing to discover what they themselves had to say about it. Secondly, the use of these types could provide a window onto how members conceptualised the ideas of equality and self-organisation which constituted the main core of their ideology. Were there different conceptualisations of solidarity according to the position that members had? And if so, how was this fact reflected in their daily reality?

While all these categories were inspired by people's own accounts of their participation in and aspirations about the group, my own 'intervention' in reconstructing the categories should not be neglected. I had a certain position while doing participant observation which had its own history in terms of what I was looking for and how I was approaching AuRA and the Sanctuary,[1] and the use of these types allowed me to draw attention to four issues that were of particular interest: members' status and power, their fields of responsibility, the type of relationship they had to other members, and their emotional investment in each other and the group.

To a great extent my understanding and construction of the typology followed Schutz's appropriation of "course of action types"[2] that reveal regular patterns of behaviour, examine motives and actions in which actors engage, and are recognised by others as "typical."[3] In this sense, the self-identification of the members as "water-carriers" had a lot to reveal about the decisions, emotions and behaviour involved in their own daily experience; yet their typology fulfilled a number of functions which remained only relatively known to me. The typology I am using is a secondary one which is greatly determined by both my field of interest and my position in and interpretation of it.[4] The types are "secondary constructions" in the sense that they do not only seek to interpret what the actors mean by engaging in certain actions, but they also seek to answer certain questions posed by the interpreter.[5] Of course any

1 Schutz 1972, 176; Schutz 1976, 17–19.

2 Schutz 1972, 187. "Course of action types," or "action-pattern types" in Schutz's terminology, focus on the "expressive process itself or [...] the outward results which we interpret as the signs of the expressive process." Ibid, 187.

3 Schutz 1972, 187.

4 Schutz 1976, 17–19.

5 Schutz 1972, 190; Dreher 2011, 503–4.

such typology remains an abstraction, but may nevertheless be a useful one through which we can conceptualise day-to-day behaviour. It can also serve as a hypothesis which may help us to approach issues of intersubjectivity between members, and also to locate the members' various positions in relation to the ideological underpinnings of the group. As Weber has said, any typology is a "means" through which a phenomenon can be better comprehended and does not constitute an "end" in itself.[6] It rather functions as an interpretive scheme for understanding the world of the Sanctuary and of AuRA.[7]

Intellectuals (Theory)

> Chara: At first, when I entered the place, I was terrified by the kindness of its people. They were all such nice and polite people. Have you noticed that? They were so willing to help you with everything. They were generous. I could not believe that. In general, I used to be suspicious [towards people]. It was at that time, while waiting for another teacher to come, that I dared to ask a few questions, and the way people replied – was so incredibly friendly and kind... A small monastery of good people. No? Aren't they so kind?[8]

When Chara first arrived at the Sanctuary, she was welcomed by what she described as a "small monastery of good people." The identification of the Sanctuary with a monastery made me wonder what kind of qualities and values she observed in it. However, she went on to describe the kindness, generosity, and friendliness of the first people she met there. The first contact for newcomers to the Sanctuary was with the 'intellectuals' of the group. On my own first visits to the place, I was advised to talk first to Danae and Ezekiel. They were two of the more prestigious members of the group, often mentioned by the other members for both their theoretical knowledge, and their practical engagement in the movement. They were responsible for the overall co-ordination of the Sanctuary and the activities of the various groups who participated in it. They provided people with all the necessary information in order for them to integrate into the Sanctuary's daily life. Newcomers were advised to contact them first and consult them about upcoming daily issues.

They were treated respectfully, or even reverentially. Their longstanding social and political activism within the movement, and their theoretical background were both recognised as significant and were honoured by the majority of the other members. Yet these qualities also created a certain distance between the intellectuals and

6 Weber 1949, 92.

7 As Schutz puts it, a typology allows for certain phenomena to "become part of our stock of knowledge about that world." Schutz 1972, 185.

8 Chara Interview Extract: Monastery, 2009.

the other members in the group, whether they were newer members or older ones. The intellectuals were charismatic figures, constituting what Weber would have called a "status group."[9] They enchanted people through rational and convincing arguments, insightful political commentaries, and theoretical analysis. In this way, they revealed the truth to their listeners. This practice had a performative function: not only was the intellectuals' versatility and their rhetorical capacity demonstrated, but also the value and purpose of the community itself was confirmed.

The intellectuals often assumed a pedagogical role towards new members, many of whom lacked any previous experience of political engagement. The following extract from my personal notes describes how one intellectual guided new members of the language courses through the basic ideological principles of the group, emphasising the importance of solidarity:

> I thought of asking Danae if I could possibly attend a lecture that was offered to the migrants at the Sanctuary. I asked hesitantly, but Danae replied kindly. She explained that this class was not with her own students. She had to replace another teacher and did not know the students well. She hoped, however, that things would go smoothly and invited me to the classroom. Four students had already taken their places. Chalil from Afghanistan, Karol and Anna from Bulgaria, and Chalil's friend, whose name I did not recall. Danae introduced herself and asked about their reading skills, as she was not familiar with their level of comprehension. She gave two of the main pamphlets about the Sanctuary to each of the students. One referred to the annual AuRA festival, the other one to the refugees' Birdhouse. The participants had to read the pamphlets and then explain to each other the parts they did not understand. Chalil explained the meaning of the 'Birdhouse' to the girls. He used to live there and could give his personal perspective. "It was not that bad living there," he said and added that his friend also used to live there.
>
> Danae focused on the role of AuRA in the daily functioning of the Birdhouse. She stressed the importance of the group's volunteer work and how members were helping the people who lived there. She was using simple colloquial language to make sure that everybody understood what she was saying. As the discussion unfolded, she raised the issue of racism: "Do you know what racism is?" she asked. "What does racism mean to you?" Anna replied first. She justified the Greeks' behaviour towards migrants. The Greeks, she said, had been accepting so many migrants and refugees, that unfortunately "they had to become racists." Her opinion was based on her own experience in Bulgaria, where many people from other countries were engaging in "illegal activities." She was mainly referring to the Roma populations in Bulgaria and the impact that stealing and other illegal

9 Weber 2013, 186–92. See also Bourdieu 2010. In this sense intellectuals had symbolic capital.

> activities had on the locals. Danae was listening carefully without interrupting her, it seemed to me because she expected reactions from the rest of the participants, which would naturally occur without her intervention.
> Chalil responded to Anna's challenging view. "When somebody is hungry, it becomes self-evident that he needs to steal," he said. Shortly afterwards, throwing a pejorative look towards Anna, he murmured: "All people are good" and then continued in a louder voice: "one needs to be in a very bad state in order to engage in illegal activities." The participants seemed rather numb during the incident. Anna continued arguing about the Roma in Bulgaria and people's feelings towards them and fear when it came to their illegality. Chalil looked sad. Karol remained silent. Danae took the floor. In a gentle voice she started to talk about the "fairy-tales of racism." Her narration in itself resembled a fairy-tale. She talked about Roma populations in Greece and people's similar accusations against them. She continued talking about the Jews, the non-existence of their state and the injustice they had to face throughout history. Gently, she asked Anna if she believed that the Jews were good or bad people. Anna responded with certainty: good. Danae then asked her what makes her believe that the Roma were inherently bad people. Anna remained silent. She did not really know.
> It seemed that Anna was trying to grasp the new perspectives that Danae and Chalil opened up to her, despite any resistance that stemmed from her previous feelings about the Roma in Bulgaria. The class was almost over, and Danae was now talking about the Sanctuary, the aims and functioning of the different groups who were involved, and of AuRA in particular. She was trying to clearly demonstrate that this is a self-organised place which undertakes self-organised projects, and that the people running around were all volunteers.[10]

It seemed to me that Danae was engaging her class in a kind of Socratic dialogue, that allowed everyone to collectively participate in answering her initial question. The discrete way in which she guided the conversation about the meaning of racism and the emotions that racism and discriminatory attitudes raised was one of the qualities that elevated intellectuals to be seen as 'enlightened teachers.' Rather than instructing, they tried to raise consciousness by discussing the issues and principles (such as anti-racism, volunteering, and solidarity) that were important to the Sanctuary and its community. Members were trusted to find their own way of inserting themselves into the new world of the Sanctuary and were presented with the opportunity to transform themselves. The old convictions, such as Anna's distrust of the Roma, might resist the new ones for a long period of time, and changing this would require time and devotion on the part of the participants. The intellectuals played a crucial role in this process.

---

10 Personal Notes: *Lesson*, 2011.

Sitting in a corner during the incident, I wondered if my position as a researcher interfered with the intellectuals' work. At times, I had the impression that my presence at the Sanctuary could be perceived as distracting. This was particularly noticeable at the end of the more strenuous days, when people would have a drink and enjoy moments of relaxation, discussing their life, their feelings, their goals and the movement's aspirations. These informal occasions allowed people to integrate and provided an opportunity for the older members to approach the newcomers and familiarise them with the movement's ideas. At those moments I felt that due to my intermediary role (that is, being situated somewhere in between the older members and the new ones, having the status of a newcomer while also aspiring to conduct research on the group) the course of this personal revealing was interrupted or partly hindered by the suspicion of the possibility of indiscreetness on my part.

The intellectuals often commented on or loudly announced my presence: "Oh the researcher is also here!" Whether this was because they thought I would scrutinise their claims or because they thought I would treat them as an object of observation, I cannot say. I had a very similar anxiety, namely that the intellectuals would raise doubts about my equal contribution to the group or even provoke suspicion among the other members about my motives. Therefore, I often decided to distance myself in order to prevent an imaginary battle between ideology and research from becoming an actual field of disagreement. For this reason, I often played the part of a non-initiated, new and ignorant member and met any moments of unease with plenty of discretion, respect and humour. On one of the festival days, after a demanding preparatory week, one of the intellectuals asked me in quite a sarcastic way: "Is everything okay? Have you researched us enough? And what have you observed? Take a seat now and enjoy your drink." It seemed as if he was suggesting that the right way to participate in the movement was by relaxing and having a drink rather than researching its practices. I gave him a smile and asked him to join me for a beer. Ironically enough, the discussion which followed centred on his own participation in protests and riots and reminded me that there is no room to escape from the movement when you are interested in it or part of it.

The intellectuals were unofficially in charge of moral education and the consolidation of the proper ethics in the community, and in general the newcomers acquiesced to their advice regarding the movement's principles, values, and customs. The intellectuals often stressed the importance of the movement's ethical order, sometimes even crossing over into the personal sphere and indicating the appropriate manners that members should follow within the community. During a party at the Sanctuary, one of the intellectuals commented on my appearance: "You are flirting with the bourgeoisie tonight my dearest and you entice your friends into the sin," he said, looking at some girls from the group who had joined me at the table. My transgression was to be wearing a red dress and red shoes with heels. The sarcastic remark, which was meant to bring me back into line with the movement's values and to warn the rest of the company of the impact of excessive signs of wealth on the movement's 'moral life' called for a return to the simplicity of style appropriate to the humility that members should and did manifest in the movement.

Another thing that the intellectuals were responsible for was the writing and editing of the texts that propagated the group's aims. According to one pamphlet about the Sanctuary, it was the coexistence of all the collectives gathered there that allowed for conditions of cooperation and active solidarity to emerge, providing the participants with the possibility to "create a model of society," as they put it, according to their vision of it: self-organised, voluntary and open to new members and the changes they bring. The Sanctuary provided a space for a variety of different people to come together in active solidarity and cooperation.[11]

Although the writing of the texts was a collective job, the intellectuals played a crucial part in accomplishing it. This was a strenuous procedure. People brought their ideas to the assembly and hours were spent in contemplation as key words and key ideas were selected and verified. Self-organisation, voluntary work and active participation were emphasised as some of the central qualities that made the Sanctuary a model for the society to come. Through their daily exchange and their active participation, the members were forming an alternative example of coexistence that functioned as a model for another possible world. However, the gathering of many different groups entailed a paradox: on the one hand, the Sanctuary was held by its members to be an open organisational structure that included a number of groups with flexible political bonds, and which emphasised the priority of self-organisation, while on the other hand, any decision had to be approved by a variety of organisations and people from various political backgrounds. The different viewpoints also had to be assimilated either by those who entered the group without previous political experience, or by those who came from older traditional and hierarchical political backgrounds.

Iakovos presented his sceptical approach during an assembly, in which people were deciding which slogans should be used at that year's festival. Some members were in favour of a slogan which included the word "barricade" in it – when Iakovos raised a serious objection. As he told me:

> No, it cannot be this slogan [...] this does not express the range [of opinions in the city]. [...] And they accepted our opinion although it was evidently in the minority.[12]

Iakovos' point was that a slogan about barricades would deter people from coming to the festival. In his opinion, even people who disagreed with the legitimisation of all migrants should be encouraged to come to the festival, and not only those who

11 Pamphlet of the Sanctuary 2010, 2.

12 Iakovos Interview Extract: Slogans, 2011.

were already sympathetic to the group's goals. In this sense, he felt that AuRA should present a welcoming face to a much broader potential audience:

> It is this metaphysical thing! Which is not good that it is metaphysical, but still we have to guess whom we may address and what kind of world [what kind of people] may be able to relate to you. It's a different world [to ours]! [13]

Iakovos appeared to give priority to the open nature of the group's projects, and in this sense, he agreed more with the new generation who were envisioning and insisting on events that would allow for more participation. There were various characteristics to the new generation's alternative vision: members should distance themselves from the old narrowly defined political identifications, they should stress the issues in flexible, non-hierarchical terms, take part in more fluid projects and welcome even seemingly paradoxical collaborations with other groups. These strategies aspired to expand AuRA's practices and goals to a greater majority of people in society, to motivate action and to encourage further recruitment. In light of this aspiration, a re-negotiation of the group's strategies was constantly taking place, and this became a site of tension between the older members who had more fixed ideas about how things should be done, and the newer members who stressed the importance of alternative strategic approaches.

From Ezekiel's point of view, re-structuring the profile of the group had necessarily to do with the kind of coalitions that the group was attempting to establish. Which organisations were to be accepted as potential allies, and which were not? In deciding this, the fact that all members' opinions carried an equal weight – though a unique characteristic of the group in terms of direct democratic procedures – could often become a burden:

> And at the same time everyone has a right of veto. This of course has tormented us enormously. This is the kind of stuff that torments us in AuRA, and it is the case in every similar libertarian endeavour [which is based on] an assembly: the here and now [the immediate] or the big picture [the general]? And how do you reconcile them? Coalitions or autonomy?[14]

The discussions about coalitions were long and strenuous. Decisions about collaboration with other groups had to take into consideration a variety of factors. What was the stance of these groups with reference to concrete political events? How could AuRA continue to denounce certain failures of other groups, while at the same time strengthening its open character by prioritising the formation of coalitions? Ezekiel explained to me some of the problems that arise when a group which could be a potential ally of AuRA took a different or unexpected stance on certain political issues.

13 Iakovos Interview Extract: The World We Address, 2011.

14 Ezekiel Interview Extract: Stuff that Torments Us, 2011.

What should AuRA do, denounce the practices, or remain silent because of the potential coalition? This could cause a great deal of turbulence as each member of the assembly not only took part in the decision-making process but also had the right to veto any decision. The way to reach an agreement on certain topics was not always self-evident, and there could be extensive discussions during the assemblies.

To give an example: The participation of the group in the gatherings of the Indignant Citizens' Movement was one issue that was extensively discussed (and I will look at it more closely in Chapter Six). While some of the older members of AuRA were wary of the non-political character of these gatherings and the danger of de-politicisation that the group might have to face, many of the younger generation stressed the importance of being part of the crucial developments that were happening on a social and not only a political level. The open character of the new generation's approach, with their readiness and flexibility to engage with something as different as the Indignant Citizens' Movement, stood in stark contrast to the hesitancy of the older generation to engage in broader popular movements that could harm or distort the image of the group.

Another important issue that many members noticed, and we will discuss this further when we look at the 'believers,' was the intellectuals' absence from the daily stress and anxiety of the group's functional life, which formed a central part of their own daily experience. The intellectuals of the group could appear to be excessively grandiose, inaccessible or remote with respect to the practical aspect of AuRA's and the Sanctuary's life. I asked Ezekiel if he felt that he had a greater responsibility in the group. He reflected for a while on my question, then seemed to respond quite emotionally:

> Well, I can say I feel the [burden of] responsibility... it goes way back in time... When you are younger, everything is better. I had the same responsibility that I do now, but more power to transform it into action and, in general, to delegate the action. Don't think that... Well, there is a criticism in the movement that some people do not move beyond theory and do not get involved in the everyday shit.[15]

One thing Ezekiel pointed out was that while the more experienced members such as himself had a lot of 'know how,' the younger members seemed to be reluctant to learn from them. On questions such as how to represent AuRA in public appearances, or the best way to engage in negotiations with the state and its mechanisms, the younger generation seemed reluctant to be guided. Even smaller issues, such as what time the music should stop at a festival, involved having knowledge about how to negotiate with the police or how to be careful not to displease the neighbourhood:

15 Ezekiel Interview Extract: Responsibility, 2011.

"Why is this so difficult? They have to learn it! We cannot have music playing until seven o' clock in the morning!" [16]

Iakovos was also aware of these criticisms and brought up the issue during our discussion, reminding me of an informal talk we had a couple of days earlier. He was aware that the new generations were reluctant to take on responsibilities, yet also felt repressed by the guidance of the more experienced members, and he gave his own account of this in terms of feeling and being "at home" at the Sanctuary, and the complications that this familiarity may have provoked between the two sides:

> We were discussing this the other day, do you remember? How much room do we give to the new people? I don't know, I feel we do… though we feel it is our own home, what should we do? Feel guilty because we feel this way? We can talk more comfortably [in the group/at the Sanctuary], say silly things […]. Others start to feel this way as well. Hercules for example has a much softer approach to things, even if he will never show up and speak during an event. Magda is another example. They are people who may disappear for ten months and re-appear, and they can [feel free to] speak! What should we do, it is their home! […] But I really do not think we suppress… well you never know; it is not simple; it may be that I pop up and take over and someone feels pushed out!
>
> Q: [I make a weird look]
>
> Iakovos: No, people have told me that I appear scary.
>
> Q: Oh, I do not think you scare anyone!
>
> Iakovos: No indeed, they have told me!
>
> Q: But anyway, we were talking about the younger members and whether they feel comfortable in assuming responsibility or undertaking initiatives…
>
> Iakovos: This is so welcomed! We want that! […] Of course, we are more relaxed, some others are not. We articulate our speech in this way because we are those who – if for example I find myself in a demonstration, and there is a journalist, and they ask who would like to talk – eh obviously. I will not seek to [talk], but I will. The newer members will not. I feel comfortable expressing the group's ideas, [but] they see the microphone and hide – we have seen that happen. And if they do speak, they get very nervous. Of course, this cannot be overcome, unless they go out and talk… it cannot be that the same people constantly speak publicly.

16 Ezekiel Interview Extract: Disputes, 2011.

Q: But is this really wanted?

Iakovos: Yes! They do not realise it, but it is![17]

There is a lot going on in the above extract, but I want to stress one thing that seems to me to be the most important; Iakovos' reference to being and feeling "at home," which took me by surprise. It was my impression that the idea of the Sanctuary as a "home" was not something that the older participants would emphasise, partly because they had experienced so many splits and organisational shifts in past political movements and structures, and partly because they did not share the enthusiasm of the newer generations who expressed this family-like idea, as we saw in Chapter Four. Another thing that struck me was Iakovos' openness and flexibility when it came to people's long absences from participating in the group. In this sense, devotion was not perceived in political terms, and nor was it compulsory. Going away for a long period of time did not deprive members of the comfort they experienced at the Sanctuary, or of the privileges (mostly emotional) they had enjoyed before their absence.

Of course, the differences between the older and newer generations cannot be restricted to these few points. On strictly political matters, the boundaries were blurred. This became clear during the group's discussions about the "barricade" slogan. Some members assumed a more assertive stance and wanted to confront issues in a more dynamic way, while others prioritised the potentiality of attracting people who were not already initiated into the movement's practices. Both sides, however, seemed to have to unlearn previous ways of engagement and organisation in order to grasp the new practices and ideas that were being produced within the context of their discussions and assemblies.

In addition to being at the centre of the administrative decision-making processes, the intellectuals also envisioned and were primarily in charge of the overall scope of the movement's goals. They had the unbearable task of conceptualising the ongoing projects of social change.[18] It was this construction of the ideological and political projects, their administration, and the ways of accomplishing them, that led to the intellectuals being somewhat paradoxically 'distanced' from the daily routine of the group.[19] This was something the other members saw as the intellectuals being 'otherworldly' in the face of daily realities.

17 Iakovos Interview Extract: Undertaking Initiatives, 2011. However, Iakovos distinguished his position from others telling me that he felt more like a sort of a 'moralist,' which in his view was incompatible with others' positions. The idea however was left unexplored.

18 Lekkas 1994, 208–9. For the role of intellectuals, see Hoare and Smith 1986a; Gramsci 2005; Said 1996b. For a typology see Chiotakis 2015; see also Weber 2004a.

19 Lekkas 1994, 209.

Throughout my notes, I humorously referred to the intellectuals as 'clergy' because of the way many of them seemed to preserve (metaphorically) the 'ecclesiastical order' of the group. They seemed bound by their ideological reasonings, their devotion to ideological goals, their rational and ethical approach, as well as the overall scope of their vision. In short, all the elements of their participation emphasised and strengthened their honourable historical commitment to the movement and announced them as a sacred paradigm of virtuous membership. In this sense, their 'charisma' seemed to stem from their place in this 'atypical' hierarchy of the group.[20]

During my time at the Sanctuary, I saw the role of the intellectuals being gradually transformed, influenced by new tendencies and new types of intellectuality that constituted an alternative approach to the political priorities that characterised the older generations. Strong leadership and guidance, devotion to ideological 'truths,'[21] and a consistent cost-benefit calculation seemed to be characteristics of the older intellectuals in the group, while flexibility, self-reflexivity, and openness to new social and political developments characterised the younger intellectuals. This new generation that gradually emerged over the late 2000s emphasised a more dialectical relationship between the group's ultimate theoretical aims and the reality of its practical engagements.[22] This new generation also turned out to be more flexible, and more receptive to embracing the demands of other members such as the 'believers,' as we will now see.

The Believers (Practice)

I chose the term 'believers'[23] to describe a rather broad category of members. Some of them were newcomers to the group and even to the movement in general, while others had been with AuRA for several years. What they all had in common was a

20 Weber 2007b, 53–54: As Weber puts it, the reason prophets never stemmed from the circles of the clergy is because their charisma was based on a personal call (*προσωπικό κάλεσμα*). In this sense, the priests act on behalf of their institution but the prophets act through their personal charisma. See also Weber 2013, 107–8. For the idea of charismatic authority in Weber, see also Weber 2005, 275–92; Weber 2019, 374–78. For more on the analogy between charismatic leadership and types of intellectuals, see the interesting article by Chiotakis 2015, 30.

21 In plural, because types of intellectuality covered broader ideological spaces, including anarchism for example. For further discussion see Chapter Six.

22 On the intellectuals' role in processes of modernisation see Lekkas 1994, 209; Gouldner 1976, 62–64.

23 For the sake of coherent presentation, I avoid putting quotation marks when it comes to the term 'believers' throughout the text. The term 'believers' however retains its metaphorical use throughout this book.

'pure' and idealised relation to the group. I met Anthi, Valia, Alkyone, Chara, Stefanos, Marc and Fedonas, to mention just some of them, at the very beginning of my research and they were happy to let me join them. Together we worked, shared our thoughts, shared emotions and co-existed. Without them, my conceptualisation of the movement in general and AuRA in particular would lack any meaning. In fact, during my time with the group I was one of them.

As we saw in Chapter Four, the believers had a great enthusiasm for being part of the group. Their kindness, endurance and faith served the daily goals of social justice and their passionate contribution imbued their presence in the group with meaning. Each day was unique, and each moment in the movement was celebrated whether they were seeking solutions to everyday problems, overcoming impasses, confronting injustice or dealing with institutional ineptitude. I asked Anthi about her decision to join AuRA:

> What I really liked from the beginning was the fact that there was an open assembly, which means that you don't need to follow a certain [political] line [...]. Your own opinion clearly has an impact on the group's opinion. For me this was a particularly important aspect. I like the group's multidimensionality, namely the fact that there are parts of the group that lean towards anarchism, other parts towards the Left, though this last part I liked less (she laughs) ...[24]

> I like all these different tendencies, even if we have to come into conflict – though this mostly happens with reference to external issues. I think that we deal with our internal issues better, primarily because of this polymorphism – I like this in the group. Other elements disturb me, for example the fact that the group has longstanding members. And the way in which some people think they have constructed the group, and as a result they feel as if it was their own estate, and this results in your own confinement. And sometimes you feel that your word does not have equal weight but maybe that's just me. There are parts of the past regarding the history of the group which remain unknown and this makes you feel that you lack... one thinks automatically that your own opinion doesn't carry as much weight as the historical members' opinion. This part annoys me.[25]

Diversity, lack of hierarchy, open assemblies; this "polymorphism" was one of the main reasons why people felt able to participate in the group. All opinions carried equal weight and everyone could contribute to the group's functioning. There were, however, other issues that Anthi was not willing to discuss: the prestige of the so-called "historical members" could create an atmosphere in which believers felt uncomfortable openly expressing their opinions. Members often described a

24 Anthi Interview Extract: Joining the Movement, 2011.

25 Anthi Interview Extract: Moments of Unease, 2011.

feeling of "not being ready yet" to express their views or equally contribute to the group's or the Sanctuary's discussions. Anthi and Valia both witnessed this during the assemblies. Valia:

> I do not speak too much [in the assemblies] because I am ashamed to talk. I have no idea, and as Anthi previously said, there are people in the group – the historical members – who know much more. I came into the group as a complete tabula rasa. I never thought about these things, I never had to organise my thoughts and express them, and that's why I have difficulties in expressing myself – not that somebody or something hinders me – it is probably me who prevents myself from… [expressing my views]. No, honestly, it has nothing to do with people in the assembly – or maybe it does, because it is true some people have a long history there.[26]

During assemblies all participants were encouraged to share their thoughts, suggest solutions and propose alternative strategies with which to address upcoming issues. However, despite this openness to contributions, a feeling of not being ready to do so inhibited some members who felt they could not compete with the "historical members of the group" (or the 'cadres' as the believers used to call them).[27] During our conversations, Valia was reluctant to speak openly about her lack of confidence in publicly expressing herself, and she did so only with Anthi's encouragement. Nevertheless, this hesitancy of the newer members to contribute due to the perceived prestige and confidence of the older members came up on a number of occasions. Power and knowledge were held to be the exclusive attributes of the intellectuals and the believers often fell into the role of ignorant, non-initiated students, who only gradually and laboriously developed their own capacities for initiatives and action.

It seemed there was an asymmetrical relation between the intellectuals as virtuous paradigms of activist engagement and the younger members who did most of the actual work. At the centre of the asymmetry was the decision-making process, as the following story from my personal notes during the field research shows:

> In the movement, self-organisation is a key word. It is to be achieved every day: the migrants self-organise; the comrades self-organise; the days self-organise; the

26 Valia Interview Extract Moments of Unease, 2011.

27 The word "cadres" was mainly used by the older generation of activists to acknowledge a disagreement with past political engagements and structures. I often had the impression that the younger participants 'borrowed' the term from the older members to indicate the 'professionalisation of activism.' It mainly focused on personal careers and advantages of cadres and functioned as a critique of further political engagement outside of activism. The 'gurus' was a teasing way of referring to the sacredness of the old historical members and at the same time tackled the adherence to older political styles.

nights self-organise – and so on and so forth. But how do people really self-organise? Is there an actual point to the endeavour or is it all just talk? Opinions differ, sceptics are marginalised, and I hesitate to share my thoughts. The following occurrence goes a long way toward demonstrating my ambivalence towards said concept. Once, during one of the festivities organised by the group, the kitchen ran out of lettuce. One of the intellectuals immediately started looking for a solution. Soon enough, he found a comrade (seeing as he could not leave his post) who was willing to go looking for an all-night grocery store. She didn't have a car of her own, though, so the guru had to find someone to give her a ride. Luckily enough for everyone involved (what good is a falafel without a lettuce salad to go with it?), he eventually also found a volunteer with a car – who, however, was too inexperienced in matters of food supplies to be trusted to pull off the feat on his own. It had to be both of them. So off they both went. It was a Friday night, way past midnight; the city streets were empty. After searching for God knows how long, the two comrades eventually (and thankfully) found a grocery store that was open. The young woman got out of the car, relieved that their search had been rewarded. It wasn't long, though, before she came back out of the store, visibly upset and – above all – empty-handed. "They're out of lettuce! Such is my luck! Vanity of vanities; all is vanity!" thought the driver to himself (it was he who told me this story). Except, when you're a member of the movement, no day (or night) is like any other: "I won't buy lettuce from this guy!", announced the girl emphatically. He has a shaven head, and there are Greek flags hanging all over the place: He's clearly a Golden Dawn[28] supporter!" Taken aback, the driver urged her to call and consult with the 'guru' – a suggestion that was followed by an endless series of phone calls. The driver could not hear what was being said on the other side of the line, but it wouldn't take much for anyone to guess that what was taking place were conference phone calls meant to produce a collectively agreed-upon solution to the lettuce crisis – to buy, or not to buy lettuce from someone who is quite possibly a fascist, that is the question. Sometime later, the young woman got out of the car once again. When she came back for the second time, she was sober,

---

28 The Golden Dawn Party (*Χρυσή Αυγή*) entered parliament in the 2012 national elections. The adherents of Golden Dawn (which is an extreme far right neo-Nazi organisation) had been very active in terms of recruiting members, especially during the crisis in Greece. After five and a half years of being on trial for the murder of a Greek rapper Pavlos Fyssas (known for his anti-racist and anti-fascist views), and the attempted murder of Embarak Ambuzid, an Egyptian fisherman and of members of the Communist Party of Greece (among various other attacks), Golden Dawn members were found guilty of various crimes and of constituting a criminal organisation in October 2020. For a map of racist attacks in Greece see Alexandropoulou and Takou 2019. For the rise of the far right, see Fragoudaki 2013.

> pensive, and had the controversial lettuce in hand. Collective decision-making? Check! Self-organisation? Check! Lettuce? Check! Mission accomplished.[29]

What the story of the lettuce crisis illustrates is what some members perceived as the asymmetrical nature of modes of participation. The believers felt the need to follow the intellectuals' requests and bow to their decisions, and the intellectuals – actually though never admittedly – were often in charge of decision making. Relations within the group were underpinned by an invisible hierarchy that did not only appertain to the making of important political decisions but permeated all daily issues on the micro-level of the community's life. The daily reality was often marked by the distance separating words from actions and goals from their accomplishment.

One question that occurred to me while I was listening to the story of the lettuce incident was: who would have found out that she had bought the lettuce from an advocate of the Golden Dawn party anyway, if she had decided to just buy it, return to the car, and not mention it to anyone? In the life of the community, however, encountering an ideological opponent is in itself of great significance. Members are often overwhelmed by the real and imaginary battles encountered during demonstrations and events, but also primarily in everyday life. These seemingly insignificant moments strengthen their will by providing a coherent context for their ideological aspirations. In such moments the utopian elements of the movement are partly realised. In this case, though, the ethical dilemma functions as a drama to be disentangled under conditions of anxiety and insecurity: Is it appropriate to buy products from an ideological enemy? At the same time, the figure of the enemy ratifies the movement's very existence, its essence and importance.[30]

Ideological elements permeated all daily routines: the adherence to an ideology means that all events, actions and interactions are filtered through the ideological prism, even when it comes to situations of lesser gravity. Even the buying of a lettuce is an ideological act, and thus, the volunteer realises that to proceed in this kind of controversial transaction may contradict the group's and even the movement's ethical and political order. Feeling incapable of resolving the dilemma on her own, the girl resorted to the opinion of the intellectuals. Their power – more symbolic than actual – was able to avert an inappropriate ideological choice.

As another interlocutor of mine revealed, her acceptance of what she called "the gurus' demands" was part of a strategy that she gradually developed to avoid any open disagreements with any of the intellectuals. Her strategy was to pretend to go along with the intellectuals' decisions while actually doing what she thought best. Most of the other believers, however, did not concern themselves with the decision making and apprehensive about the intellectuals' remarks, were content to offer

29 Personal Notes: *The Lettuce Crisis*, 2013.

30 Lekkas 2012, 96.

their labour to the objectives of the group. In this sense their bodies became *the ground for* and *the proof of* their very struggle.[31] They devoted a large part of their personal life and time to the community and were ceaselessly working in the service of the group's needs: "There is neither personal time, nor personal space... all this needs to be set aside," Anthi declared. Adopting a kind of ascetic ideal, the believers courageously suffered daily adversities and responded to them with self-denial and abnegation.[32] When they did not praise the movement, they still worked (and suffered) tirelessly for its goals.

A constant vigilance accompanied all the activities of the believers: there was a constant anxiety about who was at the Sanctuary and what they were responsible for: What kind of duties were to be fulfilled? Who was responsible for supplying the kitchen? Who was in trouble and needed to be taken care of? How did the other comrades feel? How were the relations between the members in the centre? Who needed what and how could the others provide their help and show their solidarity? All of these questions resulted in countless phone calls and discussions. The members seemed constantly ready to intervene in the Sanctuary's life. All these components had a highly ritualistic dimension.[33] The members demonstrated their engagement in the group through enactments of intense concern over daily issues. This showed a profound interest in the function of the Sanctuary and AuRA and verified the importance of the believers' role in them. Since all members participated in countless assemblies and activities, all of which demanded a lot of preparation, it took a considerable amount of time and effort for newcomers to familiarise themselves with the rhythm of the group's intensive reality. Each moment was unique, was experienced as important, and called for immediate action. Simply being physically present was an energy absorbing task.

The distribution of information among members, the daily reciprocal relations between them, the consolidation of social relationships and bonds, and the emotional investment in the activities and the life of the movement are all recurrent subjects in the literature on social movements,[34] and all these issues were present in AuRA. Emotions are the necessary fuel of participation and they orchestrate the reality of the members. Loyalty, trust, love and friendship prevailed in the believers' emotional reservoir but fear of expression, hesitancy, and at times indignation

---

31 Butler 2018, 132.

32 Lekkas 2012, 73. In his discussion of ideologues, Lekkas refers to the ascetic ideal as presented in the *Genealogy of Morals*, see Nietzsche 1989/1967, 97–163.

33 For an overview of defining rituals and ritualised behaviour see Bell 2009, 69–74.

34 For an overview of these topics see Della Porta and Diani 2006;Goodwin, Jasper, and Polletta 2001a; Goodwin, Jasper, and Polletta 2000; Goodwin, Jasper, and Polletta 2001b; Jasper 2015/1997; Jasper 1998; Srivastava 2006; Calhoun 2001; Collins 2001; Kleinman 1996; See also Ahmed 2004 and Melucci 1996b.

and anger were part of the believers' emotional reality as well, often in their relations towards the intellectuals. During long assemblies and endless discussions, I could sense the believers' longing for acceptance and approval from the intellectuals. A comment or a gesture of approval would mean they had been heard and were fully participating in the group. Recognition and having an equal say would also pave the way for a truly solidarious community.

The believers' hard work and bodily exhaustion could also be seen as part of their struggle for recognition. The believers often appeared emotionally vulnerable in light of their life in the group. Their feelings fuelled their struggles and gave meaning to their faith. The body was a sign of the priority of *praxis* (as contrasted to the words and the theory that the intellectuals represented) in the process of *making the movement*. Most of the time, the intellectuals – emotionally detached and preoccupied with large-scale planning – would hardly notice their efforts. It was these bodily enactments of faith that I was intrigued by: a self-imposed deprivation of food and sleep due to lack of time resulted in restless bodies, bodies in anxiety during endless nights of discussions and assemblies. The 'suffering' of the believers was evident in their physical exhaustion, their sleepless eyes, and their confounded speech.[35]

The believers' bodily presence ratified the strength and the cohesion of the group. Their bodies became "a site of resistance,"[36] as they drew together while aiming at a common purpose. It seemed that this communal bodily work was what provided solidarity with its strength.[37] This understanding of the bodily role is widely recognised in current discussions about social movements, resistance,[38] performativity,[39] and embodied knowledge.[40] The members' voluntarily coming together characterises their political action and imbues their coexistence with meaning, transforming them into agents of social change.[41] Butler has written about the importance of "bodily vulnerability" in the plural and diverse condition

35 For an account of body and resistance from a religious viewpoint see Davidman 2011. For body and ritual see Bell 2009, 94–117.

36 Casanova and Jafar 2016. See also Bobel and Kwan 2011.

37 Juris 2008, 65.

38 Courpasson and Vallas 2016; Bobel and Kwan 2011; Hirai 2015; Lyon 1997. Further Fassin 2012, 200–222.

39 Butler 2018; Giddens 1991, 56–63.

40 For the idea of embodied knowledge see Hirai 2015, 9; Casas-Cortés, Osterweil, and Powell 2008, 29–30; see also Csordas 1990; Gordon 1980; Foucault 1991, 25–28.

41 Butler 2018, 134–36: In her analysis, Butler tackles the 'thrill' that one may experience in this coming together in the street, and which can become misleading at an emotional level when one is confronted with the gathering together of various actors. Despite her reservations, however, her analysis centres on the element of freedom, and I am making my point from this perspective.

of co-existence. Drawing on Arendt's idea of "acting in concert" and Levinas' ideas about proximity and the ethical life, she links this *vulnerability* to people's interdependency in an interconnected world. However, vulnerable in this sense does not mean needy, as Butler is well aware. Rather, the concept emphasises the affectionate element of "being together in the world" and refers to people's capacity to act. It is this "coming together" that defines the political *praxis* within relations of mutual interdependence in a precarious world.[42] This kind of existential reading does not lack a political ground; in the context of economic and social reality, it ceases to be merely existential and enters the political realm.[43] The believers' bodily presence was tangible proof of the continual fulfilment of their ideological purposes. Deprived of their fatigue and labour, the movement would cease to exist; the gathering of bodies during events, daily practices and demonstrations indicated how much bodies mattered.

However, there is another aspect of the body that I would like to discuss. The body itself became the site of what we might call the believers' dual suffering. On the one hand, devoted and faithful to the movement, believers were unselfishly and graciously *offering* their bodies to it.[44] This offering was the very embodiment of solidarity. Its 'despair' resembled the sacrificial nature of the religious believers' faith.[45] On the other hand, the bodies of the believers ceaselessly demonstrated their desire for a *transformative power*[46] that would have direct results within AuRA and the Sanctuary: a power to begin things anew, denouncing old and established hierarchies and seeking justice not only in the outside world (society), but also inside the movement. In this sense, solidarity becomes an embodied evidence of devotion.

The believers' will to transform social and political conditions was inscribed in their bodily behaviour. The suffering of the body did not matter as long as its discipline and humbleness achieved a dual purpose: to establish solidarity and justice both outside and inside the movement. In this way, the believers demonstrated their own practical truths: they intervened in the social reality at every possible opportunity while at the same time they dynamically engaged in the movement itself in order to draw attention to its own deficiencies. This intensive bodily engagement

---

42 Butler 2018, 106–16.

43 Butler 2018, 119.

44 Lekkas 2012, 73: Drawing on Nietzsche and the ascetic ideal, Lekkas comments on the ascetic's durable, courageous and brave stance to believe in their object of faith, which often leads to the exercise of power upon her/himself. See also Nietzsche 1989/1967, 151–52.

45 Collins 2001, 33. As Collins shows, the figure of the activist-martyr in the movement is closely connected to representations of "moral power" and a symbolic dimension of the "ultimate win" of the movement. See also Fassin 2012, 216–22 for the body "as object demonstrating suffering" and the figure of the "martyr."

46 Lekkas 2012, 73.

acquires a symbolic dimension that incarnates the believers' anti-intellectualism.[47] The believers called to mind the figure of the revolutionary fighter who bodily and manually works for the purpose of revolution, as contrasted to the intelligentsia who orchestrate it, providing the "somatic participation in the struggle" in contradistinction to the "heads of revolution" as Andriakaina puts it.[48] The fighters' vigour is contrasted to the intellectuals' inclination towards "knowledge and deceit" which in turn invokes biblical images of "the serpent that deceives, the one responsible for Adam and Eve's expulsion from Eden," as Andriakaina expressed it.[49]

I perceive Anthi's frustration about the professionalisation of memberships (in terms of the 'status' of the old historical members) mainly as a feeling of betrayal, indicating how the believers' labour and devotion to the cause of solidarity was undervalued, and thus how the basic, common principles of the movement were undervalued too. I often had the impression that the recognition of the believers' contribution by the intellectuals was of value mainly in terms of the community's emotional life. The believers' ceaseless labouring aspired to have a consciousness-raising effect on the intellectuals. Through their bodies they were manifesting what the movement is, how it should function, and which ideas and ethical principles permeate it. They represented its culture and *raison d'être*. While the intellectuals were speaking their truth, the believers were performing theirs through bodily enactments. The intellectuals were urging for a return to proper ethics. The believers incarnated those ethics, by laboriously addressing the latent hypocritical tendencies of the intellectuals and their unspoken will to command. In the eyes of the believers, the extirpation of those hierarchical dissonances would render the endeavour truly solidarious and authentically self-organised.

In this sense, I do not necessarily perceive the relations between the intellectuals and the believers as one between dominators and dominated in a covert hierarchical order. However, a kind of master-slave relation in the Nietzschean sense does seem to play a profound role here.[50] The believers were the soul (in terms of enthusiasm and devotion) and the body (in terms of bodily labour) of the Sanctuary and AuRA. They enacted the theory by enacting the movement's moral and political principles. Their suffering functioned as a proof of their faith and their labour mattered in terms of the new knowledge that it was providing for the movement. They were the ones who provided the practical daily know-how. Nothing seemed impossible,

47 Andriakaina 2013, 54. Andriakaina's analysis with reference to the Greek revolution is very telling in its account of the representations of the fighter's suffering body, and the distinction between the "heads" and the "arms" of the revolution.

48 Andriakaina 2013, 59; 62.

49 Andriakaina 2013, 54; 57.

50 On the master/slave morality see Nietzsche 1989/1967, 36–56; Nietzsche 2019, 159–62; Kaufmann 1989/1967.

and the evidence for this was found in the everyday miracles that people were experiencing. Not being heard in the way the intellectuals were, however, believers had to use more cunning and artful means to make their alternative suggestions recognised and to make the intellectuals aware of the movement's ethical and practical life. In their struggle, another type, the 'others' were becoming their allies. As labourers themselves, the others constituted a prosperous 'in-between' ground where relationships could be re-experienced in an authentic way, and in this way better serve the objectives of the movement, as we will now see.

From Vulnerable *Others* to Valuable *Brothers* (The Goal)

This section is devoted to the relationship of other groups and individuals with the activists of AuRA. In the first part we will examine how the group and its members approach differences. How were the discourses about 'difference' developed in AuRA? What did people say about being different from each other? How were possible misunderstandings reconciled? In the second part we will look at the production of the sense of we-ness in the meeting of many distinct others – something that was foregrounded as the goal of the group – and people's understanding about themselves and their community within this context.

Acknowledging Differences

> Now you can turn to the individual and you recognize him as man according to the possibility of relation which he shows; you can turn to the aggregate and you recognize it as man according to the fulness of relation which he shows. We may come nearer the answer to the question what man is when we come to see him as the eternal meeting of the One with the Other.[51]

The *others* were the main reason for the group's existence. The term includes all those located either on the fringes of the group or on the fringes of society. It was often used to indicate migrants, but its use was not restricted to them. It also implied other groups and individuals who were positively disposed towards AuRA but not fully integrated in it. These included various individuals and communities that supported the Sanctuary, (such as the LGBTQ community, various feminist groups, ecological groups, conscientious objectors etc) or interacted with the Sanctuary and AuRA, as well as other anti-fascist and anti-racist initiatives. From the movement's perspective, however, these others were all to be found at the margins of any estab-

51 Buber 2002, 244.

lished social order. They were a corollary of oppression, of exclusion, of discriminatory practices, of institutional racism, of harassment and of violence.

The Sanctuary was an open space free from all social malice that welcomed all alternative attitudes. Very often however, the others occupied a marginal position within the movement. As Stefanos, a member of the LGBTQ community and friend of the Sanctuary observed, it was not only different cultural backgrounds that could lead to marginalisation and unequal treatment, but there was the more general problem of people reproducing prejudices. This was something that various collectives had to face, and it even happened at the Sanctuary. One of the incidents Stefanos experienced gave them the impetus to properly start defining the problems and openly addressing them within the framework of the weekly assemblies. The incident took place during an event at the Sanctuary, when a political refugee indiscreetly asked a friend of Stefanos if they were a boy or a girl. Stefanos:

> To ask people of our collective if they are males or females, it is not acceptable, even if you are also persecuted in your own country [as a political refugee], or even if you are local! We openly informed everyone at the Sanctuary that this is not something we can accept [as a collective]. It is something that really upset us and we wanted to discuss it, because that is the only way in which we can overcome taboos and prejudices. [...] Reporting the incident functioned catalytically in everyone's brain [they became aware of the problem], and I discovered this personally during my conversations with migrants and locals [*ντόπιους*].[52]

The implementation of the groups' aims in the Sanctuary was not free from difficulties and dilemmas. Anti-racism was a broad endeavour. Its ideological underpinnings were not limited to the category of race, and the group was supported by various other collectivities all of whom embraced a plethora of goals leaning towards social justice, anti-discrimination and egalitarianism. Very often, day to day conversation did not escape stereotypical verbal slips symptomatic of the various conflicts and misunderstandings of daily reality. During the first festival that I participated in, those verbal slips were not uncommon. An example from my personal notes may provide some insight. While setting up the festival in the park, one of the basic principles imposed on the volunteers was that of co-operation, co-understanding and consent, even when it came to minor details or tasks that one could easily handle alone. The older participants, who were primarily responsible for the gradual transformation of the park into an open, colourful festival-space would also impose – in a clear albeit polite manner – the rules of cooperation and communication among the participants. One of these rules was that everything had to be completed by at least two persons, even when the second one was essentially redundant.

52 Stefanos Interview Extract: Conflict, 2013.

> One morning, a group of women – including myself – were bolting the legs on the big benches that were supposed to become the central bars for the drinks, as Bob had told us to do. We were struggling with the strange, big tools and lacked the strength needed to finish the task properly. Omar, a volunteer from Afghanistan, saw us, took the tools from our hands and before we even realised what was going on, the job was finished! Moments later, an anxious voice was heard screaming with frustration at Omar: "No! No, no, no!... No, why are you doing this? Is your name Maria or Alkyone, I assigned this work to the girls, you are charged with another task." And then, George, a young member sitting next to us murmured: "What did you expect? As if a migrant would ever let a woman do the work!" [53]

Later, during a break, I was making notes and thinking that if any theorists had witnessed the scene, they would have quickly come to the conclusion that the movement had imperialist and hypocritical tendencies and attitudes. George seemed to place 'the migrant' in a pre-determined category, as his remark was founded on generalisations and clichés, with clear pejorative implications for Omar's culture, habits and different analytical categories. Omar would in all likelihood be categorised as being subject to the group's imperialist tendencies, encountering difficulties while trying to grasp the norms and habits of the receiving society, and having to learn what the 'Greek' was teaching him. If there were feminist theorists among us, they would no doubt have raised their own objections to the scene and paradoxically bemused, they would be unable to decide just whom they should put on a feminist trial and why. I spent some time contemplating this imaginary battle.

Exclusionary discourses and hierarchical tendencies are not to be underestimated, as Zavos witnessed during her own participant observation in an anti-racist group in Athens more than a decade ago.[54] The use of the categories 'Greeks,' 'migrants,' 'natives' and 'others' permeated the movement's language, and their use was not devoid of hierarchical connotations and racial stereotypes.[55]

Similar categories were commonly used by both locals and migrants in AuRA as well. Members of the group would identify people according to their country of origin, i.e. the Albanians, Afghans, Arabs, Nigerians, Georgians to mention only some. In this context, the Greek word for "native" is worth considering. During informal talks but during interviews as well, the Greek participants frequently referred to the "Greeks" as "ντόπιοι" [ntopioi]. Ntopios stems from the Greek word *εντόπιος* [en-topios] which means being in or from a specific place or topos. While the direct translation of the word into English is native, indigenous, or local, (the first of which in

53 Personal Notes: *As if a Migrant Would Ever Let a Woman Do the Work*, 2010.

54 Zavos 2006, 96. See also Però 2007.

55 Zavos 2006.

English may have negative connotations),[56] the Greek word *ντόπιοι* signifies a more neutral reference to the place of birth or residence. Although at the beginning of my research I didn't see any significance in the members' use of the word, over time I came to identify the fact that my interlocutors were exclusively referring to locals as *ντόπιοι*. I decided to retain the use of the word 'ntopioi,' as interchangeable with the word 'locals' since both signify the members' intention to give a value free indication of someone's place of birth or residence. Equally noticeable was the common use of the word 'migrants' with just a few cases in which somebody referred to them as foreigners, aliens, or strangers. A distinctive category was that of political refugees and asylum seekers, whom people referred to by these names, whenever it was important for their legal status to be acknowledged during assemblies and discussions.[57]

Deciding how and why it was acceptable to use some terms and not others was important within the group's anti-racist ethics and illustrated the challenging nature of its alternative vision. As a frame of co-existence for many diverse others, AuRA could not deny its mediatory function between the migrants, who were either represented by the Greeks or integrated within the specific work groups initiated by the Greeks, and the Greeks themselves as the instigators of all political activity. Although the members were familiar with these criticisms, and reflected at length on them, they mainly concerned themselves with the ways in which those criticisms were influencing the project of solidarity in its entirety. Between 'Greeks' and 'others,' 'locals' and 'foreigners,' solidarity itself seemed to allow the formation of a field of an asymmetrical field of power relations and dominant discourses. To see solidarity as "an asymmetrical act" that simply provided help to the others and resembled philanthropy[58] was, however, in the members' eyes a criticism that demeaned the group's collective efforts towards equality and authentic engagement. As we will see in Chapter Six, their emphasis on self-organisation provided a remedy to such criticisms.

From the very beginning of my participation in the life of the group, I gained the impression that the members engaged in a kind of daily, informal research which focused on otherness. My interlocutors revealed during interviews and our informal talks how and why diversity was part of the endeavour and formed part of the constant quest of the group's own becoming. They stressed the necessity of recognising the others' needs and appreciating their individuality in order for the Sanctuary to

---

56 I would like to thank my colleagues at the European University – Viadrina Frankfurt (Oder), who brought me to this realisation and rendered this note valuable for a more comprehensible account of the meaning of "ntopios."

57 See also Zavos' comments on the topic: Zavos 2006, 98–100.

58 Hoelzl 2004, 49. For a philosophical approach to the issue of solidarity see Hoelzl 2004. See also Revault D'Allonnes 2013. For the dilemma of solidarity or philanthropy within organisations and movements see also Theodossopoulos 2016 and Rozakou 2018.

become a site of truly solidarious interaction. As such, the members were constantly preoccupied with questions such as: "who are the others?", "how can we approach them in order for us to live and work together?", "what are our motives and how do they differ from theirs?" and ultimately, "which gestures, words, and what body language should be employed in order for our objectives to be better understood and supported by more people?"

The group's job was to bring together all these different perspectives and to constantly negotiate all the tensions which are expected to occur whenever so many differences intersect. The ultimate aim of these constant negotiations has been to *shorten the distance* separating the varying stances and bridge the gap between them. In this respect, participation in the group was a process of "acknowledging difference," "understanding it" and ultimately, of learning from it and re-experiencing identity and togetherness through it.[59]

It was in this spirit that it was somehow agreed that Omar could not be expected to already *know*, at the outset of his involvement with AuRA or the Sanctuary, all of the principles of co-operation and solidarity. Considering George on an equal basis, neither should he be expected to be aware of the derogatory connotations of his arbitrary comment and restrain himself from articulating it; a comment that could indicate a discriminatory attitude underpinned by social norms, but which could very well also be completely irrelevant to the incident and simply meant to serve other (less easy to detect and discern) purposes. The members would often point out that people define 'the right thing to do' on the basis of individual cultural codes, values and systems of belief, and yet do whatever serves the 'common interest' at any particular moment. And in this sense, it can be supposed that Omar's attitude was rational; following a quick estimation of how long would it take us to do the job, he spontaneously acted in favour of the economy of time.

However, even if the view that Omar was not able to cope with the sight of the girls struggling with the tools had some weight, what really mattered to the functioning of the group was the extent to which members would eventually follow the movement's aspirations; that is to say, when and how they would realise that when working with (and as) a team, women are allowed to, supposed to, and ought to bolt things together, or carry heavy things and do any other job, and that no-one should be deprived of the pleasure of being creative and offering help. What mattered was when and how members would be imbued with the idea that in the movement the most important thing is the cooperation with the other, the exchange of experience and joy. At the same time, it was important to see whether and how the locals would critically approach their own pre-established ideas. Anthi made some insightful comments on this topic:

59 Some texts that made these points more comprehensible to me are Gupta and Ferguson 1992; La Fuente 2016; Polletta and Jasper, James, M. 2001.

> This is a common base of knowledge: We are determined to be ourselves, by overcoming our differences, because if our differences become an obstacle... this is a great problem. I experience this feeling when I talk to friends who do not share similar views. They refer to people as "illegal" and "strangers" – I can go literally out of my clothes [go crazy], I cannot tame my temper, and I have a feeling I can reach my limits – and I am not against violence (she laughs)! So, you can realise what kind of limits there are implied here. But when you talk to people with whom you share a common ground, and with whom you have already agreed that diversity not only is not a problem, but it also enriches..., then even the most difficult parts of it become beautiful and reciprocal. The discussion about who is better and feels superior to the others and the like, is just a waste of time, although... no indeed, I think, it is a waste of time.[60]

In this context, the Sanctuary provided people with the chance to mingle with others and confront the prejudices and stereotypes that emerge out of this challenging cohabitation. For AuRA, differences do not constitute a problem to be resolved, but a quality to be affirmed. As such, a continual revision of all rules permeated the group. Commonly agreeing on them would allow everyone to feel truly *at home*. Other cultures, other dispositions, 'good' and 'disturbing' habits, all take their place in this new realm, where all rules needed to be re-assessed and all previous knowledge re-evaluated in order for new principles of co-existence to emerge. The affirmation of both our individual existence and the capacity to communicate and co-exist with others, "requires a deep leap in consciousness," as Melucci characteristically puts it.[61] In this sense, differences contributed to the development of the kind of egalitarian social relations that could help create the ideal society which the members aspired to become a part of. Laura:

> That's why there is the festival, which is very important, and it is one of the few festivals in Greece which unites people beyond political spaces. It gives space to migrants to come forward, and present themselves, culturally and politically, in order to be ready for the society to come.[62]

When approaching otherness, the members were ceaselessly working not merely on a project of cultural tolerance in which people accept that the others' view of the world may differ from theirs, but on one that allows people to re-experience the world through the eyes of the other.[63] These multifarious syntheses formed a 'new social contract' into which people in the Sanctuary were willingly entering. This diversity revealed the complex and interesting nature of the endeavour. In the actuality

---

60 Anthi Interview Extract: Diversity, 2011.

61 Melucci 1999, 423.

62 Laura Interview Extract: The Society to Come, 2013.

63 See on the topic Yioka 2006.

of the movement's daily life, rules were reformulated from the ground up and individual needs were discovered by exploring differences, and by re-affirming various (and not only cultural) identities in the process of collective life.

These constant explorations on the part of the group reminded me of the idea that the best way to take seriously the production of knowledge in social movements is by working "alongside them."[64] As some scholars suggest, a "relational mode of engagement"[65] between social scientists and activists is best learned within the bosom of the movement itself, and this participation opens up the road for a fruitful engagement in our study of them. This is also what allows us to pay closer attention to the "processes of production of difference"[66] and to their dismantling within local, situated settings. And indeed, the members' own interpretations of a common shared world, that of the Sanctuary and AuRA, were under constant construction and remained fluid and open to change. It is in this sense that otherness constantly demands its own affirmation. At the same time, it does not resist further problematisation as a political field of representation, where voices, powers and conflicts reproduce patterns of dominancy and exclusion.[67] I will postpone, however, the discussion of otherness through the prism of political representation until Chapter Six. For the moment, I would like to delve further into the issue of otherness as a process of acknowledging differences and re-experiencing one's own self.

Making Sense of Ourselves and Others

As I have suggested, the group itself was engaged in its own kind of daily research at the Sanctuary, into the kind of co-existence that its members and the various others who used the centre could create for themselves. The believers had an important role in this, as they spent a lot of time and effort building relations between the various groups and individuals, with the overall goal of establishing an ethical community of coexistence. In this sense, many of the theoretical issues (concerning how to approach and understand the other) that trouble social scientists were being worked out practically in the daily activities of the group. This opened up the possibility for me to take a hermeneutical approach to the way in which the group's construction of ways of coexisting engages practically with issues of otherness and selfhood.[68]

The significance of the daily routine was constantly addressed by the members themselves and it was not restricted to the Sanctuary and the groups who partici-

64 Casas-Cortés, Osterweil, and Powell 2008, 27–28.

65 Casas-Cortés, Osterweil, and Powell 2008, 20.

66 Gupta and Ferguson 1992, 14.

67 Gupta and Ferguson 1992, 17.

68 Casas-Cortés, Osterweil, and Powell 2008; Hirai 2015, 17; Riboli 2006; Kyriakakis 2004; Buchowski 2006.

pated in it. During the first years in which AuRA supported it, the functioning of the Birdhouse was considered to have been a great success. In the following comment, Alkyone describes how refugees familiarised themselves with the place, and began to follow a schedule, developing their own understanding of what collaboration, co-working and self-organisation meant:

> A very good example of this sort is the cleaning schedule – the stairs, the toilets, the basement where the showers are, and the like. Since March last year, there has been a schedule with dates and names, pairs of men and women, of men and men, and so on. There were times last year when someone wanted to pick a different day, because, I don't know, they didn't want to work or clean, they were bored, they were busy, for whatever reason, and the others said, "No, this is your day and you will do it, and if you don't, no-one will and we'll get swamped in dirt" –and they didn't care. This year, there have been many times when someone has said, "I really can't do this today, I'm bored" – this kind of thing, not that they're busy or anything – "Can you? And I'll do it when it's your turn," and they've done it without complaining and without bringing it up at the assembly. And we just happen to know it because we know migrants that are friends with the residents of the Birdhouse and they let us know – not at the assembly, but when we have a beer together, at night.[69]

Alkyone described how refugees in the Birdhouse gradually started to make sense of the cleaning schedule by understanding that the daily activities should be faced solidariously and with a sense of respect towards other people. Incidents of this sort confirm that the members' insistence on co-operation and self-organisation in their work is realistic, and that people enjoy participating in the collective life on this basis. The cleaning schedule at the Birdhouse, as well as other regular activities such as supplying the kitchen and the bar at the Sanctuary, were determining factors in people's development of a sense of belonging. During my initial research period, on one of my very first days at the Sanctuary, an acquaintance suggested we jointly clean the place. It took me some time to realise that getting people cleaning was a strategy to help people feel responsible for the place by contributing to the running of it, and also help them feel at home by familiarising themselves with the place, as well as with its atmosphere. A feeling of fulfilment accompanied these little moments of becoming useful to the group and allowed a joyful energy to suffuse the already virtuous activity of pursuing a common goal. This sense of belonging is evident in Anthi and Alkyone's description of how, in this way, migrants became an integral part of the Sanctuary:

69 Alkyone Interview Extract: Rotation, 2010.

> Anthi: Yes, ultimately the migrants managed not only to integrate into a place which ought to be mainly theirs [in the Sanctuary] – because it is not only a social centre – and parallel to this they integrate, not only into the group that is organised around them, but also into other groups that share similar sensibilities, marginalised groups in general, or groups that centre on dependencies. Anyway, they centre on all these special characteristics that groups may exhibit and do not allow them to cope with broader majorities [society]. Thus, I believe we had a very close relationship to the migrants from the beginning. We have been offering the language lessons, our work in the Birdhouse also added to that. And now since they already became an integral part of the Sanctuary, since they actively participate in it, even in the bar...
>
> Alkyone: And they want to participate very much.
>
> Anthi: It's true.
>
> Alkyone: It is not that somebody forced them to participate or even asked them to do so... "would you like to participate in the bar." No, and they already feel that they are an integral part of the endeavour.
>
> Anthi: And with a lot of them it is not only that you co-operate, but you cross the line from co-operation to becoming friends. With some of them, we have known each other for years let's say...[70]

During these minor daily activities, alliances and friendships were formed and bonds were reinforced. Although for many members, their new life at the Sanctuary was like entering into a new home and a big family, for many others friendship, as a means of socialisation, had a more important function. As a home for various others, the Sanctuary was the primary place where people could meet each other, as Luan and Rene explained:

> Rene: I came to know the Sanctuary because of Alkyone. She suggested that we could have some free language lessons there, in Greek and English. And because I wanted to learn English, I went there, and it was great. The lessons, the bar, the migrants, I met a lot of people. It is very nice because it is actually the only place we can go, as people in Greece they are a bit crazy. Going out in general is weird. People look at us strangely, or they call us names. The Sanctuary is great for us.[71]

70 Alkyone and Anthi Interview Extract: Integration, 2011.

71 Rene Interview Extract: Sanctuary, 2013.

> Luan: I have a similar story. I have met people at the Sanctuary, I have learned a lot, I have learned to play the guitar and I take Greek lessons as well. At the Sanctuary people are more open.[72]

Luan and Rene, whom I had the honour to meet later during my research, were two kind-hearted guys from west Africa. Our interview lasted for two hours. I asked if we could do the interview in English, as they spoke fluently, but they preferred to express themselves in Greek as they were participating in the language lessons at the Sanctuary and spoke Greek very well. By the time of our interview, they had already spent five and six years respectively in Greece, first in Athens and later in Thessaloniki. They attended the lessons at the Sanctuary, had a lot of friends and liked their teachers. They would often spend time at the Sanctuary after their lessons. Outside it, however, things were not the same. People looked at them strangely. They both emphasised how difficult it was to find people as generous as Alkyone or Marc outside the Sanctuary. During our conversation, I was moved by their friendliness. We still meet online, and I was pleased to learn that Rene realised his dream of moving to Germany. They were both disappointed with their lives in Greece, especially at the time of the crisis, when things deteriorated for both the local population and for migrants. I could detect Rene's eagerness to leave Greece, while his friend felt more secure in the now familiar environment of Thessaloniki.

Luan and Rene were well-known and liked among the residents of the Sanctuary. Although friendship for them seemed restricted to the Sanctuary, the familiarity and the comfort of the place reminded them of their life in their own country:

> Outside there are not so many friends. In the last month we were there every day for a beer. I talk to people and then I go home. It helps migrants a lot [to do this]. I used to have my coffee place in my country as well.[73]

During my research, I was intrigued by the meanings people attributed to friendship bonds. Friendships were complimentary to the family feeling people experienced at the Sanctuary and signified the importance that belonging to a community has in people's lives. It was the depth of these bonds and the physical presence of other people that enabled the community of the Sanctuary to flourish. Nevertheless, relationships varied in intensity, duration and level of commitment and one cannot help wondering how friendship-ties were conceptualised and affirmed in the movement.

Unquestionably, numerous factors played a distinct role in the formation of relationships and imbued people with notions of selfhood, equality, and moral engagement. Gender, class, culture, age, individual habits, as well as the personal life course of individuals led to different conceptualisations of friendship, formed in specific

72 Luan Interview Extract: Sanctuary, 2013.

73 Rene Interview Extract: Friends, 2013.

circumstances and from the participants' various standpoints. At different times, different affective capacities and emotional commitments would emerge.[74] It has often been noted that within our understanding of friendship, notions of the self are frequently reduced to the "individual, autonomous actor," a product of western liberal conceptualisations.[75] In this sense, taking for granted an assumed equality between subjects who can be friends entails an idealised perception of autonomy and is deeply problematic, as it neglects issues of class and gender.[76] Starting from a situated notion of friendship within the Sanctuary and AuRA, I tried to detect what kind of conceptions of 'choice' and 'motivation' were held by the members who thematised friendship as a central category in their understanding of membership. Within the specific context of the Sanctuary, equality was part of the social contract and simultaneously part of an ideal to be achieved in the outside world. Equal status was to be obtained on the basis of people's equal participation in the group. Individual selves as an expression of plurality were to guarantee the well-being of a greater aggregate of individuals and not to overshadow the group's overall existence.

At the same time, a variety of understandings of friendship seemed to emerge within the group. Sometimes friendship was conceptualised as comradeship, with political affiliations preceding friendly ties, and sometimes it suggested a fluid social bond formed in the course of the group's practices. In some other cases, friendship primarily arose from the act of meeting others, and was more connected to a general necessity to socialise than to any particular sense of commitment. Friendships functioned to reduce the distances between people, they fostered mutual learning and enabled people to discover each other, but also re-discover themselves within the new context of the Sanctuary. The believers seemed to actively and generously enter into reciprocal exchanges, and even longed for further commitments, all of which paved the way for relations to emerge and stabilise. They were the ones who encouraged people to participate and highlighted the importance of daily collective action. They would invite migrants and others to the assemblies, they would tell people about important moments of collective action, they would emphasise the importance of togetherness during minor daily activities such as eating and cleaning, and they would include them in collective decision-making.

Friendship functioned as a means to a good end; it was a mechanism of introducing people to their collective self and it represented a step closer to the intimate

74 For sociological studies on friendship, see Allan 1989; Jerrome 1984; Pahl 2000. For friendship from an anthropological point of view see Desai and Killick 2010; Bell and Coleman 1999; Paine 1999; Evans 2010. For historical approaches on friendship, see Silver 1990, 1989; Paine 1969.

75 Course 2010, 169; Carrier 1999, 23; See also Silver 1989, 274.

76 Carrier 1999; Course 2010. See also Uhl 1991.

atmosphere of the Sanctuary's family. The diverse rituals of the group provided opportunities for intimate and friendly interactions, ranging from daily activities to the various themed parties that were often organised at the Sanctuary. Shortly after an event for the Afghan community at the Sanctuary, Chara shared her thoughts about her experience there. Chara:

> Well, there was a party for the Afghan community. Were you actually there? No, no you were not. It was fascinating; I did not expect this at all. At the beginning, to be honest, I did not want to go, but I thought I had to go. And it was really great. There were a lot of Afghans, and they were all in a very good mood and very kind people as well. They were willing to show us their traditional dances, to present their local cuisine and because you know migrants at the Sanctuary go through severe financial hardships, some of them even have no place to live and I could see in their eyes their wish for someone to talk to them. The others did not need to say anything wise, just a simple "hi, how are you doing, I am Chara," just something simple and touch them on the shoulder. I did not feel they were expecting anything more than that, just this simple thing. And these are the people who really have an integration problem, not me. Those people, in whose eyes you see how much they need you, have an integration problem. [...] They were willing to teach you their dances, to explain their local cuisine and to buy you a drink! Someone who cannot afford to feed his family is offering to buy me a drink! It is unbelievable![77]

Having an immigrant background herself, Chara distinguishes between different levels of integration. She felt privileged having a home and coming from a relatively affluent background in comparison to those who lacked even the most basic necessities. Thus, the others' generosity in introducing her and her friends to their culture and even offering to buy them a drink made a deep impression on her. The greater the financial hardships people were faced with, the more valuable the gesture. The act of offering to buy someone a drink is symbolic of the process of constructing togetherness. Both the generosity of the migrant, and the empathy that Chara shows, are signs of mutual recognition. It is interesting that Chara affirms the offer in this way, as it could be also interpreted as a sign of flirting.

Another thing that stood out in Chara's extract was the gesture of "touching on the shoulder" as a token of recognition of the difficulties other people may have been experiencing. The gesture captures the simplicity and humbleness of the members and the Sanctuary; it is a gesture of understanding between equals rather than pity for someone less fortunate. It is similar to what Gadamer described as a process of finding or "coming-into-language" in order for people to "reach understanding."[78] It

77 Chara Interview Extract: Afghan Party, 2009.

78 Gadamer 2004, 371. See also Walhof 2006, 580.

is the engagement in this kind of mutual construction that allows members to feel that they are a meaningful part of the overall process.

Social events at the Sanctuary enabled 'differences' to be communicated, which was often a demanding and strenuous task. Gestures could be misunderstood. While 'touching on the shoulder' could be a positive gesture, it could equally become highly problematic. There were often discussions of the dos and don'ts for both migrants' communities and the members, a development of mutual knowledge that demanded a lot of time and effort on both sides. It was often advised that different populations should be approached in different ways (and certain constraints on bodily expression was a frequently discussed topic in the circles of the believers). Finding the right words and gestures to express themselves and communicate with each other was a constant struggle for all the participants. Such exchanges often revealed a mystical atmosphere, especially on those occasions when people were deprived of their 'official' roles and were left to be guided by others. In this respect, social events provided an active field of engagement in which people could acknowledge their differences and in which the members of the group and the others could come closer together, offering promises of fraternity, equality and harmonious coexistence.

At these events the others regained their dignity and affirmed a strong sense of the difference between the world inside the Sanctuary and the world outside it, where exclusion, deprivation and anxiety prevailed. During the culturally specific gatherings, roles were reversed. A community such as the Afghan migrants had the chance to act as hosts to the people and the friends of the Sanctuary. They ran the night and guided everyone through a cultural journey that amazed people and filled them with enthusiasm and hope. Another aspect that captured my attention in Chara's interview was her empathetic approach to issues pertaining to feelings of exclusion:

> We greeted them, and especially Baris the guy from Turkey, an acquaintance of Michael, you know Michael, he sat at our table at this evening. Baris looked persistently at us and I had the impression he wanted to talk to us. He did not want to only spend time with his own friends. And ultimately, he talked to us, and we met his friends as well, and I could see how happy he was. Later that night we prepared one big table out of two and all sat around together. The next morning, I learned from my friend that Baris had asked Michael if it would be okay with them if they visited the place again, and if this would be a problem for other people at the Sanctuary. These people who have to consider every single step they take, who are afraid that their very existence constitutes a problem for others, these people are the issue.[79]

79 Chara Interview Extract: Integration/Exclusion, 2009.

Chara's recognition that people can experience their very existence as a problem for others highlights the extent to which the Sanctuary and its members had to fight against the migrants' feelings of fear and hesitancy above all else.[80]

Friendship revealed people's willingness to engage and prepared them for becoming an integral and equal part of the endeavour. It not only functioned for those who wanted to take advantage of the information, language lessons and cheap alcohol that was available, but also for those who were willing to enter into the reciprocal exchange that was the first step towards a better understanding of the Sanctuary's nature and various objectives. Rene and Luan both belonged to this category of people who were actively involved. It was by actively engaging and committing, that people re-acquired their proper names and ceased to fall into the faceless categories of *ντόπιοι*, Greeks, migrants, or others. The distance between individuals, which previously characterised uneasy moments of remoteness, was reduced by properly naming the participants. At the same time, the act of naming showed respect and admiration for people's distinctive life courses, opinions and uniqueness. The affective and emotional world acquired its full shape during these interactions. Stefanos:

> It delights me that I know a lot of migrants personally. We say hello, we became friends, and I remember their names, whereas at the beginning I tended to forget or confuse their names.[81]

The example of friendship enables us to gain a deeper insight into the flaws, limitations, and prejudices of our own selves, and to achieve a more effective synthesis of the constituent elements of a successful coexistence. Friendship consists in experiencing the world on the basis of a togetherness that builds upon "reciprocal co-perception," to put it in Gadamer's words, within the frame of a dialectical relationship.[82]

As we saw in the cases of the believers and the intellectuals, diverse individuals were going through a transformative process in AuRA and at the Sanctuary, which aimed to establish a strong community which would allow all people who wished to participate in it to do so. In this sense, it was people themselves who offered an alternative example of communication and interaction, which then determined the course of friendships according to their own willingness to meet and connect with others. A compassionate self, open to influences, tolerant, flexible, diligent and devoted to others, was constructed on a daily basis, and accompanied the communal ideals of solidarity, openness, mutual understanding and generosity. This brings us

80 This reminded me of Du Bois' article and the phrase "How does it feel to be a problem?" See Du Bois 1999, 125.

81 Stefanos Interview Extract: Having a Name, 2013.

82 Gadamer 1999, 139; Walhof 2006, 578.

to the consideration of a dynamic, changing process which is realised through social relations in the community of the Sanctuary.[83] More importantly, however, a strong sense of we-ness and groupness emerge within a field of incessant elaboration of interactions and relationships.[84]

Between believers and others, solidarity reveals itself in the form of friendship, it implies mutual understanding and commitment. As the developing friendship strengthens, the figure of the other emerges as a decisive factor in the opening-up of the conscience to the comprehension and interpretation of one's self.[85] The other becomes a source of knowledge not only in terms of her/his otherness, but also with regard to the self and the world.[86] The other is the cause, the means and the physical proof of one's own transformation, and in this sense provides members with a constant reminder of the potential for creative coexistence and change.

Within this frame, the *vulnerable others* became *valuable brothers* who to a great extent endowed the Sanctuary with its meaning, and greatly determined the course of the group's own functioning.[87] Solidarity as friendship also revealed the beauty of its complex purpose. The benevolent qualities of friendship and solidarity were juxtaposed with society's depersonalised and individualistic ethics and became a paradigm of ideal cohabitation. Forming a strong and inclusive community was necessary if every diverse other was to have a fair share in the group's functional, emotional and social life. At the same time, participation and reciprocity produced new ways of thinking upon which the richness of relations and the re-writing of all rules would depend. The realisation that all members are solidarious and that the individual does not take precedence over the collective, (though nor does the collective take precedence over the individual) foregrounds the relationship of the self with every other and posits the act of communication as a means of building a new existential ethos.

The Good Comrade: *Monk-like Representations* (Utopia)

This section is intended as a short commentary on the concept of action. I do not aspire to tackle philosophical or religious questions, nor is it my intention to analyse action in metaphysical terms. I merely wish to articulate some thoughts on devotion

83 Delanty 2003, 123.

84 Brubaker and Cooper 2000. See also Dean 1996.

85 Buber 2002, 236–44.

86 Walhof 2006, 580.

87 I borrowed the analogy of other/brother from Buchowski 2006.

and commitment, which imply that beyond those qualities rests a rich field of 'unknown worlds' of action, which the members discover in the companionship of their comrades. The ideal model of the activist presented a high degree of commitment, and as the phrase "to have retreated into the movement" indicated, people withdrew from the pleasures of social life and were entirely devoted to the movement. A number of members of the group pointed out that the "comrades" played a sacred part:

> Q: What does the word comrade mean to you?
>
> Fedonas: Oh, it's a lot of things, cannot be described, no it can't be described. For me it's a feeling, it's a feeling one has towards someone, not exactly sacred, no, very... I cannot describe it.[88]
>
> Evdokia: When I was in my previous group, there was always a question-mark inside me, which proved to be warranted when I left, [in AuRA] very soon I felt like people around me were comrades in very realistic terms, and, on the other hand, in very emotional terms. I felt like the word comrade encapsulated both the political and the human [element].[89]

The figure of the comrade seemed to be shrouded in a kind of mystic atmosphere, and people continually lacked the words to describe how they felt about it. It was characterised by a pervasive feeling one could sense from imperceptible gestures, smiles and comments that indicated warmness, familiarity and expectation. The use of the word "comrade" suggested a spiritual atmosphere that seemed to mobilise people to act together. "*They are a comrade!*" By this sentence one was to understand that they were a basic figure in the movement's life, and that their life and deeds were approved of by the other members, due to their being a co-participant in the assemblies, or the Sanctuary, or on the street during demonstrations. The figure of the comrade was present in people's stories about their friends and other members. Being and acting together meant that they were all members of the ideal brother and sisterhood that they were committed to creating and the devoted comrade appealed to all members as the ideal to be reached. In their comments about the comrade people frequently spoke as if all members of the community had reached an agreement, and consensus had been achieved. However, everyone had a very different background and disagreements were part of the daily reality. In this sense, the word comrade did not so much reflect this daily reality as a less problematic togetherness. It seemed to carry more of a symbolic value, evoking the idealised qualities that people should have in the movement, and according to which everyone would

88 Fedonas Interview Extract: Comrades, 2011.

89 Evdokia Interview Extract: Comrades, 2013.

have the same understanding of and approach to the movement's objectives, and all disagreements would perish.

The idea of the comrade functions as a role model that inspires good deeds and represents the possibility not only of a different society, but also of the *different humans* who will bring it about. The comrade symbolises the qualities of the humans who *will come to be* in order to serve this different society, who will have been forged in empathy and coexistence, and whose characteristics will be morality, understanding, prudence, self-composure and struggle. To those new human beings, "solidarity among men is no longer a tenderhearted luxury but a deep necessity and self-preservation," to borrow the words of Kazantzakis.[90] Solidarity is thus not only a code of principles, but also a struggle and a moral obligation to undertake initiatives and new beginnings. Solidarious action refers to that condition in which speech and action (to use Arendt's terms) are inextricably intertwined,[91] serving as unfailing proof of devotion. Through speech and action the co-actors are becoming what Arendt described as "distinct" or unique by their coming and acting together.[92] Through the idea of the comrade, an idealistic light is cast on the dynamics of the struggle, of endurance, of physical exhaustion, and of being profoundly devoted to the cause.[93]

> The comrade is a mental construct forged through the members' embellished accounts of their fellows' solidarious actions. Comrades are intellectuals, wise and insightful coordinators. They are body and faith: an unwavering devotion. They are intellectuals and believers simultaneously: they minister to others and tend to their needs. They are fully dedicated to the cause, but also aware and accepting of the after; they bravely contemplate the finite nature of the struggle, free of arrogance or personal ambition. It is precisely this bravery that elevates comrades in the eyes of my interlocutors to the status of an embodiment of the ideal world. They are believers (they understand and respect the cause), but also nonbelievers: they doubt and question. Fighting their fights, they "stand by their God," fully

90 Kazantzakis 2007, 82–83; See Kazantzakis 1960, 70.

91 Arendt 1998/1958, 176–78; Arendt 1986, 242–44.

92 Arendt distinguishes between *otherness* and *distinctness* and she specifies that: "In man, otherness, which he shares with everything that is, and distinctness, which he shares with everything alive, become uniqueness, and human plurality is the paradoxical plurality of unique beings. Speech and action reveal this unique distinctness." Arendt 1998/1958, 176; In Greek then the two competing ideas are *διαφορά/διαφορετικότητα (distinctness) – and ετερότητα (alterity/otherness)*: Arendt 1986, 242.

93 The ideal comrade appeared to me to be a monk-like figure, and inspired me to re-read the following texts, which had a profound influence on this subchapter: Kazantzakis 2007, Kazantzakis 1960, Nietzsche and Hollingdale 1969/1961, Dimitriadis 2011, Dimitriadis 2007 and Samartzis 2017. The influence of all four works is evident throughout the text.

> aware of the moral imperatives: responsibility, sacrifice, struggle.[94] Comrades look on their companions' failings with compassion. They are Others themselves – otherworldly, alone and marginalised, in the face of the futility of their fights.[95]

The ideal comrade has a moral gravitas and a sacred, almost transcendental aura that seems almost 'monk-like' in its approach to an ascetic ideal. There is a moral surplus arising from the differentiated interactions that my interlocutors posit as the ethics of the future society. To the individualists, the opportunists, the conformists, the contented, the resigned and the fearful, the group counter-proposes what is 'right' by constructing, through speech and action, the ground of a more just society. Anthi:

> For me above all truths and above all realities is this solidarity that surpasses every other truth, that is, [the fact] that we will set every difference aside to come closer to the human being (the human being or the animal next to you) and you will fight for their sake, even if their truth or reality clashes with your own. This is what solidarity ultimately comes down to for me.[96]

Comrades never shy away from struggles or fights dictated by their conscience. Metaphorically speaking, struggle itself is evidence that something almost 'divine' is an intrinsic part of solidarity. This belief in the sacredness of solidarity is what constitutes their everyday struggle, their wisdom, their *promise of salvation or redemption* to their fellows, and by extension, their 'pledge' to humanity. Their quest for a different society and a different human evokes the ecstatic and dynamic elements of religious faith. A more just, more humane, more solidarious world is the very reality of their existence and prompts this inquiry into the questions of faith, action and solidarity. Their very struggle for it, their very faith in the possibility of it, which, despite the doubts that occasionally arise, is made stronger by the little miracles of everyday life, invariably bring to mind a quest of a religious character. At the same time, though, their discourse is so emphatically centred on the notion of 'free will' that it ends up transcending the compulsions typically inherent in the practice of faith. Ultimately, theirs is a quest that is existential, moral *and* political.

The idea of the ideal comrade relates to the old question of the nature and the characteristics of community. In the case of AuRA and the Sanctuary, the key element in the understanding of community is that it promotes neither individual selves nor the group per se. The ideal of an egalitarian society cannot rely on an action which is stripped of its actors. It rather relies on the distinctness of its members

94 Kazantzakis 2007, 82. Kazantzakis 1960 ibid, 44. It may consist in a paradox that Kazantzakis' work would inspire such an idealistic use of his writing, however, I am obliged to refer to the passages that may have had an influence on my notes and thoughts.

95 Personal notes: *Monk-like Representations*, 2014.

96 Anthi Interview Extract: Solidarity with all Human Beings, 2011.

and their contributions. In this sense, the comrades are opposed to sterile and individualistic narcissism and instead prioritise the actors' will to act and to transform themselves. At the same time, the ideal comes together with the expectation that individual and group remain a field open to further improvement. Consequently, they return their virtues back to the group, while proving that they remain flexible enough to change their surroundings, and to actively adapt to the requirements of the era. This faith in the active comrades is the essence of the model of society that the members of the group envision. It is the capacity of the members not simply to resist, but to transform themselves and to alter their living conditions.

> Q: You mean that the world can change...
>
> Alkyone: Well, if I am to be honest yes! (laughs cheerfully) Whatever others may say, yes, I know that you cannot change the whole world, [but] you can change the part of the world that you try to change. It is the conditions of our own life that we want to change- yes, those can change.[97]

I started this section by saying it is a comment on action. I will conclude it by looking at Arendt's notion of natality, which sheds light on political action by seeing it as the capacity for "beginning something anew, that is, of acting."[98] As Arendt characteristically writes:

> The miracle that saves the world, the realm of human affairs from its normal, "natural" ruin is ultimately the fact of natality, in which the faculty of action is ontologically rooted. It is, in other words, the birth of new men and the new beginning, the action they are capable of by virtue of being born. Only the full experience of this capacity can bestow upon human affairs faith and hope [...].[99]

I take the above passage in a metaphorical sense. As Benhabib comments, accurately in my opinion, there is a kind of "anthropological universalism" in Arendt's ideas of plurality, natality and action which depicts the human condition as one of "equality-in-difference."[100] On the one hand, natality (in contradistinction to mortality) is the quality that allows for a "de-centring of the subject by revealing our fundamental dependence on others."[101] On the other hand, however, it does not account for the achieving of *a priori* respect among co-actors, and cannot guarantee the removal of all differences and hierarchies.[102] Nevertheless, Arendt's idea of natality, so closely

---

97 Alkyone Interview Extract: The World Changes, 2010.

98 Arendt 1998/1958, 9.

99 Arendt 1998/1958, 247.

100 Benhabib 2000, 80–81.

101 Benhabib 2000, 81.

102 Benhabib 2000, 81.

related to the idea of action,[103] greatly reflects my understanding of the plurality of new beginnings that are cultivated in AuRA. In this sense these expectations of new beginnings allow faith and hope to remain intrinsic aspects of action.

Ideal comrades are the embodiment of the utopian in an otherwise very real world. They represent the idea that being attached to an ideology in a dogmatic fashion does not create the proper conditions within which to affirm the qualities of a solidarious whole. Solidarity itself becomes a liberating phenomenon as members discover the importance of intersubjectivity, and of the capacity and potentiality of action through togetherness. The 'good comrades' stand as an idealisation of the human condition and denote a withdrawal from daily concerns in order to better serve their faith. People in their uniqueness, those who embody their very humanity, stand as symbols and paradigms for further struggle. My understanding of the use of the word 'comrades' was that it revealed the very core of *communitas*. Without the metaphor of the ideal comrade, a crucial dimension of the utopian element in the everyday life of the people is lost. The ideal comrade is framed by real expectations, it is an aspiration, a future dimension, and a spiritual expansion of what those people are doing in the here and now of their everyday life, and as such it is a crucial symbolic dimension of the movement's becoming. For we are not here only concerned with individual or collective contributions and values, but with the people's belief in their capacity to transform themselves by uniting as comrades in the expectation of a utopia to come.

Conclusion (And a Note on Non-believers)

In this chapter I have tried to illustrate the different roles people assumed within the group, and the ways in which they interacted while working towards solidarity. Intellectuals seemed to have served the movement by appropriating issues that pertained to the institutional and organisational sphere and were responsible for the promulgation of the group's aims. The believers demonstrated their solidarity actively and practically, and of all the members of the group it was they who had the deepest connection to the people who used the Sanctuary. The others, who became fellows and brothers to the members of the group, provided the possibility for the endeavour to remain an open and flexible field of engagement that constantly produced new modes of communication and co-existence. And ultimately, there was the figure of the comrade, which functioned as a kind of role-model for the new humans in the society to come.

103 See also Kateb 2000, 135.

The typology provides a kind of the framework of the group's ideology, revealing its theory and practice, its goal and utopia. Intellectuals represented the group's theoretical constructions, which underwent constant elaboration, and were highly determined by the historical circumstances (theory); the believers represented the practical site of the movement since they were responsible for the fulfilment of the practical and vital necessities of the group (praxis); the others were part and parcel of the goal, they represented the main purpose of egalitarianism (goal); and the ideal figure of the comrade symbolised the sacred order of the ethical community to come (utopia). Indeed, any understanding of the group that would interpret the roles and relationships that make it up in strictly hierarchical and fixed terms would seem to me to be inadequate. It would be unfounded to claim, for example, that the intellectuals made use of whatever prestige they did have to keep for themselves the power to make decisions or that the believers were nothing more than 'water carriers,' (even if they did say this about themselves), or that the others had no alternative place of entertainment outside the tight circle of the Sanctuary, and their integration into it depended heavily on the locals' protection and representation.

To see the group in these limited terms would deprive us of a deeper understanding of its complex and highly idiosyncratic (in comparison to more conventional organisational structures and groups) modes of engagement. Such an interpretation would not be able to explain the group's popularity, its members' devotion, or its duration, and would leave questions of internal resistance (among members) unanswered. Equally, an understanding of the intellectuals' power as imposed primarily over the believers and the others does not shed adequate light on the complexity of the group's formation and in particular on the issues of agency and volition or individuality and collectivity. Neither would it suffice to claim that the group's internal conflicts were always resolved for the sake of the group's ultimate purpose. The long-standing presence of the group is remarkable if we consider that the natural course of similar groups' evolution very often results in their dissolution, or their fragmentation into various other smaller groups due to the inherent disputes that arise.

Different ideas of solidarity emerge out of this typology. The intellectuals were primarily responsible for supplying the group with new ideas from the outside world. By doing so they were involved in a process of overcoming past ideals and engaging in new ones, something that the new generations of intellectuals in particular brought into the movement. In this sense both a missionary and political project of solidarity permeated the macro landscape of the group. The believers, although seemingly weak and over-sentimental at times, in fact had an equal share of power, as they laboriously, though silently, kept the wheels turning and influenced the group from inside. By imbuing the group with emotions and by making a constant effort to consolidate the relationships that were continually being formed in the group, they created an inclusive atmosphere for everyone. The believers, however, would have been deprived of this transformative energy if they lacked the impetus that the presence of the others gave them. For the others were the ones who provided the believers with the opportunity to accomplish their purpose, and effectively justified the very existence of the group and its ideals. Despite the fact that both believers and others seemed to be striving for recognition from the intellectuals, they themselves were instrumental in the movement. Their efforts constituted a real experiment in developing the kind of relationships that could build towards a better society. They were indicating another way to solidarity by focussing on everyday relationships, constructing new ways of communicating their feelings, and creating an egalitarian atmosphere within which all participant members could inspire each other and collaborate together towards the creation of the society to come. It is in this sense that the believers demonstrate the effectiveness of the *charisma* of the group in achieving their aims, a charisma without leadership that constantly re-evaluates itself and is based on effort and personal work as opposed to the charismatic qualities of the intellectuals.

All the asymmetries that one confronts while looking closely at these types and their interactions are reconciled in the figure of the ideal comrade. The believers' ideal of a rigid and faithful activist and the others' hopes to find a better human company are fulfilled through the ascetic ideal of the good comrade that brings together different standpoints in the movement. Utopia is approached by inspiring the members with the strength to continue working on the project of solidarity.

Solidarity thus appears to have many different faces and facets. For the older intellectuals, solidarity is an ideal more close to a traditional understanding of doing politics and retaining the status quo, while for the younger intellectuals it presents a more fluid vision imbued with the ethical atmosphere of everyday life, while still promoting a broader socio-political understanding. Solidarity is manifested as sacrifice in the believers, as friendship between brothers, and even as a kind of challenging cohabitation for some of the more sceptical members, as I will further examine in Chapter Six.

However, before moving on there is one more type we need to consider. All of the different subgroups we have looked at so far did not only interact with each other but were also engaged in an ongoing conversation with the outside world, and this included what we may call 'non-believers' – those who resisted a durable relationship with the group. Non-believers is admittedly a broad category, including all sorts of different individuals whose reservations about the group took different forms. For our purposes, however, we can take non-believers to be those people whose participation in the group was of a temporary nature, as opposed to the more faithful members of the group.

The effect that the non-believers had on the group was to provoke a constant vigilance regarding the competing values within the broader leftist space. A good example of this vigilance revolved around the issue of volunteering. During recent years, and largely because of the crisis, volunteering at places like the Sanctuary had become very popular. Later, as the public discourses on solidarity deepened, and as social participation began to receive more praise, a new set of formal and informal rules and regulations for volunteers would be introduced as part of a new state policy for the evaluation and recording of NGOs and other organisations.[104] The most common consequence of this gradual regularisation of volunteer work was the granting of certificates to verify volunteer jobs. However, the Sanctuary and AuRA lacked the kind of administrative organisation to do this.

> Friday night. I was waiting for a friend to come to the cafe at the Sanctuary. I was sitting at the small bar talking to some acquaintances about the current political issues. A very young pretty lady entered the Sanctuary. She was observing the place intensively and reminded me of the curiosity the newcomers displayed when they entered the place. I thought she was a student. "Excuse me I am interested in volunteering and the like...", she almost whispered, as if unsure of herself.[105]

The way she asked the question, in slang terms, made it sound as if she had come to engage in some sort of drudgery. I wondered what she could possibly mean by "and the like." Her conversation with Emanuel (one of the older members of the group) lasted a couple of minutes. It turned out that the young lady was in need of a certificate proving some months of 'social and political engagement.' The members of AuRA were well familiarised with this sort of request. Proof of some months or years spent doing volunteer work could be a valuable indication of someone's public virtue and good work ethic when it came to seeking employment. For this reason, some of the young volunteers who requested to participate in AuRA's projects did so because they needed a certificate of participation in return. In this way, a kind of 'bureaucratisation syndrome' arose alongside the popularity of solidarity during the crisis.

Neither individual members, nor the assembly as the collective body for decision making, were in charge of certifying volunteers. While members recognised people's frustration with this incapacity of the group to grant such certificates, at the same time they maintained a clear position regarding the group's main principles, that solidarity was not to be reduced to a piece of bureaucratic evidence of someone's seemingly virtuous social and political public life, which they could then use to help them pursue their individual careers. Solidarity was a commonly agreed, informal contract among participants. Being a part of the movement meant actively experiencing the life of the group. Understanding, emotion, empathy, and long-term commitment all played their part in the contract, individual ambition did not.

Within the group, volunteering was not seen as a means to an end, and the people who stayed with the group did so out of a sense of solidarity with the cause, not to

104 On this topic and on the refugee crisis in 2015 see Rozakou 2018, 237–44.

105 Personal Notes: *I Am Interested in Volunteering and the Like*, 2013.

help them later in pursuing their individual careers. The policy of rewarding volunteers with certificates was seen by some members of the group as a way of blackmailing people into some sort of social and political participation, people who invariably had little commitment to, energy for, or authentic engagement with the causes they volunteered for. The institutionalisation and bureaucratisation of solidarity through the issuing of certificates also had the effect of introducing people into the movement who were primarily concerned with rigorously performing defined tasks in order to gain their certificate, a lack of engagement which could undermine self-organised initiatives and projects. Members of AuRA were suspicious of what they saw as this prioritisation of the self over the community, and the different 'ethos' that such a treatment of volunteering would bring into the movement.[106]

Solidarity in all its facets was to be actively experienced within the community, in all the various ways we have examined so far. It was a gradual learning of coexistence, a re-shaping of one's own self through the group and its practices. It was based on benevolent feelings, friendship, strong emotional bonds and had as its focus the raising of one's consciousness with reference to otherness, diversity, and co-existence. The hope was that this could transform inflexible social structures from within by changing individual perceptions and by de-marginalising certain populations that were excluded from social and institutional life.

The most common reaction of the members to requests for certificates was they lacked the authority to issue them and that this kind of individual evaluation was beyond the members' scope. Members of the group often had to explain in a polite manner to potential volunteers that offering one's time, energy and skills to the group was not going to be repaid by any kind of certificates, and that the group's work was highly dependent on individual contributions that come from a recognition of the importance of the group's goals and a real need to support them.

106 On this topic see also Rozakou 2018, 241–42.

6. Solidarity in a Time of Crisis

This chapter focuses on the second period of my research at the Sanctuary in late 2012 and early 2013, a time during which the Sanctuary and the members of AuRA had to deal with various challenging situations. The recent financial crisis that had broken out in Greece suggested that the forthcoming years would be marked by debts and recession, as well as changes at the social and political level. There was widespread talk of the need for financial support from the European Central Bank (ECB), the European Commission (EC) and the International Monetary Fund (IMF) – the so called 'Troika' – and the need for major changes at all levels.[1] Redundancies, reduction to pensions and increases in taxes were among the measures that the government introduced in order to escape bankruptcy, all of which heavily affected the population. Gradually the consequences of the financial crisis began to appear on the micro-level of daily life: rising prices, unemployment, the closure of businesses, higher taxes, an increase in homelessness, and increasing levels of household debt.

At the same time, political mobilisation was dynamically growing, a fact that was evident from the increasing number of general strikes, protests and riots aimed at the institutions and politicians who were thought to be responsible for the crisis.[2] Thus, from out of the crisis, solidarity appeared as a remedy with multiple functions. First, solidarity was evident in the communication and organisation between people, and ultimately the systematisation of collective action: solidarity nets, citizens platforms, neighbourhood committees, movements of solidarity, initiatives of solidarity, pharmacies and clinics of solidarity, assemblies that focused on the consequences of the crisis, and movements for the free distribution of products.[3] All

1 For an overview of the crisis internationally and in Greece see Sakellaropoulos 2014, 17–83; see also Hadjimichalis 2018, 2020.

2 For more on the protests and events of the period, see Diani and Kousis 2014. See also Karyotis and Rüdig 2018.

3 For an account of the multiple projects of solidarity during the period see: Arampatzi 2018; Chatzidakis, Maclaran, and Bradshaw 2012; Rakopoulos 2014b, 2014a; Gritzas and Kavoulakos 2016; Hadjimichalis 2018, 267–80; Cabot 2016, 281–92; Rozakou 2016; Tsilimpounidi and Walsh 2014.

these activities, however large or small in scale, enabled the communication between groups and individuals that were organising themselves in order to fight the consequences of the crisis. Secondly, solidarity acquired an ethical as well as a political character and demonstrated the necessity of engaging in struggle if change was to be achieved. As the political system and its institutions failed to effectively represent broad social strata, these kind of 'social reflexes' were more and more dynamically activated.

The wide range of collective actions that people undertook and the multiple projects that arose during these periods created certain new conditions which the Sanctuary and the members of AuRA had to deal with. The members had to constantly revise the group's priorities in response to the ongoing crisis and its consequences, both inside and outside the borders of their own community. The effects of the crisis were evident in the Sanctuary in the increasing signs of tiredness, of physical and emotional exhaustion, and in the misunderstandings and quarrels that arose between people. They were all symptomatic of the process of routinisation, to recall Weber's terms.[4] In the following pages I will look at some of the specific problems that arose in the Sanctuary and the ways in which people tried to negotiate them. This will allow us to see how the various different stances on solidarity – that were related to the members' various roles – resulted in different suggested solutions under the weight of the crisis. First, however, let us look at one of the main issues of the period that will shed some light on the group's orientation and role within the new socio-political landscape: their participation in the Indignant Citizens Movement (or Indignant Movement).

Solidarity's Mass Appeal: A Great Momentum or the Dissolution of a Vision?

The financial crisis was accompanied by a generalised feeling of social and political impasse. A sense of general uncertainty sharpened the political debate and contributed to an atmosphere of frustration and indignation. New austerity measures were constantly announced, wages and pensions were cut, and new taxes were constantly introduced. It was not only the national debt and the country's uncertain future, but also individual debts and the overall deterioration of living conditions that created a suffocating atmosphere. The first years of the crisis were marked by extensive general strikes, protests and riots, a fact that showed that the civil society was active and resistant to the political and social failures that people experienced

4 Weber 2019, 378–79. Routinisation indicates processes which deprive charisma of its initial, exceptional qualities, and reduces it to more plain, everyday matters. Ibid, 378 and see also the editor's note on *Veralltäglichung*.

first-hand. Some scholars have noted the emergence of new forms of contestation, and the emergence of a new political subject, that stemmed from these grassroots movements.[5]

The Indignant Movement of May 2011 was one of a number of public forms of contestation during this period.[6] Other important moments of the period were the hunger strike of 300 migrants that started in January 2011 and ended in March 2011,[7] various protests during 2012 and the closure of the state media in 2013.[8] The hunger strike in Thessaloniki and Athens, in which 300 migrants took part, raised issues of migrants' legalisation and brought to the fore the multidimensional face of the crisis. While the migrants' demand for legalisation was rejected, a special status of tolerance was granted to them. Migrants who had been residents of the country for ten years could obtain legal documents, and there was a reduction of pension credits which would permit them to continue to live and work in the country.[9] The hunger strike was supported by various NGOs and smaller collectives, while during the hunger strike the Initiative for Solidarity was established by a variety of groups. Karyotis and Skleparis identified this moment as the first organised effort by migrants to form a collective identity and act on behalf of migrants in general.[10] Subsequently, the unexpected shut-down of the national TV and radio stations in June 2013 provoked protests that lasted for months. Supporters occupied the Hellenic Broadcast Company (ERT) buildings for several months while the workers continued broadcasting over the Internet.[11]

In AuRA there was an ongoing discussion about all these events. The group were in favour of taking action on the occasion of the ERT's shutdown, and actively supported the migrants' hunger strike. The end of the hunger strike was celebrated as a victory not just for the migrants, but for everyone who was working to help those most affected by the crisis. Solidarity continued to grow and continued to gain in political significance. The case of the Indignant Movement, however, raised a number of issues within the group regarding the extent to which they should get involved. While some members treated the movement with great suspicion, fearing its depoliticised character, others reported that the Indignant Movement made them realise that something must be done. Rafael:

5 Hadjimichalis 2018, 283; Arampatzi 2018, 51–52. For a periodisation of protests at the time see Karyotis and Rüdig 2018.
6 Arampatzi 2018; Simiti 2016; Theodossopoulos 2013; Douzinas 2011, 155–65.
7 Karyotis and Skleparis 2014.
8 See for an overview and comparatively for other countries Hadjimichalis 2020, 138–70.
9 Karyotis and Skleparis 2014, 154. See for relevant material Clandestina, January 19, 2011.
10 Karyotis and Skleparis 2014.
11 Hadjimichalis 2018, 256–58.

> In May 2011 the Indignant Movement arises in Greece and in Thessaloniki. I would like to say a few things: it has changed me very much mainly in terms of how much and in what ways I started to get involved [in the movement]. That is, I have actually decided to become involved in political matters and I was not the only one for whom this change happened. There were also other people who in the spring of 2011 essentially decided that the way things were going we would have to deal with a lot more issues.[12]

Rafael belonged to a younger generation of emerging intellectuals in AuRA. Although he had a friendly relationship to AuRA and the Sanctuary before this event, the gathering of the Indignant Citizens was a binding process that would initiate his long-term participation in both AuRA and the Sanctuary. For Rafael it was necessary to follow the same direction as the majority at this point, and he participated in the gatherings and public discussions which took place at the White Tower in Thessaloniki. In the case of AuRA, he saw a chance for greater political participation and the transformation of the means of engagement and mobilisation. In this sense, solidarity could be re-invented and radicalised through the crisis and AuRA had the chance to dynamically engage in the forms that collective action was taking. The crisis and the broad mobilisation it provoked were treated by second generation intellectuals such as Rafael as an opportunity for the movement's aspirations to be more easily communicated to the broader public, and to involve a previously ignorant social majority in what was until recently thought of as the province of certain people who belonged to groups with strong ideological underpinnings.

However, the participation in the Indignant Movement was an issue that also found resistance in the bosom of the group and reflected some of the movement's bewilderment towards the new modes of protest. Rafael described his personal struggle to convince other comrades of the importance of harmonising the group's goals with what was happening "out there":

> I became quite actively involved, I tried along with other comrades from the Sanctuary, especially with David to convince some people that this thing, what was happening was important, because the people of the Sanctuary and AuRA were rather cautious about it. There has been this ongoing discussion about the movement's – and the movement's vanguard – contact with broader popular masses. There was however an intervention there, on our part, and that also showed in texts by *αγανακτισμένοι* [the Indignants] in Athens and Thessaloniki. That is, from the very first text [of the Indignant Movement] migrants seemed to join [the movement]. That is to say that many may have overlooked this fact because [from the outside] it may have looked like there were also "others," like especially in Athens, on the upper square, who were [chanting] patriotic or

12 Rafael Interview Extract: Indignants and Mobilisation, 2013.

> national and nationalistic slogans, but the texts were all ours, they belonged to the movement, and of course this bothered the Golden Dawn.[13]

The Indignant Movement provoked a lot of discussion regarding its appearance, unity and the scope of its overall course. This was a time when various protests and demonstrations were taking place across Europe, asking for more democratic policies and demonstrating against austerity measures. Although the Occupy movements and gatherings cannot be subsumed under one and the same category (as their demands, characteristics and natures vary), what they did bring to the fore, as Hadjimichalis observed, is a very tangible demand for democracy and the realisation that a great distance separates the state and its institutions from society and its citizens.[14]

In Greece this was a time when the parliament were deciding on further austerity measures and a general feeling of impasse and frustration was translated into the condemnation of the politicians who had lost public support.[15] The calls for public gatherings started to multiply in May 2011. It was claimed at the time that this was a response to the Spanish invitation to the Greeks to "wake up."[16] These calls initially focussed on individual participation at gatherings, and discouraged the involvement in parties, unions and other political organisations since, as a common saying of the time put it, these were "not to be trusted." However, when Syntagma Square, located in front of the parliament in Athens, was occupied two separate groups quickly formed. The upper square, right in front of the parliament building, was a landscape of Greek flags and infuriated citizens who claimed not to have any political affiliation and engaged in a variety of symbolic acts of disapproval: cursing at the parliament and the politicians, and showing their palms against them – a pejorative gesture which is a known sign of disrespect in Greece – chanting anti-European, anti-austerity slogans, and trying to hinder various politicians from entering the building.

On the lower square a different atmosphere developed as people from leftist and anarchist groups were attempting to follow more direct-democratic procedures, calling people to join public assemblies and to formulate concrete demands through public discussions and exchanges among the various participants. The gatherings lasted for a long time and various working teams emerged with specific responsibilities (a social media group, a first aid group, and groups for food, security, entertainment, cleaning, etc) to help organise the occupation of the square.[17] This organisational aspect of the gatherings was often attributed to the broader leftist

13 Rafael Interview Extract: Participation in the Indignant Movement, 2013.

14 Hadjimichalis 2018, 248.

15 Fragoudaki 2013, 99–108.

16 Sotirakopoulos, June 15, 2011.

17 Hadjimichalis 2018, 256–58.

and anarchist space.[18] This systematic effort to orient the movement to address real problems contrasted greatly with the unfocussed patriotic and nationalistic atmosphere on the upper square. Nevertheless, the two worlds coexisted.

As Marilena Simiti puts it, although it would be hard to claim there was a collective identity or common ground that leant the Indignant Movement coherence, protestors on both sides found themselves to be mutually co-dependent, as their presence on the square was highly determining of the overall course of the movement and its success.[19] As was often argued, the Indignant Movement was based on the strength of self-organised, but often uncommitted or poorly organised crowds which bore no clear political or ideological agendas.[20] Overt political identifications were considered hazardous at the time of the crisis, and people partaking in these gatherings often demonstrated no clear political identification.[21]

However, while a clear political/ideological distinction emerged in Athens between the lower and the upper Syntagma Square, in Thessaloniki the boundaries were more blurred. People in AuRA were faced with multiple dilemmas regarding whether to attend the gatherings at White Tower. Iakovos raised his objections to such a participation:

> Q: Could you please tell me about the gatherings at the White Tower?
>
> Iakovos: Oh no! Okay it is simple. Yes, it is positive, people getting out on the streets is positive. Masses out on the streets that's not much better. Obviously, those people participating in it, or at least a great majority of them, – not those who are there every day, – they are people who would like to do something, something very close to nothing, however. They are not people who will go on strike, or oppose their bosses, or even members of the parliament or anyone with whom they have a clientele relationship, because they are afraid.[22]

Iakovos' initial unwillingness to discuss the subject eventually gave way to a well-formed opinion about why he abstained from participating actively in the Indignant Movement. There was a feeling that the people who gathered on the square were those who for years had enjoyed privileges and now felt infuriated at the loss of them. However, these gatherings were not accompanied by an agonistic culture. Even if demonstrations were a positive development, the anger of the 'masses' was not necessarily always itself positive. Iakovos linked this development to the political

18 Ibid.

19 Simiti 2016, 37.

20 At the time this fact had positive connotations. See Douzinas 2011, 151–153; 232–237.

21 It would be wrong to consider all participants to be 'ideologues,' as many participants had no previous political engagement. See also Papataxiarchis 2017, 211; Hadjimichalis 2018, 257.

22 Iakovos Interview Extract: Indignant Gatherings, 2011.

culture that prevailed in Greece during the Metapolitefsi. The optimism that characterised political life during the 1980s was based on the guidance of charismatic leaders. One of the reasons that Iakovos was cautious about indignant gatherings was that he saw a similar desire for a leader to emerge. This, according to Iakovos, had certain consequences:

> The last three generations have been taught not to fight for anything, it is this [idea] that "daddy will save them." And as a society we will pay for this, there is no way we won't pay for this. The question is how high the price will be. And many among these people who get out and shout – yes, fine, it is a good thing that they get out and shout – but what they are shouting about is their fatherlessness (*ορφάνια*): "Dad why did you abandon us, where are you?" And that's what makes them susceptible to electing a new dad.[23]

The metaphor of the "fatherlessness" of the ideologically uncommitted crowd captured the hesitation of many members to regard the Indignant Movement as one that would function as an agent for real change. The Left seemed rather numb regarding these spontaneous gatherings and doubts about joining the movement were raised from all sides of the left-wing spectrum.[24] The state of being "fatherless" indicated the participants' political immaturity, something that was seen by Iakovos as a repetition of old attitudes that centred on benefits and privileges (referring mainly to the 1980s and 1990s).[25] As Iakovos sees it, the people on the square were to a great extent people who were not used to assertively demanding anything. They exhibited an individualistic approach, were still dependent on the clientele relationship to their party or union and did not have any real interest in changing either society or themselves. The gatherings indicated that many people – deprived of their past privileges, frustrated and afraid – were joining collective action out of despair about the future. In this sense, mobilisation was not only emotionally charged (indignant), but also lacked political awareness.

Another problem that Iakovos saw in these gatherings was that the impeachment of parties, unions and organisations raised serious concerns about the political future of the country. Many people who were participating in the gatherings insisted on their non-adherence to any party or organisation, a fact that raised doubts about whether they could achieve anything, something that Iakovos was concerned could lead to a decline in democratic values. As a commonly used phrase during the Indignant gatherings pointed out, people joined the gatherings as 'citizens' ("I came here

---

23 Iakovos Interview Extract: Fatherlessness, 2011.

24 Sotirakopoulos, June 15, 2011.

25 This is linked to the culture of metapolitefsi and the critique we analysed in Chapter 1. See for example: Tsoukalas 2017/1993; Pappas 2010. See also the analysis of similar discourses in the case of the indignant movement in Theodossopoulos 2013.

as a citizen"), a phrase which connoted a politically neutral form of participation. Joining the movement as a citizen indicated the absence of any ideological motive. It is in relation to this, that Iakovos spoke about the cultivation of a populist mentality during the gatherings:

> Okay, over the last few days there has been a more nationalist atmosphere in Thessaloniki. But I cannot, I cannot, I will be on the sidelines, observing, but I cannot attend the assemblies [in White Tower]. And I cannot do what others do, suddenly speaking up against all parties – because someone is an anarchist or whatever [and they say]: "I came here as a citizen" and "I don't belong to any party!" I do not belong to any party either but damn! I don't think of parties as an evil thing. Parties, organisations, unions are processes [...]. But it is there that you experience struggle and everyday reality. Direct democracy does not mean, "all of us gathered here let's organise a foodbank!" [...] Okay, if someone feels like learning something out of it, they will, but if they have the inclination to do something very close to nothing, they won't get any further than that and in all likelihood they will salute the messiah who will emerge from that.[26]

For Iakovos, the importance of political representation is at stake here. The overall condemnation of the political system would never come out of the crisis if the resistance it gave rise to was that of the Indignant gatherings. On the contrary, it seemed that the predominant demand was precisely for political protection. On the one hand, the squares allowed contradictory groups to gather together. On the other hand, the way the ideal of 'Greekness' and nationalism were revived by some of the Indignant Citizens could not but be misleading and dangerous. In this sense the potential consequences of the depoliticised character of the gatherings (which could go in the direction of populism, nationalism and even violence) were not to be underestimated.

Rafael, on the other hand, brought to the fore a more positive element of the Indignant gatherings, which in his opinion should not be neglected, namely the movement's potentiality for raising awareness. While recognising the reasons why many of his comrades treated the Indignant Movement with contempt, taking into consideration the nationalistic, xenophobic, even racist tendencies that it exhibited, he focussed instead on the advantages it might have for the broader leftist space. Namely, these collective gatherings at the White Tower in Thessaloniki introduced a lot of "non-initiated" people into the world of movements and direct action:

> People without previous contact with the movement suddenly found themselves participating in direct-democratic assemblies. For us – who have known what an

26 Iakovos Interview Extract: Representation, 2011.

> assembly is since student years – this may not seem that important. What happened at the time for hundreds or thousands of people was mind-blowing. It may have otherwise been immensely problematic, but to have someone participating in an assembly and [to hear them] say, "please let him speak," something which does not even happen in left-wing assemblies in many cases, was unbelievable![27]

The statement "let him speak" was often heard during the public assemblies at the White Tower. During the popular assemblies, people announced their willingness to express themselves publicly and an equal amount of time was offered to them in order to present their ideas. In those moments, when people were too loud or disagreements came to the fore, somebody from the crowd would shout loud: "let him speak." The phrase represented the kind of ethics that 'change' required. The gradual cultivation of a different culture took place through assemblies and direct democratic procedures in the squares. The new culture implied dialogue, respect and despite, or even because of, the fact that it emerged from such a controversial setting, it further empowered the belief that people and society can change from the bottom up. Moreover, it verified AuRA's own calling: they were among the first to invite people to gather together, to build platforms of communication and to unite people against the consequences of the crisis. The 'moment of the Indignants' was experienced as one of great momentum not only for the group's engagement in political action, but for the course of the movement in general. The movement's future was here at stake. It was a moment in which the ideal of solidarity was gaining ground among the various actors who strove for equality, justice and democracy.

During this period a variety of organisations and neighbourhood assemblies emerged to address the problems caused by the crisis (debt committees, anti-memorandum initiatives, the 'we don't pay' movement, neighbourhood committees). At the same time, various hangouts, social spaces, and squats became an active part of the political and social life of the city. However, the popularity of the extreme far right Golden Dawn party increased as well.[28] Their presence in neighbourhoods and schools became evident as racist attacks against migrants, citizens, and various alternative spaces multiplied during these years.[29] The causes of the increase in the various forms of extremism that flourished during this time are not to be sought solely in the financial dimension of the crisis.[30] As we already examined in Chapter Three, there was a plethora of social, political and ideological reasons for the prevalence of nationalism and racism throughout the previous decades, and under

27 Rafael Interview Extract: Let him speak, 2013.

28 Henley and Davies, June 18, 2012. In the June 2012 elections the Golden Dawn party received 6.97 percent of the vote.

29 Alexandropoulou and Takou 2019. See also the related campaign HumanRights360, n.d.. See also Papataxiarchis 2014.

30 Fragoudaki 2013.

the pressure of crisis these were reactivated.[31] As Pantazopoulos comments, the old nationalistic rhetoric about the uniqueness of the nation and the protection of national identity re-ignited feelings of cultural insecurity ("πολιτισμική ανασφάλεια") in those who felt themselves to be suffering under the crises, making them prone to radicalisation.[32]

In Thessaloniki, anti-fascist organisations decided to take action at schools and inform pupils what fascism and racism is. An old acquaintance of mine, Apostolis, a participant in an antifascist solidarity assembly stressed the need for unity and strategy in the organisation of their activities. The latter should not be restricted to the "distribution of texts," written in what he described as a "wooden language," but should seek creative ways to engage younger people in a consideration of the subject of fascism. However, as he told me, in Thessaloniki the activities of the Golden Dawn were still limited, for two reasons in particular:

> First of all, it is the character of right-wing politics in Thessaloniki in general, which already absorbs many extremist elements. And the second reason, I believe, is the university, which is placed right in the city centre and functions protectively.[33]

During our meeting he described the proliferation of squats and social spaces, at least five places similar to the Sanctuary that had flourished since 2011, along with various anti-racist organisations and local movements, as well as four anti-fascist assemblies, all of which were making a considerable effort to collectively meet and find a common strategy to act against fascism. Stefanos was also participating in the same antifascist assembly as Apostolis. I asked him about the influence that the antifascist assembly could exert on society:

> During a demonstration that we organised, people were appearing on the balconies, supported us, applauded, people from the neighbourhood joined the demonstration spontaneously. We saw people responding and I finally felt that I am not alone with the adherents of Golden Dawn![34]

The social centres, squats and hangouts that emerged in Thessaloniki during this period were not only places where people pursued their political interests, or where collectives had their meetings. Most of them hosted a variety of activities capable of attracting a range of people. The youth organisations of the political parties started to initiate similar centres as well, all-inclusive spaces where a variety of activities (similar to those at the Sanctuary) took place. Instead of staying enclosed in the political office of their party, they established parallel spaces that functioned as a pole of

---

31 Fragoudaki 2013, 86–99.

32 Pantazopoulos 2012.

33 Apostolis Interview Extract: Anti-fascist Mobilisation, 2012.

34 Stefanos Interview Extract: The Impact of Anti-fascist Assemblies, 2013.

attraction for many of their followers. What all these relevant spaces had in common was that they combined political participation with entertainment, cultural festivities, book presentations, and they aspired to become alternative spaces where people could gather.

However, despite all this mobilisation, the first signs of weariness also appeared inside the Sanctuary during 2012–2013. The key words in the conversations I had in 2013 were particularly illustrative in this respect, as we will see: fatigue, whining, violence, racism, institutionalisation syndrome. I asked Rafael for his opinion on what happened and what had changed?

> As for what's happened: It started out with great momentum; moving into a new place – and a place that is so beautiful and historic as that – always gives people strength; it unites people, it brings them together. Moreover, at the time, it was run by people who, before the crisis, had some certainties and enjoyed the sweet life in a way –"yes, there are many problems [in the world], but there's also a social contract, there's a consensus, [and] the migrants may be oppressed but we'll get through this." And the people that frequented the Sanctuary also enjoyed spending time there; they were fairly educated, with university degrees, with money to spend. The migrants had not yet become very familiar with it, but as the years passed by, various things happened. One of them is that, obviously, as time passes by, the groups and collectivities that support and participate in it start to disagree with how certain things are done. That is, in any case, I mean, even if there were no crisis, when something has been up and running for three, four years, like a living organism, it is impossible for a group – let alone for an individual – to never disagree with anything, to never say, "I don't like this" [or] "This doesn't work for me." This may lead to detachment, that is, someone may stay around without really bothering with the affairs of the Sanctuary and [those of] the group and [with] how many people the group brings [to the Sanctuary]; and it may even lead them to altogether withdraw [from the Sanctuary].[35]

Rafael analysed the issue in a rather dispassionate manner and distinguished between what happened with the people who initiated the Sanctuary, its friends and supporters, and what the migrants themselves introduced. What Rafael considered to be important for the members was the fact that the social and financial background of many of the members allowed their participation, and the overall atmosphere in the Sanctuary allowed for its success, for unity, cohesion and broader participation.

In the same manner, he explained to me the situation with the migrants. The migrants found a place where they could find shelter. Lacking strong friendship or family bonds and lacking a community which would be able to organise them, they

35 Rafael Interview Extract: What has Changed, 2013.

visited the Sanctuary mostly for socialisation and companionship. But many of them were unwilling to engage politically in the groups of the Sanctuary, and often failed to understand exactly what the Sanctuary was about. This caused a lot of disagreement and quarrels between locals and migrants, as everyone was missing the point about what the ultimate purpose of the Sanctuary actually was.

> Then, there are the migrants who have found out about the Sanctuary, who come over to have some beer because there are cheap drinks there. But we should keep in mind that these people are people who usually don't have strong social ties with other people – with Greeks or other migrants; they don't have a strong community here, they don't have many things to do other than go to the Sanctuary with their friends or by themselves and have some beer. [...] This would often lead to friction, to minor quarrels, maybe even to bigger ones, among them or between them and the people tending to the bar, because there was often a failure to make it clear to one side or the other what exactly the Sanctuary is about. And when – every time there's a fight, and there are also other people present, everyone knows that this drives people away. I mean, if someone who's never been to a place before sees other people fighting, yelling at each other, why would they want to go back to that place? The crisis made all this even more intense, because the migrants are looking for a place that is more... protected in every way, [they want] to feel like they have a place they can call their own.[36]

Rafael's account made me wonder about the different perceptions of this crisis at the Sanctuary. While he was presenting the situation, he seemed rather detached, as someone who would like to deal more with finding solutions to the problems rather than discussing the problems themselves. While he wanted to acknowledge the positive dimension of the crisis outside the Sanctuary and seemed ready to give all possible solutions to the problems, other members did not share this optimism. Those within the circles of the believers, having spent a lot of time and effort trying to embrace all the people and activities in the Sanctuary during the previous years focused on the lack of consensus in the Sanctuary that led to an unbearable emotional fatigue.

Reflections on the Crisis

While the intellectuals were preoccupied with the grand political issues of the time, the believers, the others and the friends of the centre were showing signs of what we might call 'routinisation': disagreements, quarrels and frustration – all have entered into the daily routine. This was particularly evident in four areas. First of all, there

36 Rafael Interview Extract: Migrants at the Sanctuary, 2013.

was a proliferation of similar spaces in the city that threatened the popularity of the Sanctuary. The second area concerned the political profile of the Sanctuary following the rise of SYRIZA.[37] Another was related to what members called the "lumpenisation" of the group: the fact that just because people participated in the centre, it did not necessarily follow that they were political aware. Finally, there was the problem of incidents of violence at the Sanctuary, arising from disputes between migrant communities or individuals, or between members of the group and migrants.

> Q: In 2010, 2011... the atmosphere was different, whereas now everyone – including myself – seems to be of the opinion that there is a downswing. Do you have an explanation for it, besides the socio-political situation, which has obviously played a part? How did this turn happen?
>
> Laura: I don't know if I can completely separate it from the political situation, because when there is – when things suddenly change and you're left unemployed, you have a really hard time making ends meet, and it also affects your mood; it's only natural that it would affect your mood, that you wouldn't feel like going out, or you may not have the money to go out. So I guess you end up cutting back on the time you devote to your social space, because you probably have to spend time looking for a job, for example, or getting another postgraduate degree so you can find one [a job]; [...] precisely because you have all these problems to deal with, you probably feel like going someplace where everything is better, so you can temporarily escape your problems and avoid facing new ones; and precisely because the Sanctuary, for example, is neglected – but it is not always neglected because that's what we wanted, [but] because of objective circumstances – it has probably reached a point where it has become a new problem. I'm not saying that it's bad [it has turned into something bad], but it has become a new problem – not a huge one but going there would still feel like being burdened with more of the same [with another problem]. So, you avoid going there altogether so that you only have your own problems to deal with.[38]

The pressures people felt under the crisis appeared to become a crucial factor in their everyday experience at the Sanctuary, particularly in their experience of time. Previously the members' perception of time was closely connected with the detailed scheduling of the group's needs. Time was experienced with joy and certainty while the spaces of engagement (the assemblies, the groups, the various thematic sessions and the Sanctuary in general) gave a feeling of safety, and boosted the desire to return, as people felt relaxed and enjoyed the familial feelings that these spaces engen-

---

37 The SYRIZA party (Coalition of Radical Left – Progressive Alliance) came second in the elections of 2012.

38 Laura Interview Extract: What has Changed, 2013.

dered. But it was not only a lack of time, but also emotional exhaustion that affected both people's private life and the life of the Sanctuary. The Sanctuary became a place where all problems overlapped and going there began to feel like a threat to one's own inner cohesion. A feeling of dissolution prevailed:

> Q: What does it translate into? What do you observe to have happened?
>
> Laura: Into [a lack of] human resources. [It means] that where there used to be fifteen of us, now there are many who have focused on 'solidarity for all' in the area of healthcare, [or] on some other area that SYRIZA is responsible for, and they can no longer help at the Sanctuary. Because, whether we like it or not, you also count as – we need people; there are not enough people volunteering at the Sanctuary; we need people to tend the bar, to take care of the assembly-room, to clean up, even [to come up with] new ideas at the assemblies. All that stuff. That's pretty much how things are. And there's also the emotional fatigue [that comes with it]; there's nothing positive coming out of it, especially since 2011 nothing positive has come out of it for the movement in general or any other similar endeavour; there hasn't been anything that could make us say, "at least, we got something out of it" or "we took a step forward." [...] I mean, we may all be aware of these issues, but we're not actually doing anything [about them]. [Is it because] we can't? [Because] we're unable to? [Because] we're tired? We aren't always able to do something about them, even though the majority is aware of them.[39]

The rise of SYRIZA, and the multiple emerging projects that drew people away from the Sanctuary were two recurring points in people's accounts during this period. Social clinics, collective kitchens, and a whole range of other initiatives responding to the crisis were added to the already heavy schedule of the Sanctuary's members. The SoCliSo healthcare project, for example, provided a mediatory service for all of those who had no access to health care due to a lack of official papers or insurance. Another constant concern was the number of projects hosted inside the Sanctuary. The 'solidarity for all' mindset had resulted in certain people – few in number – shouldering all responsibilities by themselves; they were the only ones who strove to address every concern that would arise, to meet every need that would come up, to contribute to every event, to implement every suggestion, to participate in every action. Inadequate staffing was a prominent issue at the Sanctuary; it led to a drop in the quality of the voluntary services provided, had a negative effect on people's vitality and investment in the endeavour, and gave rise to irritability, and friction between individuals. There were already too many issues that needed to be dealt with, and only a handful of people actively involved in addressing them – and the crisis had only made

39 Laura Interview Extract: Emotional Fatigue, 2013.

things worse by constantly breeding new ones. Unemployment, lack of energy, lack of motivation, lack of investment. A kind of 'institutionalisation syndrome' was often mentioned in unofficial conversations between the members. Laura:

> This mood plays a huge part, I think, as does the fact that many people have focused on the more central political issue. Okay, for better or for worse, a great many people have focused on SYRIZA. This 'solidarity for all'[40] thing – which I have yet to decide whether it is a good thing or a bad thing – has also absorbed many people from the Sanctuary.[41]

In addition to all this, the members of the initiative also had to deal with a major political turn of events. The results of the June 2012 election established the left leaning political party SYRIZA as a potentially governing party. As many outside the Sanctuary argued, AuRA was no longer a marginal socio-political entity; their initiatives and actions were now – at least partly – endorsed by a party that could end up being voted into power. People outside the Sanctuary started to identify its members as affiliated with or sympathetic to SYRIZA, which posed a threat to their previously undisputed autonomy. Their initial 'above and beyond all politics and ideologies' motto could be partly undermined if a minority party of the Left which embraced and supported the actions of grassroots initiatives and movements started to gain increased electoral support. SYRIZA's new position as an influential party in the country was likely to drive away people who subscribed to radical political views within the Sanctuary.

As Evdokia pointed out, this 'accusation' that the group was under the protection of a party which recently won power was highly inconsistent with the Sanctuary's or AuRA's real nature. As she mentioned, various collectives participated in the Sanctuary from time to time, even anarchist ones, and in her opinion to link the very recent rise of SYRIZA to the functioning of AuRA would be inaccurate and rather unfair:

> If you want my opinion, there is no connection to SYRIZA. What's happening, for better or for worse, is that SYRIZA's popularity has grown a great deal. So, SYRIZA's members have increased as well, and they are people who are young and relatively active, let's say, who also take part in movement-oriented action [*κινηματικά πράγματα*]. In this sense the most popular space for them are not other hangouts or squats [she names other places, for example of an anarchist orientation]. I think this criticism comes mainly from anarchists, from this side, because they are annoyed even by the presence of parties. [...] And this debate, apart from the existence of SYRIZA, which is vexing [to some] in and of itself because SYRIZA is the

40 Solidarity4all was also a relevant initiative; see www.solidarity4all.gr.

41 Laura Interview Extract: Solidarity for All, 2013.

> most active among all those political groups – as opposed to KKE-m-l,[42] for example, which is not active, [as] it only turns up once, at the festival – revolves around issues of informal hierarchy, I think; they [the critics] see those they view as sitting at the top of that informal hierarchy, as supporting SYRIZA in theory, because none of the people I can think of is an actual member. So, SYRIZA is quite heavily criticised here [in the Sanctuary], as it is ANTARSYA[43] as well.[44]

According to Evdokia's viewpoint, the debate about AuRA's alleged adherence to SYRIZA, namely the claim that certain members of the group were closer to the political ideas of SYRIZA, was irrelevant. This did not constitute a problem when SYRIZA was a small party, but with its rise in popularity the debates became more heated. From the very beginning of AuRA, the attraction of broader political spaces that focused on the migration issue fostered its reputation. The Sanctuary was also perceived to a large extent as a 'neutral political zone' that focused on migrants, and as such attracted people from a wide range of left-wing positions to participate in its annual festival. Hence, it was obvious to Evdokia that SYRIZA's members would be sympathetic towards somewhere like the Sanctuary, whereas they would probably feel less sympathetic towards anarchist social spaces.

So far, we have examined the complications that arose at the Sanctuary and AuRA regarding two of the problems that I identified during the second period of my research: first the members' physical and emotional exhaustion due to the number of projects that were initiated during this period, and second the political profile of the Sanctuary in the context of the rise of SYRIZA. I would now like to turn to what some members called a process of "lumpenisation" that the Sanctuary was undergoing, before finally looking at the problem of violence at the Sanctuary. As we have seen, the financial crisis and the austerity measures that were introduced to deal with it created problems that members of the group had to confront. Two of the main areas the activists focussed on were healthcare and food initiatives. A voluntary kitchen was initiated at the Sanctuary to provide meals to all those who needed them. The kitchen provided an opportunity for people not only to benefit from the distribution of free meals but also to discover and familiarise themselves with the Sanctuary. The meals were prepared by volunteers, and the people who came for free meals (for example homeless people, migrants and others) were themselves welcomed to become part of the initiative. This cultivated a feeling of 'going home for food' and attracted people to the Sanctuary. Rafael, however, elaborates on some of the complications that this development brought about:

42 KKE m-l Communist party of Greece (Marxist-Leninist).

43 Anticapitalist Left Cooperation for the Overthrow. They first participated in elections in 2009.

44 Evdokia Interview Extract: Political Memberships, 2013.

> The kitchen used to attract more people too, but those people too were lumpen or very poor or homeless; and achieving an osmosis between these two worlds is not always as easy as that. We are talking about people who not only come over to eat or drink, but also – because that's the purpose of the Sanctuary and [that's] how it is structured – begin to become involved with the affairs of the Sanctuary, but this hasn't come to pass through a coherent political process.[45]

People who had not previously participated in any political or social endeavours and had little knowledge about processes of political engagement were being invited to participate in the running of the place. Rafael interpreted this as a kind of "lumpenisation" of the Sanctuary: lacking the time to achieve a necessary "osmosis" between different worlds through political processes (assemblies, personal interactions), the voluntary kitchen created more problems than it solved. Being part of the assemblies, having a say in the function of the Sanctuary, and being willing to help with the various tasks that had to be accomplished were all part of being a member. Even in this case however, Rafael detected a positive development regarding the affirmation of solidarity in its "tangible meaning." Solidarity was to be affirmed by those non-initiated people in its practical dimension:

> For me, this is a good thing, in the sense that it's better for a place like this to be built, first and foremost, on [the concept of] need; these people come to realise, in a very basic, yet very authentic way, that solidarity is something tangible, that "this place offers me food, so [in return] I'll stay here and cook." And from that you can move on to the political dimension of it all. [This often happens] in a way that can make many people in the movement, [many people] from the Sanctuary, take it as an abuse of a right; let's say, "Why does this guy come here more often?" [or] "Why does he stay longer than his shift?" [or] "Why does he open the bar when it's supposed to be closed?" "We agreed to do this thing a certain way, [so] why don't people do it this way?" And this is often also followed by complaints and dis-involvement on the part of the people of the movement, because they say, "I can't work things out with these people," or by dis-involvement on the part of the newcomers, because they feel offended.[46]

Lacking the time to build long-term relationships between participants, or to familiarise themselves with the basic principles either of the Sanctuary or AuRA, the success of the collective kitchen-initiative was called into question. By the time of our discussion there was an ongoing argument about who was in charge of the Sanctuary, who was supposed to have its keys, and who had access to it. Many people were in a difficult financial position and considered the Sanctuary as a place to return to at

45 Rafael Interview Extract: Osmosis Between the Worlds, 2013.

46 Rafael Interview Extract: Misunderstandings, 2013.

night. There were some cases, when people stayed in the Sanctuary overnight, which greatly annoyed some members. Not everybody in the assembly approved of those practices, mainly because people staying there overnight raised the broader issue of who had responsibility for the Sanctuary. Taking responsibility for the Sanctuary, however, was a collective practice in which all members participated, not just the responsibility of one or two privileged members. In this sense, it was agreed that the Sanctuary should open and close at certain hours. Even they who had the responsibility for keeping the café open did so as a team and not as individuals. When individuals arbitrarily took the initiative to open the Sanctuary themselves, this blurred the boundaries of trust. Decisions were not to be made by individuals, they belonged to the relevant assembly.

Rafael further stressed this incompatibility between newcomers' perceptions of the Sanctuary and those of the existing members, who prioritised the proper organisation and function of the Sanctuary, based on communication and mutual understanding among its members. With the arrival of the newcomers, rules and principles which were indisputable during the previous years now had to be discussed anew. This situation was perhaps similar to what is known as the "free-riders" problem which brings out rival tendencies as to how it should be approached.[47] On the one hand, it shows the limits of anti-hierarchy when it comes to the banning of certain participants, while on the other hand it brings to the fore various favouritisms on the part of the members themselves.

For Evdokia, sticking to the rules of the Sanctuary was of crucial importance. This would not only restore equality and horizontality in the way decisions were made but would also suggest a way of eliminating violence and various unpleasant incidents that people had to deal with. For example, she pointed out that the proper time for the Sanctuary to close every night should be eleven or twelve o'clock. In previous years when a better atmosphere prevailed at the Sanctuary, there was no need for such restrictions. As the conditions changed, the regulars had to adapt and change their habits. Staying later at nights would increase the risk of having to deal with unpleasant events. I asked her about violence in the Sanctuary and she distinguished between two types: violence between migrants themselves and violence against the Sanctuary and its members.

> And there is also the violence against us. Of course, it would be better to specify what type of violence we refer to [what we mean by violence] in each case. That is to say, in my opinion, the incidents of theft were violence. I mean, it may be true that nobody hit me, but there's this feeling that you cannot be yourself in a space

47 Hadjimichalis 2018, 266.

> of your own. You cannot feel at ease, you cannot trust others, you're wary of those around you… and this is, in itself, violence.[48]

Incidents of theft were often occurring at the Sanctuary, and this kind of violence though not physical, was damaging to the cohesion of the group and the Sanctuary. Feelings of not being safe or not feeling at home made the Sanctuary's friends hesitant about going back there. Rene and Luan described some of the efforts made by members of the Sanctuary at the time and sympathised with them. "It is not easy." Rene told me, "Well, there is a lot of quarrelling during this time. And not only quarrelling. They steal a lot as well." Who are they? I asked… "Mostly Arabs, they drink and have fights and steal a lot." Luan wanted to bring some balance to the discussion, as the statement sounded too strong:

> If you don't have the money to eat, and you know that if you sell a phone that you found on a table, you will get some euros, well, I understand, they are in a bad situation. They do not have anything to wait for in Greece. […] Out of a hundred migrants in Greece, maybe only two have a good life.[49]

For both Rene and Luan, quarrels and racism were a fact that prevailed over the last year in the Sanctuary and greatly troubled its members. Their feeling of being at home there was greatly undermined by such incidents. But as many members explained to me, these behaviours were closely related to the fact that many migrants did not intend to stay in Greece and for this reason were not interested in forming bonds or being integrated in the Sanctuary. During this period members of the Nigerian community, and people from Senegal and Somalia were coming to the Sanctuary. The Afghan community that used to be present and active at the Sanctuary during its first years distanced themselves from its activities for reasons that remained unknown. But when it came to individual memberships, there continued to be a sense of discontent among the members at the group's failure to involve the migrants in the more politically oriented, decision-making processes, and incidents of violence were directly linked to these issues. Racism was another problem that was discussed intensively during this period, and we will now briefly look at that issue.

Now Comrades, What about Racism?

Racism at the Sanctuary was another issue that did not come up in discussions during the initial period of my research, although of course, racism as a social problem

48 Evdokia Interview Extract: Violence, 2013.

49 Luan Interview Extract: Theft Incidents, 2013.

was always the main issue that AuRA tackled. This seemed to have changed, however, by the time of my second period of research when people started to suspect racist attitudes within the Sanctuary itself.

> Q: I've heard people talking about racism at the Sanctuary lately.
>
> Laura: Oh yes? That they are racist towards migrants (sighs). Oh yes (worried) and it is not... To me, it was shocking; [...] I was on my way to the ERT premises, and I ran into one of the migrants, and we started talking. He asked me, "How are you? Where have you been?", stuff like that. [And then] I asked him: "What about you? Do you still go to the Sanctuary? Do you attend the classes?" He said: "No, why should I? Everything is run by the same two people, and they [these two people] are racist to us. It's not the place it used to be. I don't feel like going there [anymore]". And it was extremely shocking to hear someone say these things. And, more or less, the problems started when certain people with a tendency to be domineering became involved. [...] Let's say we have experienced the extreme case, namely, to be told by an immigrant – anyway he was constantly creating problems – that "this place is only for migrants, and you should leave." But yes, it is difficult for him to understand that the Sanctuary is for everyone, it is for us all to coexist and now we have to deal with this extremity that migrants think that the Sanctuary is a racist place! However, there are always certain people who claim they deal with a racist attack.[50]

Many members of AuRA would often say they experienced a feeling of being 'lost in translation' whenever they tried to explain to an outsider the role of AuRA, its voluntary work and the limitations their action often met. But how could the different demands and interests of the various participants at the Sanctuary be reconciled? Which voices or needs had to be prioritised? These questions help us to understand the two main causes that Laura identified as provoking accusations of racism. In the first case there were some people, who were newly arrived but who quickly acquired power because of their constant interfering with the daily running of the Sanctuary, yet who lacked the political awareness to understand the nature of the place and the people who used it. The effect of these newcomers was part of what Rafael and other members were referring to as the "lumpenisation" of the Sanctuary. Lacking the time to develop their awareness through contact with the various populations in the Sanctuary (through the kind of processes we have examined so far), they tended instead to become domineering. They decided upon various issues or handled certain situations independently, and outside of any ways which had been decided upon by the members of AuRA or of the Sanctuary's assembly. In the second case, there were migrants claiming that the Sanctuary was only for them and often felt offended

50 Laura Interview Extract: Racism, 2013.

by the presence of locals. Many migrants were not familiar with the Sanctuary being a part of a broader movement and that all sorts of people came and went for all sorts of reasons.

The discussion with Evdokia was extremely useful in clarifying the complexities involved in discussing the issue of racism within AuRA, as well as highlighting some of the contradictions involved in the endeavour of coexistence at the Sanctuary itself.

> Q: The other [part of my question] is if there are some racist or xenophobic tendencies within the Sanctuary.
>
> Evdokia: (Shocked) To tell you the truth, I've never heard that before.
>
> Q: No?
>
> Evdokia: Ok, wait... You've heard that [there are xenophobic/racist tendencies] from whom towards whom? From us towards the migrants? And whom did you hear that from, migrants or Greeks?
>
> Q: Does it matter?
>
> Evdokia: It does, yes, I can explain; I can explain, and you can tell me afterwards, if you want to.
>
> Q: From both sides, in any case.
>
> Evdokia: Ok, look, to tell you the truth, I'm a little shocked to hear that. I mean, I've never heard it before. I've heard migrants say that, and it's a misconception of who we are and what we do; that is, the migrants often find it hard to understand that this thing is self-organised, [that] none of us get paid for what we do, [that] we're not an NGO, [that] we're not associated with the state, nor with the police. I mean, we sometimes find ourselves in a very difficult position – especially the legal support group, who have had migrants say: "Get me papers, and I'll give you €3.000,00; why won't you do that?
>
> Q: And this is taken as racism?
>
> Evdokia: This is taken as racism or as: "You're not helping us, so something's up, why are you doing this?" And we're trying to explain to them that: "Guys, we can't

> do that, we don't have the authority to do that, we are not the state, that's not what we do."[51]

This extract is illustrative of a moment when I felt like I had offended my interlocutor by unintentionally giving her the impression that I meant to question her morality. Asking questions about racism provoked a defensiveness on her part, as if it was my intention to judge whether the group was truly anti-racist or not. I understood, however, her reaction as closely related to the rule of not talking about internal family issues.[52] So, who broke the silence in the family? Keeping quiet about family difficulties is a way of protecting comrades from outside interventions. Openly expressing the emotions that accompany these difficult situations means betraying the internal order of the family. When somebody "breaks the silence" and challenges the adequacy of the chosen strategies this can affect the coherence of the group and endangers people's commitment and devotion to it.[53] Evdokia who had been part of the endeavour from the very beginning, seemed to me to be trying to protect those who may be affected by the accusations of racism. Be it real or imagined, the very act of talking about the issue threatened the family as a whole.

There was another factor that made such claims hard to talk about: the political circumstance. The rise of the Golden Dawn, the increased number of attacks against migrants, and the attacks on places similar to the Sanctuary, both in Athens and in Thessaloniki, served as a catalyst for the decision of antifascists and antiracists to combat harassment, violence and racism. To suggest that such tendencies were to be found in the Sanctuary itself would mean that they had to deal with a similar threat in the very core of their own ideology.

Regardless of whether Evdokia had, until that moment, truly been oblivious to the matter or whether her reaction was due to a combination of the pressure of being interviewed (the pressure to present oneself positively) and the stress of having been blindsided by an unfavourable question, she started bringing up cases of miscommunication. Some were similar to the situation Laura had described, where AuRA was mistakenly thought to have an institutional authority and people thought that they should be able to obtain documents or other types of legal services there. Others stemmed from misinterpretations that occurred during daily interactions, for example cases of flirting and rejection, where sexism appears to be an overlapping factor further confusing the issue. Evdokia:

---

51 Evdokia Interview Extract: Racism, 2013.

52 Srivastava 2006. Srivastava's research on an anti-racist group sheds light on how emotions and ideas of family prevent members of anti-racist organisations from talking openly about disturbing issues, and how this protection net further promotes the family ideal, which however remains selective. For the idea of family in similar organisations, see Kleinman 1996.

53 Srivastava 2006, 76.

> Moreover, there is – I'll explain, I'm laughing because [not only have I heard other people say it, but] I've also had it happen to me; I've had an African guy hit on me, and when I told him, "You know... It doesn't work like that," the very next thing he said to me was: "You won't give it to me because I'm black, right?" I mean, come on, why would you say something like that to me. And, if I'm not mistaken, it's also happened to Andria, as well [another member]. I mean, these are... they are cultural things, which, for me – for most of us, I think – have nothing to do with whether you're Arab or black, obviously; they have to do with how you approach a given context. [...] I'm simply defending myself. Now, if this is taken by the other person as a reaction [that is] due to him being who he is, I think that, unfortunately, there's not much I can do about that. I mean, [that's how I would react] even if I had a Greek guy do that to me. And I have had a Greek hit on me in a distasteful, even aggressive way; I kicked him out of the Sanctuary the same way [I would have if he were an immigrant]. I mean, it's only human; it's a matter of whether you're crossing my personal red lines, no matter where you come from, no matter your cultural background.[54]

At the time of the interview, Evdokia did volunteer work in the café at the Sanctuary, and, along with other women, she had often felt bothered by people's notion that her tending the bar meant that she was sexually available, so to speak. In her description of the situation, we can see how culture counterbalances ethnicity: the problem is not so much about where you come from, but rather what you have learned since entering a new cultural setting. This, however, applied to both migrants and Greeks. The failure to acknowledge women's equal status in the Sanctuary, and even sexist and aggressive behaviour towards women could pose a serious threat to the functioning of the Sanctuary. Applying race as a category of discrimination in order to silence responses to sexism was a tactic that further undermined the equality between participants. To simply repress feelings of anger towards sexism or racism was for Evdokia, as for others, not an acceptable strategy. However, dealing with problems like violence in the Sanctuary often led to it being explained by a kind of cultural or religious contextualisation. As Alkyone told me:

> It may be that people who turn out to be violent at the Sanctuary may have been raised in a different way, maybe all this behaviour was tolerated, in [their] religion and the society they used to live in, but now they have to eliminate violence from their everyday life... let's say, at all costs.[55]

This kind of contextualisation often seemed like a strategy for dealing with feelings of frustration and anger so that they did not lead to disputes. Members' insisting

54 Evdokia Interview Extract: Sexism, Racism and other Vicissitudes, 2013.

55 Alkyone Interview Extract: Violence, 2011.

that people who used the Sanctuary become actively involved in it, required that they unlearn past habits that were no longer appropriate to life at the Sanctuary. Notions of autonomy and self-organisation could not remain a vague, abstract ideal, but had to be a practical reality for both migrants and locals, if the Sanctuary was to flourish.

> We are not racists. We are not. I believe that we are not. That we bear some part of that that originates from the outside world is obvious, yes, we do. [...] Because they are reproduced. Well, look. If you mean, let's say, that, during an assembly, there's a likelihood that I won't take the opinion of an immigrant into account as much as that of a comrade, who's been here for the past ten years and all that, maybe. If it ever does, it will have to do with each individual's level of experience, just like – and I'll be perfectly honest with you – I'd give more consideration to David's opinion than to yours, let's say – not that I wouldn't value it, but when it comes to a matter this... – And the same goes for myself, meaning that, my opinion may be given great consideration when it comes to the Sanctuary, [but] it won't be heard when it comes to how we handle matters related to the Municipal authority of Thessaloniki; that is another group's responsibility, is what I'm saying. I mean, there's such a broad range of positions and activities that we can't have everyone be responsible for everything. But this is a matter of task delegation, it doesn't have anything to do with – I mean, when the Nigerian community came to tell us that they wanted to protest the killing of their fellow Nigerian, the Greeks [in the assembly] didn't say a word; it was the Nigerians who did the talking. All we did was tell them when the stores would be open so their protest could attract as many people as possible. Now, that we all bear the influence of the outside world, because that's how we are brought up – [we are brought up] in a capitalist, patriarchally structured society and all that – [is true], yes...[56]

The opinions of long-standing members seemed to matter more when it came to the Sanctuary's internal issues, and the same went for the migrants when it came to issues relating to them. There was also a distinction between people who had a different ethnic background and had the intention of staying in Greece, and therefore showed a greater interest in being part of an endeavour such as the Sanctuary, and others whose residency in Greece was short-term and who did not focus on creating any bonds either with people or with places like the Sanctuary. For example, people who did not join the language courses or any other activities in the Sanctuary, or people who just came for the cheap alcohol in the café (as many members claimed), were thought of as visitors for whom the Sanctuary would have no further value. As Evdokia claimed, people who had a real interest in it clearly showed their intentions: they actively participated and sought to promote the Sanctuary's principles by respecting the rules and integrating into its activities and life. One example of

56 Evdokia Interview Extract: Their and Our Affairs, 2013.

this was the Nigerian community – which was quite active in the Sanctuary at this time – announcing its intention to engage in a dynamic protest on its own initiative and strive for what it considered to be important. They were interacting with the Sanctuary without, however, creating a relationship of dependency to it.

The issue of racism was just one element in a more general reassessment of the group's objectives and concerns that took place during the period of the crisis. The question of racism revealed both the complex social and political climate within which the group operated during this period, and the overall atmosphere of unease, annoyance, and suspicion that existed within the Sanctuary. It seemed as if AuRA would have to re-adjust its practices and discourses if a greater number of people were to follow its calling. While the formation of a physical space such as the Sanctuary had been very innovative in so far as it offered a place where people could combat racism by familiarising themselves with the object of their fear, the central idea of 'bringing people together' lost some of its impetus during the crisis. This may partly have happened because other similar spaces multiplied, or from a lack of energy and optimism resulting from the crisis, or for a range of reasons such as those I mentioned above.

What, then, were the priorities of the group in this radically changing landscape? And how could they face the multiple dilemmas that emerged from the crisis, both outside and inside the group? A self-assessment that would redefine the group's future course and the role of the Sanctuary under the new conditions of the crisis was necessary. This self-assessment involved various understandings of solidarity that were transformed into ideas and suggestions about the development and the course of the Sanctuary and AuRA. Let us now examine these suggestions further.

Attempts at Re-Enchantment: Solidarity in Perspective

So far, I have examined the main problems that AuRA and the Sanctuary were faced with during a period that was marked both by the financial crisis in Greece and a kind of internal crisis in the Sanctuary itself. I would now like to look at some of the possible solutions that members suggested to overcome these problems. How could the Sanctuary become more like it used to be? How did members deal with the effects of routinisation that were reflected in the exhaustion, the quarrels, the fights and the unwillingness of people to return there? I will identify three different approaches that the members advanced regarding possible solutions to the problems they were faced with during this period: 'mission solidarity' (a movement-oriented approach), 'solidarity as challenging coexistence' (a sceptical approach) and 'solidarity in between' (an affective interaction approach). These approaches do not oppose each other but rather overlap. The solutions, or better the emphasis on different elements of possible solutions, take into account three factors. First, the members' position and role in the group. Second, the familiar problems those members came across on a daily basis. And finally, their understanding of the movement's ultimate goal, one aspect of which is solidarity. What is important here is the field of interest that various members have, their overall conceptualisation of the movement (or the absence of such a conceptualisation) and their conceptualisation of solidarity. How, then, did the members envision their attempts at re-enchantment?

Mission Solidarity: A Movement-Oriented Approach

Some members of the group saw the crisis, both inside and outside the Sanctuary, as creating a fertile ground for new political opportunities. It provided a call to transform the ways in which they were engaging in their struggles. It was an invitation to rethink outdated political commitments and modes of organisation, and instead to form broader coalitions and to dynamically engage in what was happening beyond their own specific groups. Even the new problematic popularity of the Sanctuary was treated positively by some members, as they focussed on the way it revealed a variety of new alternative spaces in the city. When the Sanctuary opened, it was a very innovative idea. It provided a safe space of interaction with multiple activities on offer, capable of engaging a variety of groups and organisations. Some years later a variety of similar alternative places were opening up in the town. This fact strengthened the conviction that more and more people were becoming sensitised to the social and political issues and were willing to engage in collective action and initiatives of solidarity. Even if this meant that previous members and sympathisers of the Sanctuary had changed their preferences and begun attending different places instead, this was still a success in terms of the movement in general. Rafael:

> And let's emphasise this again. One good thing is that there are several such places in the city, centres, squats, and hangouts, a fact that might help explain where these people gather [if they are not in the Sanctuary]. But I also think that we need to find a way to bring the hangouts into contact with each other more systematically. There was a meeting, we met on the occasion of the sudden shutting down of certain squats in Athens, but we have to further work on that.[57]

The Sanctuary was never in danger of suffering great internal losses, or extensive fragmentation or dissolution. However, various ideological shifts had taken place; older members were replaced by new ones, and new ways of operating the Sanctuary seemed to be necessary. The rise of the second generation of intellectuals did not mean that older members were defenestrated, nor was there any vociferous opposition to them. This new generation of intellectuals focused on the gradual transfor-

57 Rafael Interview Extract: Hangouts and Contacts, 2013.

mation of the Sanctuary's means of organisation and engagement and were calling for unity according to principles of openness and flexibility. As every single volunteer mattered, their view was to be preserved within an open perspective. Rafael had certain ideas as to how this was to be done:

> But you cannot just say: "I want more people" [at the Sanctuary], it's not enough. You must find a way, through an aggressive management, through a campaign, to bring people in – I won't say [bring people in] again, I don't care about again – to bring people into the Sanctuary, [...] to thicken its lines. We are not an organisation so we cannot make those who come [to the Sanctuary] stay there by following a line, or through strict discipline but this is our advantage. That this way someone may feel more inclined to come [to the Sanctuary], to engage in something in a less committed manner but be consistent, in a free way, but consistent. [To realise] that what is happening here is important. Nobody here tells you that you have to believe this or that, or says "here, this is our brochure and get informed" and I think this is the direction we should take from now on, we have to get more people engaged [...].[58]

In order for the Sanctuary to regain its liveliness it had to be filled again with people. Independently of the antagonism that may have existed between different alternative spaces in the city, the preservation of the Sanctuary was to be achieved through a systematic effort to bring back people whose interest in it may have waned. The strategy employed to try to achieve this involved increased cooperation with other centres, and a promotional campaign that would allow more people to become familiar with the place. Ideological factors took a back seat, as commitment to the Sanctuary at this point meant encouraging a greater number of memberships. Rafael:

> However, I don't want to sound too bleak, so let me say this: Even though during 2012–13 there were [...] minor theft incidents, [and] even though certain collectives – or certain people that used to contribute a lot – withdrew from the Sanctuary, there were also things that changed for the better. That is, we held many events, many more events than [we did] during 2011–12; [we held] theme nights involving movie showings on a regular basis; [we held] very successful events aimed at financially supporting various endeavours; we had new people show up, new collectives, and [we held] some events that, especially from February onwards, restored the importance of the Sanctuary in the city.[59]

Rafael avoids excessive emotionality. I could say he was expressing his ideas with a 'political calmness.' He identified the problems, eagerly proposed solutions and

58 Rafael Interview Extract: Thicken the Lines, 2013.

59 Rafael Interview Extract: Events, 2013.

focused on the role of his group as part of the movement's overall function and goal. If all the minor, fragmented, local endeavours succeeded, then this would constitute a successful movement, a powerful discourse challenging the prevalent one. This is the moment that led me to ask him "what is the movement for you?"

> Hmmm, what is the movement to me, you ask? To me – because I get the feeling that a lot of people would probably disagree – it is a palette (*παλέτα*) of all those lesser or greater things that take place in the city, and not only in the city, but also in society, whether they are political, labour-related, movements for rights, for anti-racism, anything one can imagine, or movements for the environment, which sort of function like communicating vessels. They have a strong street presence [...], they take action and they want to change the world towards a certain direction, and let us put it in general terms: towards a society of equals, a society of equality because whether you call this society classless, communist, anarchist, or discrimination-free, at the end of the day it is a society of equality; that's where all these things lead, whether there is joint action or not, whether their means and strategy differ from each other, or not, eventually that is the goal.[60]

The conceptualisation of the movement as one that strives for a society of equals beyond any minor ideological labels that may be attached to it allows for a better understanding of what we have called the 'open character' of the second generation of intellectuals. It is a perspective that seeks to overcome the preoccupation within leftist politics with minor divisions and factions rather than the overall objective of their common political goal. This ideological strictness now seemed outdated. The way the old politics focused on minor details of how action should be undertaken and according to which theoretical paradigm, did not serve the overall purpose of either the movement in general or AuRA in particular. However, since the movement includes different leftist traditions and a variety of demands, its unity is always going to be disputable to some degree. Rafael:

> In my definition of the movement, I include things which extend from black anarchy and the Communist Party of Greece, to bourgeois collectives, who in times of crisis realise that certainties they used to have, were actually not that certain. The LGBTQ movement is part of it and a last relevant comment: I read recently on twitter (on the occasion of the ERT incident) – no matter what we say, no matter how much we fight with each other, anarchists, the anti-capitalist Left, the communist Left, the radical Left, all that space, or better all those spaces, we all feel that we all belong to the same community, that is, when we curse at each other, we curse at people who are on the same side of the fence as we are. They are the people who get out on the street to oppose the others. It doesn't suffice to protest and to

60 Rafael Interview Extract: What is the Movement, 2013.

> complain from home, obviously there must be some action involved. All this is the movement.[61]

This idea of multiple but united spaces replaces the traditional idea of single unified space that characterised leftist politics over the past years. Here the idea of 'weness' indicates a kind of emancipated identification. It is a general inclusiveness that seeks to liberate individuals from various ideological and political compulsions by embracing difference, non-unanimity and controversy. In this way a whole range of political tendencies are able to harmoniously find their place in this broader multifarious construction. Since, however, the strategies of various groups may still differ and the movement may still appear highly fragmented, various questions emerge: How assertive should any given group within the movement be? What form should this assertiveness take? How are all the minor differences that separate one group from the other to be overcome? Collectives now had to deal with all these kinds of questions in an internal dialogue with themselves as well as with those other groups who they were working alongside.

However, Rafael's answers seemed to be consistent with the contradictory nature of the movement. Namely, that all its diverse aspects contributed to a united vision of a society of equals. By accepting and embracing its internal contradictions the movement changes its character in two significant ways. Firstly, collective action is directed towards a greater vision of social unity and not just a range of more specific aims, and secondly, all individual projects gain a sense of themselves as part of a common struggle against exploitation, inequality, poverty, and injustice. In this sense, solidarity appears as part of an overall mission that dynamically engages the priority of the intellectuals in consolidating a common identity that is formed through multiple interactions and "continual investments."[62] The inclusion of all the various collectives under the broad definition of the movement, as well as the emphasis on commonalities within it, seeks to overcome ideological obstacles, and to focus instead on openness and horizontality as a way of gaining a new vitality and advancing all of the movement's shared aims. In this sense, solidarity is a movement-oriented approach in the service of a common vision, signifying the unity of all struggles against those who stand 'on the opposite side of the fence,' and foregrounding the broader coalitions that have to be achieved if the movement is to flourish.

61 Ibid.

62 Melucci 1989, 34.

Solidarity as a Challenging Coexistence: A Sceptical Approach

We have seen how what I have called the 'movement-oriented approach' prioritised the preservation and revitalisation of the Sanctuary as part of the movement's overall goals and mission. I would now like to discuss the second approach that members adopted towards the problems that arose at the Sanctuary, what I have called a more 'sceptical approach.' This approach differs from the first in that it prioritises people's own experience within the various groups and activities that made up the Sanctuary. This approach foregrounded self-criticism and paid close attention to the nature of individual contributions as well as horizontal cooperation with other similar groups on specific tasks.

> It takes time in order for us all to be able to coexist together. The truth is that it is difficult, when culturally you are completely different people, and needs effort from both sides, and maybe we also do not approach them properly, and they do not approach us at all. Well, I have seen a lot of efforts on the migrants' side to get more involved, and it needs work, it needs effort from both sides in order to understand the different issues that concern us all.[63]

For the believers, solidarity had always been a kind of ideal to be aspired to, something that people tried as hard as they could to achieve on a daily basis, but under the crisis this very enthusiasm itself came into question. In these new conditions, solidarity involved first of all the challenge of just co-existing from day to day. People had to accomplish this continuous, strenuous process first, if their ultimate aim was to be accomplished. Thus, while still taking into consideration the broader social and political situation, members had to increasingly pay attention to the micro-politics involved in all the groups and coalitions that emerged between different spaces and under various political labels. In this sense, even groups of an anarchist orientation were not to be excluded from the new open dialogue about the common problems that the new alternative spaces in the city were all faced with:

> Laura: One of the positive things I can mention about the Sanctuary is that it succeeded in uniting with other spaces. It may be that the job being done at the Sanctuary with relation to the migrants was not that good anymore...
>
> Q: Oh, is that so?
>
> Laura: Yes, this past year, it has not been good, but we have been doing a good job when it comes to our relations with other hangouts because we have all realised that we all have to deal with the same problems. Thessaloniki is not that

63 Laura Interview Extract: Group Engagement, 2013.

> big of a city, and we all – all people who engage in similar social spaces – meet in the same places and we had to deal with the same problems, fights, incidents of theft. So, this led to a process of acknowledging that we are not rivals and that it goes without saying that we should not speak in such terms, that we have to talk to each other, to exchange opinions, to exchange ideas on how each space faces each problem. [...] For example, in the case of the collective kitchen things did not work out, everyone went on their merry way, so to speak, but in the case of the groups who give the language-lessons things panned out very successfully and that will also show in the anti-racist festival where we will organise a discussion panel all together.[64]

The close cooperation between the different spaces that multiplied during the crisis, was not always linked to the vision of a unified movement, as it was for Rafael. Laura focuses on the here and now of the daily struggles that necessitated a constant exchange among various groups that dealt with similar problems. Through this fermentation process, a culture of exchange was developed between the various centres, squats and social spaces. The idea of political fermentation (*πολιτική ζύμωση*) often came up in conversations with my interlocutors, and while this process of developing the movement by bringing different groups and individuals together was a positive one, it also entailed a constant negotiation of the group's boundaries and a continuous self-reflection on its own practices. One issue that groups dealt with differently was that of violence, and whether they offered a 'second chance' policy. Some spaces adopted very strict regulations when it came to incidents of violence or fights, but many members of the Sanctuary were sceptical about this tough approach and were more in favour of giving people a second chance:

> At other centres, for instance, they are much stricter when it comes to giving people a second chance. If you do something wrong once – if you steal something or get drunk and break a bottle or I don't know what – you'll definitely be expelled from the place. [She names a certain place with an anarchist background]. I don't know if they hold an assembly and ask you to present yourself there – I have no idea – but I [do] know that they are very strict. We, on the other hand, at the Sanctuary, we don't have a standard way of handling things like this. Of course, not all cases are the same, but it always also depends on the assembly's decisions. Sometimes, we try to be less strict, [to be] lenient and to give people another chance. Basically, that's what we would do in most cases; we'd be extremely lenient and give people another chance.[65]

64 Laura Interview Extract: Coalitions, 2013.

65 Laura Interview Extract: Second Chance Policy, 2013.

The group's lenient stance is contrasted to the comparatively less tolerant stance adopted by other similar groups. The Sanctuary seemed to favour a second-chance policy: when someone behaved in a problematic manner, they were not immediately expelled, but instead were given the chance to become aware of their problematic behaviour and its impact on the function of the Sanctuary. Helping people understand what the Sanctuary was about and what it aspired to achieve supported the emancipated, free and equal manner of people's participation in it. It was not about limiting anyone's freedom or policing their behaviour, but rather showing people that there are certain rules that everyone should follow if they are to coexist successfully. Laura:

> It must also be made clear to them why they were given another chance – that it wasn't a favour or your decision, but the assembly's [decision]. And it might be that we gave someone another chance but didn't work hard enough on getting them not to behave like that again, that is, [on getting them] to better understand what the Sanctuary is about. And what I believe plays a very important part at the end of the day is whether and how you approach and communicate with these people – with other people in general – on a personal level; it's not simply a case of [they should not end up thinking] "you, you're oh so perfect; you participate in the assemblies, and you have a political theory, and you're punishing me [you think you are entitled to punish me]". The most important thing is that [you understand that] "I'm not here to simply lecture you; I'll sit with you afterwards and have a beer with you" – or anyway, a juice, so they don't drink alcohol – "and spend time with you and treat you as an equal." I think that's what's most important at the end of the day...[66]

These decisions about how to deal with people do not stem from any theoretical or ideological concerns. What was important was that discussions affirmed the common goal of the group, which was mutual understanding and coexistence, and did not create power relations among the members. People had to be approached in an appropriate way in order to not offend or discriminate against anyone, and the important thing about the assembly in this respect was its nature as a community of equals, much more than any of its ideological underpinnings. The aim of the assembly was not to introduce a method of correction as much as to induct people into the way the group conducted itself. Contrary to the anarchist group's attitude towards similar events, the aim here was a mutual agreement reached through meaningful communication and mutual understanding. This personal, communicative approach allowed the migrants not only to feel like they were, but also to actually become, an integral part of the Sanctuary.

66 Laura Interview Extract: Second Chance Policy and Equality, 2013.

Q: You mean you've seen it working first-hand...

Laura: Yes, I have. [I have seen first-hand] that when we sit or don't sit – that it also requires that kind of work, sitting [and talking] with you [them][...]; Personal contact is very important. Because it's not simply about giving the other person a lesson from a... from a... how do we say... because you have more power and authority [than them], but, on the contrary, [it is] about being their equal; and you may be able to teach them Greek or cook for them, but they, too, have something to give you (back). And, from what I've gathered, a great number of migrants want to do something [to be helpful], but they don't know what, and we need to help them find it. Of course, there are also those – as is the case everywhere – who only come over to drink, to see a girl, etc but this happens everywhere."[67]

Acknowledging the problems and finding creative ways to respond to them were among the priorities of many members. Stressing the importance of equality by engaging in a personal struggle to affirm people as equals and interact with them accordingly was among the strategies that many members promoted. This is what the Sanctuary was essentially about: an invitation to people to come together and contribute, for each has something to offer to the other simply by the fact of being different from them. In this framework, otherness is seen as a gateway to the world; it represents the very essence of communication. And friendship appears here as a strategy towards this aim. Stefanos:

We have to organise more themed parties, local cuisines and music from various countries. In this way, with events and documentary presentations which show how other people live in other countries, with debates... I believe in this way friendships arise, and we are able to overcome our prejudices and taboos.[68]

Some issues, however, remained unresolved: On what terms do the migrants participate in the group? What tasks are they assigned? And how does their status as migrants affect their participation?

One way they participated was in the multicultural festivities that took place at the Sanctuary – parties that involved music, dance and food from the migrants' home countries. At the festival the migrants' participation was often restricted to a show-casing of ethnic cuisine, which they would prepare and sell there. The truth is, there was often a gap between theory and practice when it came to the migrants' participation in the movement – a gap that occasionally resulted in friction.[69] Whereas

67 Laura Interview Extract: Personal Contact, 2013.

68 Stefanos, Interview Extract: Overcoming Prejudices, 2013.

69 Further on this topic, see also Zavos 2006.

the group was in control of their own affairs and made all the decisions regarding the social, financial and political issues that concerned them, the migrants' role was often restricted to the participation in activities emphasising their cultural background. And when their involvement was centred around their customs and traditions, how could the perpetuation of exotic representations of them be avoided? Could it even be argued that such events undermined the anti-racist foundation on which the endeavour was built?

> Q: What was the role of AuRA and what was the migrants' role at the Sanctuary?
>
> Laura: As a group we are there in order to offer an alternative line of thought to that of society. It is not only what they [the government] want to represent to you as existent and real. There is also a counter-discourse, and actually it is a positive counter-discourse, there is an alternative suggestion. Over the years that AuRA has been active the anti-racist/immigration issue was mainly... everyone else tends to forget about it. Yes, the group gives voice to all those whom the system cannot deal with (*να σηκώσει*). And, of course, one can say that AuRA speaks in the name of the migrants, [and that it does so mainly] without them. It is not exactly like this. Migrants are an integral part of the group. And you try to integrate more, you search for communities willing to participate, or you search for unions, in order to become united against the government.[70]

The members of the group were hardly unfamiliar with these criticisms; in fact, they made a consistent, conscious effort to address them. The key to the success of the endeavour lay in the participation of the migrants themselves; and therefore, even fragmented and short-term migrants' memberships were considered of great importance, despite the difficulties this constantly changing membership could raise. At the same time, the migrants' customs and traditions were also an integral part of the endeavour, as they strengthened the conviction that all otherness should be embraced within the society to come.

However, criticisms were raised from within the leftist spectrum which were reminiscent of an old controversy that Butler called the "merely cultural" debate: the orthodox, left-wing idea that the political is sacrificed on the altar of the cultural.[71] Butler criticises the more rigorous Marxist attempts to safeguard a materialist approach as opposed to the fragmented – albeit dynamic – approaches of social movements in what is thought to be a "cultural" resistance. This is evident in what came to be broadly defined as 'identity politics.' In this sense, the perception of the "cultural Left" as a relativist and politically paralysing movement that affirms identities and particularities while sacrificing the materialistic aspect of a rigorous Marxism,

70 Laura Interview Extract: Counter-Discourses, 2013.

71 Butler 1996, 268.

is an anachronism that strips the Left of many of its vital elements.[72] It has not only led to political sectarianism and accusations of who can best serve the "real business of politics," but also rouses conservative viewpoints which seriously undermine the political dimension of social movements' actual work.[73] These kinds of benevolent attempts at political 'fratricide' are evident in Rafael's and Laura's discussion of the movement and in the criticisms that are raised against what is perceived to be a 'soft political struggle,' a criticism that could be said to apply in the case of AuRA.

Rafael's definition of the movement in terms of a heterogeneity of polymorphic aspects could be considered radical, when compared to what other comrades might have expected the movement to be. As we have seen in Chapter Three, elements of what is perceived to be the movement remain rather fluid and change periodically according to different alliances. The inclusion of many contradictory elements in the definition of the movement only stresses its multi-dimensionality and raises its capacity and strength. Moreover, it opens up perspectives that overcome dichotomies that bear no fruits either in theoretical terms, or in the practical outcome of the common struggle. The tendency to 'forget' about the real rivals, that is to say the opposite political spectrum, or even the state and its mechanisms, while spending time analysing what the real business of politics should be, obscures the unity of the movement's various elements and the way in which all still contribute to a shared goal. By striving to accomplish the overall goal against exploitation, inequality and injustice, the question of representation is relativised: who promotes the interests of whom is not as important as the fact that interests are indeed promoted. Laura's definition of the movement starts from the slogan "it's not an image [not for show], and you will only understand what it is if you take to the streets":

> I mean, no matter what people tell you, no matter how hard you try [to understand what it is] through theory, [...] unless you take to the streets and become one with others – always in a positive way – and change things together with others, you cannot understand what 'movement' means. Apart from being large-scale – it's not ideologically uniform – it is also built on that concept – the concept of solidarity, [the idea] that we're all together in this, we struggle together. We have a common goal. And that's the only way things can change: through movements. There's no other way to change them. And, of course, only if you take to the streets – only if you do that.[74]

To summarise, what I have called the sceptical approach describes the efforts of some members of the group to deal with issues of coexistence relating to the daily

---

72 Ibid.

73 Ibid.

74 Laura Interview Extract: What is the Movement, 2013

life at the Sanctuary. This approach remains highly self-reflective regarding the everyday activities activists undertook in the Sanctuary, in particular relating to their coexistence with other groups and individuals, and to the role of the migrants in the Sanctuary. The main solutions emphasised a constant promotion of solidarity, cooperation with other centres and a focus on the interactions taking place in the Sanctuary. What people considered important was a systematic, horizontal communication between various groups and spaces about certain key tasks.

Solidarity in Between: An Affective Interaction Approach

A third stance focussed exclusively on the coexistence of the various members, on the unlearning of past practices and on trying to approach new people based on a genuine interest in the other.[75] According to Alkyone, what was missing in other interpretations of difficult situations and events in the Sanctuary was a true, heartfelt engagement with the others. In this approach, the morality of the solidarious coexistence is emphasised, boundaries fall apart, and otherness is affirmed like a family.

> The bar was being run by familiar faces and there were many people present–teachers and students from diverse countries. Most of them were lifelessly sitting around the tables and the atmosphere was not particularly high-spirited. Looking for Alkyone, I found myself at the centre of the room observing and being observed by the people around me. Every now and then, someone would say something funny in their language. I felt awkward; I thought to myself that things had changed, that the former vitality of the place had dissipated into discomfort. Gradually, though, the mood began to change; a few hours later, people were eagerly rearranging the tables – which had hitherto been arranged in a way that made the crowded little place look unintentionally mournful – and dancing in frenzy to the uplifting music blasting from the speakers. At some point, I lost sight of Alkyone and another member informed me that she was in the middle of settling a fight in her perpetually level-headed way. A day later, as we were discussing it, she reacted to someone's remark that such things should not be happening at the Sanctuary by saying: "He's not entitled to comment on this; come hold Ali's head over the bucket while he throws up, make him a coffee, make sure no-one else gets drunk, have him drink a little lemon juice, go clean up the toilet, take him to bed, go find a blanket, and then you can tell me what we should do about it."[76]

What Alkyone meant is that some members seemed unmindful of the very real fact that the migrants were present among them and in need of their attention, and oth-

75 "Affective solidarity" is a term used by Jeffrey Juris see Juris 2008.

76 Personal Notes: *Quarrels*, 2013.

ers were too often overly engrossed in taking care of people. However, taking care of people was not merely a practical detail of secondary importance to the theoretical projects of the group. It was the centre of people's interaction and was constantly endowed with emotional investment. What bothered Alkyone was that many members were too caught up in theory to handle the here-and-now situations without arrogance, whereas, on her part, she was *actively* engaged in this endeavour – she lived with these people, she spent time with them, knew them and cared for them. After the party, I told her I had not realised there had been a fight; her answer was, "Yes, we're discreet." She had gathered together those involved and had calmly requested the drunk man's friends to take him home, make sure that he was okay, and then come back to have more fun if they felt like it.

Alkyone, engaged in activities promoting the establishment of a "sensitive or affective interaction," as she called it. When we would walk down the street, she would greet numerous migrants (whom she knew by name), take them by the arm, ask them how they were doing, and have a brief, cordial chat with them. She never made it out to be a big deal, and would not comment on it unless I asked her, "Who was that?" in which case she would reply with a brief yet concise biographical outline of the person we had encountered: "He's Orhan's brother, they came from Afghanistan, the other one tried to cross the border – long story, you have no idea!" She knew each case individually and was genuinely invested in all of them, because, as she would say: "we can change society; if we care enough, we can."

Alkyone's approach could be described as an all-embracing affective stance, and many members' efforts to approach others through interaction, emotion and mutual understanding could be understood in this way. It is an approach that involves a laborious exercise in surpassing the borders of one's own self while discovering the potentiality of true transformation through making a connection with others. It calls for the responsible affirmation of others and the recognition of human interaction in its spontaneous, fallible and even controvertible dimensions. It insists on the authenticity and meaningful construction of an in-between relationship, despite any cantankerous omen, that may stem from this coexistence. Alkyone's constant effort to reveal the universe of choices that the members of the group had, and the actual choices they made in the here and now, reminded me of Sartre's description in "Existentialism and Humanism" of the kind of "quietism" that ideologies allow, an avoidance of the actual work which is to be undertaken, which mainly serves those who refuse to assume responsibility.[77] In contrast to this, Sartre argues that without any hope for a future to come, or for things to get better, everyone chooses for her/himself in which way s/he may act, and at the same time this very choice is a commitment that "involves mankind in its entirety."[78] If God is dead, man carries

77 Sartre 2007, 47.

78 Sartre 2007, 57.

the responsibility to choose among a universe of choices, and what *one is,* is nothing more than "a series of undertakings" and "the sum, the organisation, the set of relations that constitute these undertakings."[79] It is a kind of existential point of view that places people at the centre of their own life by stressing the importance of choice, commitment and constant decision-making and that allows them to constantly reflect not only on others' actions, but also on their own.[80] It is an approach that centres on one's own responsibility in the daily making of the world, as individuals are free to choose in every instance their own contribution to the cause they decide is important.

Most of the time, Alkyone did not consciously realise her own decisive contribution to the cause, and yet she *actively practiced* the precepts of the group on a day-to-day basis, rather than just contemplating a future change that will somehow come about without the contribution of the people it directly concerns. For Alkyone, the resolution of the problems of daily coexistence did not come about automatically; it was a constantly ongoing process, and it was continually negotiated, challenged, agreed on, and assimilated. It was a never-ending learning process for everyone involved, where nothing was given a priori and where even the conflicts arising within the bosom of the group still reflected the members' efforts to jointly make sense of the new, uncharted territories they encountered daily.

I have to admit that I myself was greatly inspired by the courage and endurance of this approach, but in the end, it is the complementarity of all three approaches that is most evident, a fact that to a great extent explains the popularity of the endeavour as a whole. While all three approaches communicate and overlap at certain points, they each have a particular focus that distinguishes them from the others. The focus was strategic and political-oriented for many of the new intellectuals. Coalitions and horizontal communication were favoured by many sceptics, who, however, did not circumvent personal contact and the importance of in-between relationships. And then there was the 'affective interaction' between people which demonstrated a more existential understanding of solidarity. This is not to imply that the intellectuals neglected emotion, that the sceptics disregarded the advantages of having concrete tasks and an overall strategy, or that the members who took a more existential approach neglected the movement's ideals. The three approaches obviously communicated and were under constant deliberation and we should not overemphasise the uniqueness or importance of a certain position. It was the general atmosphere of openness, the fluctuating ideas of solidarity that strengthened the fragmented visions that each position was claiming. The approaches certainly do not exhaust the multiplicity of standpoints that various individuals had with reference to concrete,

79 Sartre 2007, 49.

80 Sartre 2007, 66–67.

daily or general issues. Rather, they indicate three general fields of concern and reveal the distinct priorities of various members of AuRA and the Sanctuary, and their particular modes of engagement.

In this sense a more political stance, one that preserves the overview of the functioning of the group in the context of the movement as a whole, is promoted in the 'mission-solidarity' approach, a more sceptical stance is advanced in the in-between space of the political and the personal realm, while the micro-level of interpersonal relationships in the daily reality of the group is central for the existential stance. If these strategies favour one or the other factor, it is as a means of improvement and not as a single policy that would by itself save the Sanctuary and its members from dissipation. All three, however, are indicative of the new direction of the movement, and of the emergence of a political Left that is abandoning many of its previous characteristics. What they emphasised instead was horizontality, difference, solidarity, openness, and the importance of practically engaging with, and responding to, the demands of a changing society.

Conclusion

Solidarity: Spaces In-between

From early on, it has been clear to me that the choice of the word 'endeavour' to describe this undertaking was not accidental. The Sanctuary started out as – and, to all intents and purposes, continues to be – an experiment. The people involved attempted to build something without any guidelines as to how they should go about it, driven by a well-intentioned eagerness and a range of experience drawn from their different individual backgrounds.

The Sanctuary and AuRA provided familiar spaces where participants experienced warmth and fulfilment, and where members were not hemmed in by the hierarchical structure of a unified ideological project but could fulfil a desire that had pre-existed the formation of the Sanctuary and was woven through the rather marginalised groups to which some of the comrades had previously belonged (we encountered a number of these groups in Chapter Three). The Sanctuary cultivated an atmosphere within which processes of what Giddens called the "democratisation of everyday life" could develop.[1] This allowed for long-term satisfaction and a developmental perspective on the relationships, freedom of choice, mutuality, compromise, negotiation, sharing of wishes, acceptance of the uniqueness of the other, trust and transformation that the members experienced.[2]

The creation of a home for both migrants and locals was central to the group's 'open and pluralistic' perspective. This emphasis on openness and anti-hierarchical organisation replaced more rigid forms of political organisation. Although inspired by older ideological projects, the Sanctuary and the groups who used it were constantly imbued with new ideas. The innovation at the heart of the Sanctuary lay in the members' efforts to bridge the communication gap between themselves and the wider society.

The daily fermentation of individuals and collectives meant that the members could undertake action spontaneously, based on the changing conditions of their

1 Giddens 1993, 95.

2 Giddens 1993, 94–95.

everyday reality, rather than having to follow a group's pre-formed agenda. This was one of the most basic elements of the alternative nature of the endeavour; a constant attempt to emphasise the autonomy of individuals. With no-one dominating or taking charge in the Sanctuary the emphasis remained on everyone's freedom to choose and define the course of their own participation. The cultivation of characteristics such as autonomy, responsibility, flexibility and openness were central to the reconfiguration of members into political subjects who were capable of altering their own living conditions.

The group's ideology was also reflected in the roles people were assuming and the way that tasks were delegated to its various members. As we saw, the intellectuals were largely responsible for the ideological aspect of the group's functioning, the believers were responsible for the strengthening of the relationships within the group, the others were part and parcel of the group's overall goal in the making of the sister and brotherhood, and the good comrade served as a metaphor for ideal selfhood in the better world they were all working towards. This typology was completed by the non-believers that stood at the periphery of the group and provided a sense of the wider context within which the members of the Sanctuary and AuRA acted.

The group's goal of everyday transformation was not restricted to the group itself but expanded into the broader society through events, projects and activities that rendered their anti-racist endeavours visible and present in the heart of the city. The members' aspiration was to create a "single world out of many," an open world in which anyone could participate and the construction of this new world was the ongoing intention of the alternative community that was itself in the making within the Sanctuary. The community of the Sanctuary encompassed a field of relationships capable of reinforcing individual participation and action in a way that did not undermine the collective to which everyone belonged. With its emphasis on personal bonds, relationships and friendships that transcend political, religious, ethnic and cultural boundaries, the project provided an alternative vision for society: one without inequality, discrimination and racism, in which individuals have a fair share in the distribution of wealth, amenities and public and private care.

Within the frame of this alternative vision, the group engaged in a constant dialogue with broader social actors, citizens, communities and individuals and promoted actions and initiatives that sought to combat racism and discrimination on the one hand, and to build safe spaces in the city where various populations could come together on the other. Up to the moment of the foundation of the Sanctuary, the existence of these kinds of spaces was sporadic and short lived. Nevertheless, the idea of a broader space that brings together various populations – migrant communities, groups that focus on human rights, and various marginalised populations – persisted. What was truly innovative about the Sanctuary was the formation of a physical 'space' where people are encouraged not to have the status of a visitor, but rather of a participant. This made me wonder what the development of AuRA would have been like without the foundation of the Sanctuary.

The Sanctuary bears the imprint of an era in which a different understanding and practicing of the political became necessary. It demonstrated people's need to construct spaces where the political could acquire both a more concrete, but also a more adaptable meaning; something it did through all the multi-faceted processes of socialisation that the Sanctuary made possible: the festivals, the events, the courses, and all the individual meetings people had with each other. The Sanctuary seemed to me to open up a new way of engaging in politics, signalling the priority of interpersonal relationships in the forming of the different society its members were envisioning.

It was a place that aspired to bring the familiar into contact with the unfamiliar, the local into contact with the foreign, and where identifications of 'us' and 'them' could be united in a differentiated sense of 'we-ness' which the members constructed through their everyday interactions. In this sense, AuRA attempted to become an intermediary between public affairs and individual concerns with the aim of bringing the personal close to the political, rendering 'the private matters' of its various participants public, and the 'public matters' their priority. The alternative nature of this endeavour then, was that it aspired to become what we could call an 'in-between' space.[3] This idea stems from Buber's conceptualisation of a "third genuine alternative" which surpasses both individualistic and collectivist approaches and strives to fit in the realm of "in-betweenness":

> "Between" is not an auxiliary construction, but the real place and bearer of what happens between men; it has received no specific attention, because in distinction from the individual soul and its context, it does not exhibit a smooth continuity, but is ever and again re-constituted in accordance with men's meetings with one another; hence what is experience has been annexed naturally to the continuous elements, the soul and its world.[4]

This focus on the real efficacy of meetings and interrelationships resonates strongly with the intentions of the Sanctuary and of AuRA, as does the emphasis on plurality. The Sanctuary was located in between the social and the political world, in between real and ideal relations, in between the old and new approaches to activism. It emphasised differentiation, multiplicity and multi-belongingness the plurality of which contrasts strongly with previous more unified conceptualisations of belonging. An in-between space is a space that is also under an ongoing process of ex-

3 The term is greatly inspired by Buber's ideas, however, I recently came across Leontidou's very different usage of term, referring to southern Europe's semi-peripheral cities and their urban organisation. See Leontidou 1996.

4 Buber 2002, 241.

change: the influence of changing social and political contexts flowed into the group from the outside, and what flowed out was the individual contributions that people made through their engagement with solidarity. These relationships between the world inside and outside the Sanctuary and AuRA accounts for much of their charismatic qualities. The group's charisma stemmed not from any leaders but from the members' emotional investment and commitment to their project.

At the core of this in-between space lies the idea of solidarity – and indeed it too is a multifaceted idea: for many it constitutes a political enterprise, for others it is part of a social vision, for some it was a strange, cantankerous cohabitation of a familiar place, while for still others it denoted the familiarity of a home and the warmth of friendship. Nevertheless, the members all believed that solidarity can be 'learned' and that it is in this way that it forms the central, inclusive dynamic of the group, and of the individual comrades acting together. The notion of solidarity, then, is closely related to the idea of action, and we have seen how it fuelled people with the creative energy and the impetus to act. This notion of action seems quite close to the Arendtian conception:

> Action, the only activity that goes on directly between men without the intermediary of things or matter, corresponds to the human condition of plurality, to the fact that men, not Man, live on the earth and inhabit the world.[5]

The idea of action, then, relies on the idea of being in the world with others. Throughout this book I have been exploring my interlocutors' understandings of solidarity, and the type of actions that it leads to; it is a type of action where those others participate together in the construction of a better world. Solidarity was at the same time both an abstract goal and the sum of all the group's activities. It was to be achieved by as many different means as there were different individuals.

Solidarity, then, had multiple distinct and dispersed aspects. It served as a matrix for the cultivation of an ethic of everyday life, constituting a frame within which daily tasks were accomplished. For some members, such as Anthi, it formed a spiritual transformative journey, especially in the early stages of their engagement with it. For others, such as Valia, it functioned as a call that invited both individual and collective participation and signalled a period of transformation under the vision of change that the group shared. Indeed, solidarity has assumed various forms according to the position and the roles that individuals held in the group (it was a politically driven aspiration and a mission, it was friendship and connectedness, and it was a daily exercise in acknowledging who the other participants were). In the later stages of the group's development, when they were struggling with both internal and external problems, solidarity provided a constant source of inspiration to restore the sense of enchantment that prevailed in the earlier stages of the group's development.

5 Arendt 1998/1958, 7.

Solidarity was fragmentary, dispersed, an aim to be achieved, an ideal to be realised in the symbolic universe within which individuals made sense of themselves and others, of their goals and vision. In this sense, we could say that solidarity was for the activists, what the "amorous subject"[6] is for lovers: the core of meaningfulness and the impetus to act.

Concluding Remarks on Method: Critically Engaging in the Group

There were two main goals that I felt I had to fulfil throughout this study. Firstly, when researching this group, I wanted to keep the emphasis on the processes of community building and on the way the members felt about and understood their own participation in it. Secondly, I wanted to recapture the atmosphere of the Sanctuary, both the place itself and people's experience of it. This atmosphere is important within activist environments, yet it often goes unnoticed (or is even intentionally ignored) because it is overshadowed by the more obvious political commitments. In this sense this study showed how a group and even whole movements can be approached from a different perspective, focussing on those characteristics that may often go neglected: emotion, attachment, devotion, and shared meanings and values. These were some of the concerns that I have had to negotiate in doing this research.

A long-term research process such as this one involves an ongoing process of reflection, which reveals a lot about our own prejudices, the limited scope of the knowledge we acquire, and the way we adjust to the significance of new and changing findings. But this should not be understood as simply a linear development or improvement. It is more of a transformative dynamic, informed by three fields, – the personal, the social and the political – which produces new elements and findings as it goes on. For example, I had certain biases when I started my research, and when re-reading the text now I sometimes sense the distance there was between the group and my impressions of it. But rather than this making the early research redundant or outdated, it means it can preserve what one participant referred to as "nostalgic remnants" for later contemplation. Looking back over my text now, I notice how the first chapters reflect the enthusiasm of the new experiment of the group, something that changes and becomes more complicated later on when the social and political conditions which the group had to contend with created a distance between how things should evolve and how they eventually did. Following the members through their own changing understandings of their action and their reflections on their beliefs, enabled me to gain a valuable insight into their real life, through a kind of real time experience of people's own becoming.

6 Barthes 2002.

The same is true of the spaces the group occupied. Being in and studying the group meant familiarising myself with multiple fragmented places as they were formed and inhabited and experienced by the participants: places such as the Sanctuary, the festival, the assemblies, the sites of various smaller events as well as all the locations in which the interactions that made up everyday reality took place. And this is not to mention the group's participation in 'external' events such as demonstrations and protests. Participating in the day to day activities of the group, meant following them around, from place to place, through all their gradual processes, and gaining glimpses of their self-reflexive moments.

Looking through the movement's own lenses, however can be tricky, as one is often left enchanted by the movement's idealised view of themselves.[7] It was not my intention, however, to echo the group's own views uncritically, or to propagate their message. My intention was to understand both the individual members and the evolving collective and to question why and how their practices, discourses and actions interwove the notion of solidarity with notions of a new plausible world, and how both were realised in their own daily reality. This does not imply an uncritical stance on my part. Rather, it demonstrates my conviction that being critical does not mean 'putting others on trial' according to our own objective standards of research, something that would only demonstrate a woeful ignorance of our own ideological standpoints, but rather means attempting to really understand the group and its members by 'walking in their shoes,' that is to say, by experiencing first-hand the reactions, expectations, aspirations, failures and achievements that the group goes through. I think that a productive participatory space of dialogue between anthropology and movements can be opened up in precisely this way.

In this approach, *unlearning* is an indispensable method that involves both the researcher and the group being researched. The idea of critical unlearning stems from the suggestion that one "has to unlearn their own privileges,"[8] but applies just as much to the prejudices of the researcher who believes themselves to be capable or justified in explaining the actions of others. And indeed, the results of these "unlearning processes" were constantly evaluated and re-assessed by the participants themselves: they were demonstrated and thoroughly discussed in their assemblies and unofficial talks. Motives, patterns of behaviour and conflicts were constantly placed under their own microscope as they gradually elaborated on the know-how they were developing, regarding the various issues they had to face. As one participant revealed, "we did not construct the Sanctuary with the guidelines of a detailed manual!"

What was important, then, in researching this process, was to emphasise the priority of their actual learning in the here-and-now and the importance of the par-

7 Casas-Cortés, Osterweil, and Powell 2008, 46–47.

8 Spivak, Landry, and MacLean 1996, 4.

ticipants' daily interactions with each other as opposed to a simple dependence on their previous experiences, knowledge and habits. In this sense, to understand AuRA meant not only understanding the processes of individual transformation that were realised within the frame of the group, but also the processes of gradual and radical learning that were taking place in the bosom of the Sanctuary.

This is closely related to the idea of learning as actual "self-transformation."[9] Learning within this activist setting takes the form of what Marvakis and Petritsi call a "dynamic relatedness."[10] In the context of actual everyday interaction, learning calls for a cognitive and physical engagement which transcends traditional educational approaches and invites people to immerse themselves in the group. All things had to be experienced anew in order for people to learn how to cope with unknown situations and unexpected events while adhering to commonly agreed values and principles. The group's overall goals – the amelioration of society, the direct opposition to the practices of the state, the promotion of anti-racism – are essentially founded on the conviction that a different society is possible. This conviction manifests itself – sometimes implicitly, sometimes explicitly – in the way that people in the group and the centre learn to coexist harmoniously and in solidarity despite the difficulties they encounter. The members' different cultural and political backgrounds, and their different individual knowledge and experience, appeared to enhance rather than hinder their initiatives by allowing different perspectives to infuse their projects with creativity and spontaneity. As my interlocutors stressed, "*solidarity is us*" – a statement that was meant to highlight the personal labour and conscious engagement which revealed the authentic meaning of solidarity.

Some questions may be left unanswered, particularly that of how 'equal' and 'solidarious' the endeavour really was? The question is much justified and welcomed. But let me stress this once again: It was not my concern if the people in the group I was researching were 'anti-racist' or 'anti-nationalist' enough, or if they were pursuing their ideology in their right way. What I was concerned with was the meanings they attributed to their action, and how this was realised in their daily lives. In this sense, borrowing again from the religious analogy, it was not my business to judge one particular denomination as opposed to another in order to find out which are the better Christians, but to understand how AuRA and the Sanctuary worked and what made them what they were.

This study was inspired by many scholars, various disciplines (anthropology, sociology, political science, philosophy and psychology) and also by real life and action. It aspired to give a 'micrography' of the places and the people it delved into. However, its uniqueness is to be found not only in the distinctness of the places and the people it looks at, but also in those characteristics that makes it applicable to broader

9 Marvakis and Petritsi 2014.

10 Marvakis and Petritsi 2014, 136.

phenomena. One such phenomenon is ideology. By providing a sort of map of the ideological elements of the group I studied, I provided a possible means of analysis that, though avoiding going into detail about the specific content of this ideology, recaptured its main characteristics by adopting other means of analysis such as metaphors. This, I think, allowed me to bring to the fore crucial components of the construction and the function of the group, and the complexity of its vision, without however entering into a strictly political discussion and examination of the content of its ideology.

I have often been asked if I would follow the same method while conducting research on different ideological groups and movements; for example, on groups from opposing ideological backgrounds. It is difficult to answer, but I hope that yes, I would. Being immersed in an ideology as a researcher does not necessarily distance us from our own ideological standpoints, but the latter should be kept in brackets if we want to be able to do research at all. It is this bracketing of our beliefs, prejudices, previous misconceptions and convictions that will enable us to see through the others' eyes and delve into the others' worldview, something that is necessary if the research is indeed a search for meaning, and if the social scientists' job is to reconcile what appears to be an objective reality with the multiple, idiosyncratic subjective realities of the people, groups and worldviews that compose and create it. This cannot be achieved through a 'rigorous objectivity,' as I have stressed throughout this book. Rather, it involves a constant exercise of 'self-reflection' which allows us not only to embrace our own new alternations in a constructive way, but also to identify and try to understand the alternations of others.

Going Back to the Field

I was in Thessaloniki, quite lonely and melancholic after a long return journey from Berlin. The annual festival was on, but I was unsure about whether to show up. The previous year I did not show up at all, as I was quite confused, stressed out about the political situation in Greece, and felt ambivalent about the group and my book. It was Friday evening and Alkyone called me three times to encourage me to join her for the first day of the festival. The preparation week was already behind the members, and I could imagine how much stress it must have been for everyone, working right up to the opening hour. I was a bit hesitant to show up and respond to people's questions about where I had disappeared to again, to catch up on small talk, and to have to excuse myself for my prolonged absences. I decided, however, as I usually do when I am confronted with my anxieties, to get ready and go.

Within a couple of hours, I found myself in the festival kitchen, together with old friends, exchanging our experiences of the past year, laughing together and meaningfully bridging the gap of time and distance since we had last seen each other. Relieved, I thought how much it does not matter in the life of the group, where you were before, and what are you going to do next. For the friends of the movement and the members of AuRA every small contribution had its meaning in the here and now of their activities and tasks, and every presence was taken as a new beginning. My friends welcomed me warmly in the self-made kitchen, where in a while we would together serve the visitors to the festival, contributing in our own way to this annual event. The movement, after all, is everything that one's body, mind and will could transform into action.

References

Agelopoulos, Giorgos. 2013. "Πολυπολιτισμικότητα «αλά γκρέκα»: Από το 1980 στο 2009." [Greek Versions of Multiculturalism 1980 to 2009.] *Science and Society: Review of Political and Ethical Theory.* 30: 75–103. https://doi.org/10.12681/sas.644

Agelopoulos, Giorgos, Pavlos Pantazis, and Nikos Rotzokos. 2014. *Φαντάροι.* Το Κίνημα για τον Εκδημοκρατισμό της Θητείας και οι «Ένστολοι Πολίτες.»[Soldiers. The Movement for Democratisation of Military Service and 'The Civilians in Uniform.'] In *Η Ελλάδα στη Δεκαετία του '80. Κοινωνικό, Πολιτικό και Πολιτισμικό Λεξικό.* [Greece in the 1980s: Social, Political and Cultural Dictionary], edited by Vasilis Vamvakas and Panayis Panagiotopoulos. 2nd ed., 617–19. Athens: Epikentro.

Agelopoulos, Giorgos, and Nikos Rotzokos. 2010. "Το Κίνημα για το Στρατό τη Δεκαετία του 1980: Πολιτικές, Ιδεολογικές και Οργανωτικές Διαστάσεις." [The Movement for the Army in the 1980s: Political, Ideological and Organisational Aspects.] In *Η Ελληνική Νεολαία στον 20ο Αιώνα. Πολιτικές Διαδρομές, Κοινωνικές Πρακτικές και Πολιτιστικές Εκφράσεις.* [Greek Youth in the 20th Century: Political Pathways, Social Practices and Cultural Expressions], edited by Vangelis D. Karamanolakis, Ioanna Papathanasiou, and Eudokia Olympitou. 1st ed., 345–68. Athens: Themelio.

Ahmed, Sara. 2004. *The Cultural Politics of Emotion.* Edinburgh: Edinburgh University Press.

Alexandropoulou, Ilektra, and Eleni Takou, eds. 2019. *Ο Μαύρος Χάρτης της Ρατσιστικής Βίας.* [The Black Map of Racist Violence.] Athens: Topos.

Allan, Graham. 1989. *Friendship: Developing a Sociological Perspective.* Hemel Hempstead: Harvester Wheatsheaf.

Alonso, Luis E., Carlos J. Fernández Rodríguez, and Rafael Ibáñez Rojo. 2015. "From Consumerism to Guilt: Economic Crisis and Discourses About Consumption in Spain." *Journal of Consumer Culture* 15 (1): 66–85. https://doi.org/10.1177/1469540513493203

Andriakaina, Eleni. 2005. *Παίζοντας με τα Όρια. Θεραπευτικές Κοινότητες και Χρήστες Ναρκωτικών.* [Playing with Boundaries: Therapeutic Communities and Drug Users.] Athens: Vivliorama.

Andriakaina, Eleni. 2009. *Πέρα από τον Θετικισμό και το Μεταμοντερνισμό: Εκθέσεις στην Ιστορική Κοινωνιολογία.* [Beyond Positivism and Postmodernism: Essays in Historical Sociology.] Patra: Opportuna.

Andriakaina, Eleni. 2013. "The Promise of the 1821 Revolution and the Suffering Body: Some Thoughts on Modernisation and Anti-Intellectualism." *Synthesis* 5: 49–70.

Arampatzi, Athina. 2018. "Constructing Solidarity as Resistive and Creative Agency in Austerity Greece." *Comparative European Politics* 16 (1): 50–66. https://doi.org/10.1057/s41295-016-0071-9

Arendt, Hannah. 1970. *On Violence.* New York: Harcourt Brace & World.

Arendt, Hannah. 1986. *Η ανθρώπινη Κατάσταση (Vita Activa).* Translated by Stefanos Rozanis & Gerasimos Lykiardopoulos. Athens: Gnosi.

Arendt, Hannah. 1990/1963. *On Revolutions.* New York: Penguin.

Arendt, Hannah. 1998/1958. *The Human Condition.* With an Introduction by Margaret Canovan. 2nd ed. Chicago, London: The University of Chicago Press.

Arendt, Hannah. 2006. *Between Past and Future: Eight Exercises in Political Thought.* Harmondsworth: Penguin Books.

Arvanitis, Lefteris. 2014. "Δολοφονία Καλτεζά. Η Αστυνομία Χάνει τη Μάχη της Συναίνεσης."[The Kaltezas Killing. The Police Are Losing the Battle of Consent.] In *Η Ελλάδα στη Δεκαετία του '80. Κοινωνικό, Πολιτικό και Πολιτισμικό Λεξικό.* [Greece in the 1980s: Social, Political and Cultural Dictionary], edited by Vasilis Vamvakas and Panayis Panagiotopoulos. 2nd ed., 122–23. Athens: Epikentro.

Askouni, Nelly. 1997. "Απέναντι σε Δύο Αντιθετικές Φιγούρες του «Εθνικού Άλλου»: Στοιχεία από μια Ανάλυση του Λόγου των Εκπαιδευτικών." [In Front of Two Opposite Figures of the "National Other": Elements from the Teachers' Discourse Analysis.] In *«Τί ειν' η πατρίδα μας;» Εθνοκεντρισμός στην Εκπαίδευση.* [What Is Our Homeland? Ethnocentrism in Education], edited by Anna Fragoudaki and Thalia Dragona. 2nd ed., 283–322. Athens: Alexandria Publications.

Atkinson, Paul, and David Silverman. 1997. "Kundera's Immortality: The Interview Society and the Invention of the Self." *Qualitative Inquiry* 3 (3): 304–25.

Avdela, Efi. 1997. "Η Συγκρότηση της Εθνικής Ταυτότητας στο Ελληνικό Σχολείο: «Εμείς» και οι «Άλλοι»." [The Formation of National Identity in the Greek School: "We" and "Others."] In *«Τί ειν' η πατρίδα μας;» Εθνοκεντρισμός στην Εκπαίδευση.* [What Is Our Homeland? Ethnocentrism in Education], edited by Anna Fragoudaki and Thalia Dragona. 2nd ed., 27–48. Athens: Alexandria Publications.

Avgeridis, Manos, Effi Gazi, and Kostis Kornetis. 2015a. "Εισαγωγή." [Introduction.] In *Μεταπολίτευση. Η Ελλάδα στο Μεταίχμιο Δύο Αιώνων.* [Metapolitefsi: Greece on the Verge of Two Centuries], edited by Manos Avgeridis, Effi Gazi, and Kostis Kornetis, 9–26. Athens: Themelio.

Avgeridis, Manos, Effi Gazi, and Kostis Kornetis, eds. 2015b. *Μεταπολίτευση. Η Ελλάδα στο Μεταίχμιο Δύο Αιώνων.* [Metapolitefsi: Greece on the Verge of Two Centuries.] Athens: Themelio.

Avgeridis, Manos, and Glistras Dimitris. 2017. "Η Εξωκοινοβουλευτική Αριστερά στη Δεκαετία του '70. Τα Πρώτα Βήματα μιας «Άλλης Αριστεράς.»" [The Extra-Parliamentary Left in the 1970s: The First Steps of a Different Left.] Interview by Manos Avgeridis. Aired May 7, 2017, on Kokkino 105,5. http://www.askiweb.eu/index.php/el/component/content/article?id=231:callforpapers

Balabanidis, Giannis. 2015. "Ρηχός Εξευρωπαϊσμός: Η Αντιφατική Υποδοχή της Ευρώπης ως Κληρονομιά της Μεταπολίτευσης." [Shallow Europeanisation: The Contradictory Perception of Europe as a Legacy of the Metapolitefsi.] In *Μεταπολίτευση. Η Ελλάδα στο Μεταίχμιο Δύο Αιώνων.* [Metapolitefsi: Greece on the Verge of Two Centuries], edited by Manos Avgeridis, Effi Gazi, and Kostis Kornetis, 225–45. Athens: Themelio.

Balibar, Étienne, and Immanuel Maurice Wallerstein. 1991. *Race, Nation, Class: Ambiguous Identities.* Translated by Chris Turner. Radical thinkers. London, New York: Verso.

Bampilis, Tryfon. 2015. "Ουίσκι σε αφθονία. Μεταπολίτευση, Διεθνής Καπιταλισμός και Εθνογραφικές Πτυχές της Νεωτερικότητας στην Ελλάδα." [Whiskey: Metapolitefsi, International Capitalism and Ethnographical Approaches of Modernity in Greece.] In *Μεταπολίτευση. Η Ελλάδα στο Μεταίχμιο Δύο Αιώνων.* [Metapolitefsi: Greece on the Verge of Two Centuries], edited by Manos Avgeridis, Effi Gazi, and Kostis Kornetis, 317–31. Athens: Themelio.

Barthes, Roland. 2002. *A lover's discourse.* Translated by Richard Howard. London: Vintage.

Bauman, Zygmunt. 1993. *Postmodern Ethics.* Oxford: Blackwell.

Becker, Howard S. 1997. *Outsiders: Studies in the Sociology of Deviance.* New York, London: Free Press.

Behar, Ruth. 2003. "Ethnography and the Book That Was Lost." *Ethnography* 4 (1): 15–39.

Behar, Ruth. 2012. *The Vulnerable Observer: Anthropology That Breaks Your Heart.* 12th ed. Boston: Beacon Press.

Bell, Catherine M. 2009. *Ritual Theory, Ritual Practice.* Oxford: Oxford University Press.

Bell, Sandra, and Simon Coleman. 1999. "The Anthropology of Friendship: Enduring Themes and Future Possibilities." In *The Anthropology of Friendship*, edited by Sandra Bell and Simon Coleman, 1–20. Oxford: Berg.

Bell, Sandra, and Simon Coleman, eds. 1999. *The Anthropology of Friendship.* Oxford: Berg.

Benhabib, Seyla. 2000. "Arendt's Eichmann in Jerusalem." In *The Cambridge Companion to Hannah Arendt*, edited by Dana R. Villa, 65–85. Cambridge: Cambridge University Press.

Berger, Peter L. 1961. *The Precarious Vision: A Sociologist Looks at Social Fictions and Christian Faith.* 1st ed. New York: Doubleday & Company.

Berger, Peter L. 1969. *A Rumour of Angels: Modern Society and the Rediscovery of the Supernatural.* Garden City, New York: Doubleday & Company.

Berger, Peter L. 1983/1963. *Πρόσκληση στην Κοινωνιολογία. Μια ανθρωπιστική Προοπτική.* [Invitation to Sociology: A Humanistic Perspective.] Translated by Eleni Tselepoglou. Athens: Boukoumanis Editions.

Berger, Peter L. 1990/1967. *The Sacred Canopy: Elements of a Sociological Theory of Religion.* New York: Anchor Books.

Berger, Peter L. 2004. *Questions of Faith: A Sceptical Affirmation of Christianity.* Oxford: Blackwell.

Berger, Peter L. 2011. *Invitation to Sociology.* New York: Open Road Integrated Media. https://play.google.com/store/books

Berger, Peter L., Brigitte Berger, and Hansfried Kellner, eds. 1974. *The Homeless Mind: Modernization and Consciousness.* Harmondsworth: Penguin.

Berger, Peter L., and Thomas Luckmann. 1991. *The Social Construction of Reality: A Treatise in the Sociology of Knowledge.* Reprint. Harmondsworth: Penguin.

Bergson, Henri. 1977. *The Two Sources of Morality and Religion.* Translated by Ashley Audra & Cloudesley Brereton. Notre Dame, Indiana: University of Notre Dame Press.

Bhabha, Homi K. 2012. *The Location of Culture.* Routledge classics. London, New York: Routledge. https://play.google.com/store/books.

Bhambra, Gurminder K., and Victoria Margree. 2006. "Reappraising Identity Politics: The Need for a 'Tomorrow'." *Journal of the Interdisciplinary Crossroads* 3 (3): 493–512.

Bobel, Chris, and Samantha Kwan, eds. 2011. *Embodied Resistance: Challenging the Norms, Breaking the Rules.* Nashville TN: Vanderbilt University Press.

Böll, Sven, Böcking David. 2011. "Mythos Vom Faulen Südeuropäer." *Spiegel*, May 18, 2011. Accessed January 20, 2023. https://www.spiegel.de/wirtschaft/soziales/euro-krise-mythos-vom-faulen-suedeuropaeer-a-763366.html

Bonnett, Alastair. 1993. *Radicalism, Anti-Racism, and Representation.* London: Routledge.

Bonnett, Alastair. 2015. "Constructions of Whiteness in European and American Anti-Racism." In *Debating Cultural Hybridity: Multicultural Identities and the Politics of Anti-Racism*, edited by Pnina Werbner and Tariq Modood, 173–92. London: Zed Books.

Botsiou, Konstantina. 2015. "Ν.Δ. και ΠΑΣΟΚ, 1974–1985: Η «Ευρώπη» ως Πολιτική και ως Ταυτότητα." [New Democracy and PASOK, 1974–1985: 'Europe' as Politics and as Identity.] In *Μεταπολίτευση. Η Ελλάδα στο Μεταίχμιο Δύο Αιώνων.* [Metapolitefsi: Greece on the Verge of Two Centuries], edited by Manos Avgeridis, Effi Gazi, and Kostis Kornetis, 211–24. Athens: Themelio.

Bourdieu, Pierre. 2006. *"Συμμετοχική Αντικειμενοποίηση."* [Participant Objectivation.] In *Η Προσέγγιση του Άλλου. Ιδεολογία, Μεθοδολογία και Ερευνητική Πρακτική.* [Approaching the Other: Ideology, Methodology and Research Practice], edited by Giannis Kyriakakis and Martha Michailidou. 1st ed., 27–51. Athens: Metaixmio.

Bourdieu, Pierre. 2010. *Distinction: A Social Critique of the Judgement of Taste.* Translated by Tony Bennett. London: Routledge.

Brubaker, Rogers, and Frederick Cooper. 2000. "Beyond 'Identity'." *Theory and Society* 29 (1): 1–47.

Buber, Martin. 1996/1970. *I and Thou.* Translated by Walter Arnold Kaufmann. 1 Touchstone ed. New York: Simon & Schuster.

Buber, Martin. 1996. *Paths in Utopia.* Syracuse, New York: Syracuse University Press.

Buber, Martin. 2002. *Between Man and Man.* Translated by Ronald Gregor -Smith. London: Routledge.

Buchowski, Michał. 2001. "Communism and Religion: A War of Two Worldview Systems." In *The Academic Study of Religion During the Cold War: East and West*, edited by Iva Dolezalova, Luther H. Martin, and Dalibor Papoušek, 39–57. New York, Oxford: Peter Lang.

Buchowski, Michał. 2006. "The Specter of Orientalism in Europe: From Exotic Other to Stigmatized Brother." *Anthropological Quarterly* 79 (3): 463–82. https://doi.org/10.1353/anq.2006.0032

Bulmer, Martin, and John Solomos, eds. 1999. *Racism.* Oxford: Oxford University Press.

Butler, Judith. 1996. "Merely Cultural." *Social Text* 52/53 (15): 265–77.

Butler, Judith. 2018. *Notes Toward a Performative Theory of Assembly.* 1. pbk. Cambridge, Massachusetts, London, England: Harvard University Press.

Cabot, Heath. 2015. "Banality of Solidarity." Occasional Papers 7. Accessed November 25, 2023. https://www.academia.edu/25419638/Cabot_Banality_of_Solidarity

Cabot, Heath. 2016. "'Contagious' Solidarity: Reconfiguring Care and Citizenship in Greece's Social Clinics." *Social Anthropology* 24 (2): 152–66. https://doi.org/10.1111/1469-8676.12297

Calhoun, Craig. 2001. "Putting Emotions in Their Place." In *Passionate Politics: Emotions and Social Movements*, edited by Jeff Goodwin, James M. Jasper, and Francesca Polletta, 45–57. Chicago, London: University of Chicago Press.

Carrier, James G. 1999. "People Who Can Be Friends: Selves and Social Relationships." In *The Anthropology of Friendship*, edited by Sandra Bell and Simon Coleman, 21–38. Oxford: Berg.

Casanova, Erynn Masi de, and Afshan Jafar. 2016. "The Body as a Site of Resistance." In *The SAGE Handbook of Resistance*, edited by David Courpasson and Steven P. Vallas, 139–55. London, Thousand Oaks, California: SAGE Publications. https://play.google.com/store/books

Casas-Cortés, María Isabel, Michal Osterweil, and Dana E. Powell. 2008. "Blurring Boundaries: Recognizing Knowledge-Practices in the Study of Social Movements." *Anthropological Quarterly* 81 (1): 17–58. https://doi.org/10.1353/anq.2008.0006

Castells, Manuel. 1983. *The City and the Grassroots: A Cross-Cultural Theory of Urban Social Movements*. London: Edward Arnold.

Chainides & Apostolakis, Dimitris. 2000. "Θέλω να Πάρω τη Φυλή μου και να Φύγω." [I Want to Take My Tribe and Leave.] Track 4 On *The Barefoot Prince*. [Ο Ξιπόλυτος Πρίγκηπας.] Music & Lyrics: Dimitris Apostolakis, Compact Disk, Chromodiastasi EPE.

Chatzidakis, Andreas, Pauline Maclaran, and Alan Bradshaw. 2012. "Heterotopian Space and the Utopics of Ethical and Green Consumption." *Journal of Marketing Management* 28 (3–4): 494–515. https://dx.doi.org/10.1080/026725X.2012.668922

Chiotakis, Stelios. 2015. "Διανοούμενοι: Οριοθέτηση και Τυπολογία μιας Πολύσημης Έννοιας." [Intellectuals. A delineation and Typology of a Multifarious Concept.] *Science and Society: Review of Political and Ethical Theory* 7: 1–38. https://doi.org/10.12681/sas.626

Christopoulos, Dimitris. 2001. "Το Τέλος της Εθνικής Ομο (οι)ογένειας: Παραδοσιακές και Νέες Μορφές Ετερότητας στην Ελλάδα." [The End of National Homogeneity: Traditional and New Forms of Alterity in Greece.] In *Μετανάστες στην Ελλάδα.* [Migrants in Greece], edited by Athanasios Marvakis, Dimitris Parsanoglou, and Miltos Pavlou, 57–80. Athens: Ellinika Grammata.

Chryssochoou, Xenia. 2009. "Στρατηγικές Ένταξης των Μεταναστών: Απόψεις Ελλήνων, Βορειοηπειρωτών και Αλβανών στην Αθήνα." [Migrants' Integration Strategies: Opinions of Greeks, Albanian Greeks and Albanians in Athens.] In *Μετανάστες και Μειονότητες. Λόγος και Πολιτικές.* [Migrants and Minorities: Discourse and Policies], edited by Miltos Pavlou and Athina Skoulariki, 439–55. Seira meleton / KEMO 3. Athens: Bibliorama.

Clandestina. 2011. "300 Migrants in Hunger Strike in Greece." *Clandestina*, January 19, 2011. Accessed October 25, 2023. https://clandestinenglish.wordpress.com/2011/01/19/300-migrants-in-hunger-strike-in-greece/

Clifford, James. 1983. "On Ethnographic Authority." *Representations*, no. 2: 118–46.

Clifford, James. 2010. "Introduction: Partial Truths." In *Writing Culture: The Poetics and Politics of Ethnography*, edited by James Clifford and George E. Marcus. 25th ed., 1–26. Berkeley, California, London: University of California Press.

Clifford, James, and George E. Marcus, eds. 2010. *Writing Culture: The Poetics and Politics of Ethnography.* 25th ed. Berkeley, California, London: University of California Press.

Clogg, Richard. 1995. *Συνοπτική Ιστορία της Ελλάδας 1770–1990.* [A Concise History of Greece.] Translated by Lydia Papadaki. 1st ed. Athens: Istoritis, Katoptro.

Clogg, Richard, ed. 2014. *Greece 1981–89: The Populist Decade.* Studies in Russia and East Europe. Basingstoke, Hampshire and London: Palgrave Macmillan.

Coffey, Amanda. 1999. *The Ethnographic Self: Fieldwork and the Representation of Identity.* London, Thousand Oaks California: SAGE Publications.

Cohen, Anthony P. 2015/1985. *The Symbolic Construction of Community.* Series Editor Peter Hamilton. London: Routledge. https://play.google.com/store/books

Collins, Randall. 2001. "Social Movements and the Focus of Emotional Attention." In *Passionate Politics: Emotions and Social Movements*, edited by Jeff Goodwin, James M. Jasper, and Francesca Polletta, 27–43. Chicago, London: University of Chicago Press.

Courpasson, David, and Steven P. Vallas, eds. 2016. *The SAGE Handbook of Resistance.* London, Thousand Oaks, California: SAGE Publications. https://play.google.com/store/books

Course, Magnus. 2010. "Making Friends, Making Oneself: Friendship and the Mapuche Person." In *The Ways of Friendship: Anthropological Perspectives*, edited by Amit Desai and Evan Killick, 154–73. Oxford: Berghahn.

Craib, Ian. 1993. *Modern Social Theory: From Parsons to Habermas.* 2nd ed. New York: Harvester Wheatsheaf.

Csordas, Thomas J. 1990. "Embodiment as a Paradigm for Anthropology." *Ethos* 18 (1): 5–47.

Dalakoglou, Dimitris, and Georgios Agelopoulos, eds. 2017. *Critical Times in Greece: Anthropological Engagements with the Crisis.* 1st ed. London: Routledge. https://play.google.com/store/books

Daliou, Sofia. 2015. "Κοινωνικά Κινήματα Πόλης και οι Χωρικές Διαστάσεις τους: Η Περίπτωση των Αυτοδιαχειριζόμενων Κοινωνικών Κέντρων στη Θεσσαλονίκη." [Social Movements in the City and Their Urban Dimension: The Case of Self-Organised Social Centres in Thessaloniki.] Bachelor's Thesis, Aristotle University of Thessaloniki, Polytechnic School. Accessed August 10, 2020. http://ikee.lib.auth.gr/record/136439/files/DALIOYDE.pdf

Davidman, Lynn. 2011. "The Transformation of Bodily Practices Among Religious Defectors." In *Embodied Resistance: Challenging the Norms, Breaking the Rules*, edited by Chris Bobel and Samantha Kwan, 209–19. Nashville TN: Vanderbilt University Press.

Dean, Jodi. 1996. *Solidarity of Strangers: Feminism After Identity Politics.* Berkeley, California, London: University of California Press.

Delanty, Gerard. 2003. *Community.* London: Routledge.

Della Porta, Donatella, and Mario Diani, eds. 2006. *Social Movements: An Introduction*. 2nd ed. Malden, Mass., Oxford: Blackwell.

Demertzis, Nikos, ed. 1995. *Η Ελληνική Πολιτική Κουλτούρα Σήμερα*.[The Greek Political Culture Today.] Athens: Odysseas.

Denzin, Norman K. 1991. *Images of Postmodern Society: Social Theory and Contemporary Cinema*. London: SAGE.

Denzin, Norman K. 1997. *Interpretive Ethnography: Ethnographic Practices for the 21st Century*. Thousand Oaks California, London: SAGE Publications.

Denzin, Norman K. 2016. "The Reflexive Interview and a Performative Social Science." *Qualitative Research* 1 (1): 23–46. https://doi.org/10.1177/14687941010010010 2

Dermentzopoulos, Christos, and Manos Spyridakis, eds. 2004. *Ανθρωπολογία, Κουλτούρα και Πολιτική*. [Antropology, Culture and Politics.] Athens: Metaixmio.

Desai, Amit, and Evan Killick, eds. 2010. *The Ways of Friendship: Anthropological Perspectives*. Oxford: Berghahn.

Diamandouros, Nikiforos P. 2014. "Politics and Culture in Greece, 1974–91: An Interpretation." In *Greece 1981–89: The Populist Decade*, edited by Richard Clogg, 1–25. Studies in Russia and East Europe. Basingstoke, Hampshire and London: Palgrave Macmillan.

Diani, Mario, and Maria Kousis. 2014. "The Duality of Claims and Events: The Greek Campaign Against the Troika's Memoranda and Austerity, 2010–2012." *Mobilization: An International Quarterly* 19 (4): 387–404. https://doi.org/10.17813/maiq.19.4 .d865w28177575673

Dimitriadis, Dimitris. 2007. *"Lethe" Und Andere Stücke*. Translated by Torsten Israel. Berlin: Theater der Zeit.

Dimitriadis, Dimitris. 2011. *Λήθη: Πέντε Θεατρικοί Μονόλογοι*. [Oblivion: Five Theatrical Monologues.] Thessaloniki: Saixpirikon.

Douzinas, Costas. 2011. *Αντίσταση και Φιλοσοφία στην Κρίση: Πολιτική, Ηθική και Στάση Σύνταγμα*. [Resistance and Philosophy in the Crisis: Politics, Ethics and Stasis Syntagma.] 1st ed. Athens: Alexandria Pubications.

Dreher, Jochen. 2009. "Phenomenology of Friendship: Construction and Constitution of an Existential Social Relationship." *Human Studies* 32 (4): 401–17. https://doi.org/10.1007/s10746-009-9130-4

Dreher, Jochen. 2011. "Schutz, Alfred." In *The Wiley-Blackwell Companion to Major Social Theorists*, edited by George Ritzer and Jeffrey Stepnisky, 489–510. Oxford: Wiley-Blackwell.

Du Bois, W.E.B. 1999. "Of Our Spiritual Strivings." In *Racism*, edited by Martin Bulmer and John Solomos, 125–29. Oxford: Oxford University Press.

Durkheim, Émile. 2008. *The Elementary Forms of the Religious Life*. Translated by Joseph Ward Swain. Mineola New York: Dover Publications Inc.

Ellis, Carolyn. 1995. "Emotional and Ethical Quagmires in Returning to the Field." *Journal of Contemporary Ethnography* 24 (1): 68–98.

Emmanouil, Dimitris, ed. 2016. *Κοινωνικές Τάξεις και Κατανάλωση. Οικονομικές Τάξεις, Στρώματα Status και Πρότυπα Πολιτιστικής και Υλικής Κατανάλωσης στην Αθήνα.* [Social Classes and Consumption: Economic Classes, Status Strata and Patterns of Cultural and Material Consumption in Athens.] 1st ed. Athens: Alexandria Publications.

Evans, Gillian. 2010. "The Value of Friendship: Subject/Object Transformations in the Economy of Becoming a Person (Bermondsey, Southeast London)." In *The Ways of Friendship: Anthropological Perspectives*, edited by Amit Desai and Evan Killick, 174–95. Oxford: Berghahn.

Fassin, Didier. 2012. *Humanitarian Reason: A Moral History of the Present.* Translated by Rachel Gomme. Berkeley, California, London: University of California Press.

Featherstone, Kevin, ed. 2006. *Politics and Policy in Greece: The Challenge of Modernisation.* London: Routledge. https://play.google.com/store/books

Fine, Gary Alan. 1993. "Ten Lies of Ethnography: Moral Dilemmas of Field Research." *Journal of Contemporary Ethnography* 22 (3): 267–94.

Fine, Gary Alan. 2003. "Towards a Peopled Ethnography." *Ethnography* 4 (1): 41–60.

Fine, Michelle. 1998. "Working the Hyphens: Reinventing Self and Other in Qualitative Research." In *The Landscape of Qualitative Research: Theories and Issues*, edited by Yvonna S. Lincoln and Norman K. Denzin, 130–55. Thousand Oaks Calif., London: SAGE Publications.

Fitili, Magda. 2015. "Λωτοφάγοι και Ηρόστρατοι: Μνήμες του '40 στον Πολιτικό Λόγο των Κομμάτων κατά τη Δεκαετία του '80." [Lotus-Eaters and Herostrati: Memories of the '40s in the Political Discourse of Parties During the '80s.] In *Μεταπολίτευση. Η Ελλάδα στο Μεταίχμιο Δύο Αιώνων.* [Metapolitefsi: Greece on the Verge of Two Centuries], edited by Manos Avgeridis, Effi Gazi, and Kostis Kornetis, 29–39. Athens: Themelio.

Foucault, Michel. 1990. *The History of Sexuality 1: The Will to Knowledge.* Translated by Robert Hurley. Harmondsworth: Penguin.

Foucault, Michel. 1991. *Discipline and Punish: The Birth of the Prison.* Translated by Alan Sheridan. London: Penguin Books.

Fragoudaki, Anna. 1997. "Οι Πολιτικές Συνέπειες της Ανιστορικής Παρουσίασης του Ελληνικού Έθνους." [The Political Consequences of the Ahistorical Presentation of the Greek Nation] In *«Τί ειν' η πατρίδα μας;» Εθνοκεντρισμός στην Εκπαίδευση.* [What Is Our Homeland? Ethnocentrism in Education], edited by Anna Fragoudaki and Thalia Dragona. 2nd ed., 143–98. Athens: Alexandria Publications.

Fragoudaki, Anna. 2013. *Ο Εθνικισμός και η Άνοδος της Ακροδεξιάς.* [Nationalism and the Rise of the Far Right.] 1st ed. Athens: Alexandria Publications.

Fragoudaki, Anna, and Thalia Dragona, eds. 1997. *«Τί ειν' η πατρίδα μας;» Εθνοκεντρισμός στην Εκπαίδευση*. [What Is Our Homeland? Ethnocentrism in Education.] 2nd ed. Athens: Alexandria Publications.

Fuller, Timothy, and Michael Oakeshott, eds. 1996. *The Politics of Faith and the Politics of Scepticism*. New Haven and London: Yale University Press.

Gadamer, Hans-Georg. 1986. "The Relevance of the Beautiful." In *The Relevance of the Beautiful and Other Essays*, edited by Robert Bernasconi. Translated by Nicholas Walker. 3–53. Cambridge: Cambridge University Press.

Gadamer, Hans-Georg. 1999. *Hermeneutics, Religion, and Ethics*. Edited and translated by Joel Weinsheimer. New Haven, London: Yale University Press. https://play.google.com/books

Gadamer, Hans-Georg. 2004. *Truth and Method*. Translated by Joel Weinsheimer and Donald G. Marshall. 2nd ed. London, New York: Continuum.

Gauchet, Marcel. 2011. *Η Απομάγευση του Κόσμου. Μια Πολιτική Ιστορία της Θρησκείας*. [Le Desenchantement du Monde: Une Histoire Politique de la Religion.] Translated by Anta Klampatsea. Athens: Patakis.

Gazi, Effi. 2015. "Μεταπλάσεις της Ελληνικής Εθνικής Ιδεολογίας και Ταυτότητας στη Μεταπολίτευση." [Transformations of Greek National Ideology and Identity in the Metapolitefsi.] In *Μεταπολίτευση. Η Ελλάδα στο Μεταίχμιο Δύο Αιώνων*. [Metapolitefsi: Greece on the Verge of Two Centuries], edited by Manos Avgeridis, Effi Gazi, and Kostis Kornetis, 246–60. Athens: Themelio.

Geertz, Clifford. 1973. *The Interpretation of Cultures: Selected Essays*. New York: Basic Books.

Giakovaki, Nasia. 2006. *Ευρώπη μέσω Ελλάδας. Μια Καμπή στην Ευρωπαϊκή Αυτοσυνείδηση, 17ος -18ος Αιώνας*. [Europe via Greece: A Watershed in European Self-Consciousness, 17th -18th Century.] 1st ed. Athens: Vivliopolio tis Estias.

Giddens, Anthony. 1991. *Modernity and Self-Identity: Self and Society in the Late Modern Age*. Cambridge: Polity.

Giddens, Anthony. 1993. *The Transformation of Intimacy: Sexuality, Love and Eroticism in Modern Societies*. Oxford: Polity Press.

Giddens, Anthony. 2001. *Οι Συνέπειες της Νεοτερικότητας*. [The Consequences of Modernity], edited by Gerasimos Lykiardopoulos. Translated by Giorgos Mertikas. Athens: Kritiki.

Gilroy, Paul. 1999. "The End of Anti-Racism." In *Racism*, edited by Martin Bulmer and John Solomos, 242–49. Oxford: Oxford University Press.

Gilroy, Paul. 2002. *There Ain't No Black in the Union Jack: The Cultural Politics of Race and Nation*. London: Routledge.

Giovanopoulos, Christos, and Dimitris Dalakoglou. 2011. "From Ruptures to Eruption: A Genealogy of Post-Dictatorial Revolts in Greece." In *Revolt and Crisis in Greece: Between a Present yet to Pass and a Future Still to Come*, edited by Antonis

Vradis and Dimitris Dalakoglou, 91–114. Oakland, California, Edinburgh: AK Press & Occupied London.

Gkintidis, Dimitrios. 2017. "Free Money, Spoiled Recipients: The Capitalist Crisis as a Moral Question Among Greek Technocrats." In *Critical Times in Greece: Anthropological Engagements with the Crisis*, edited by Dimitris Dalakoglou and Georgios Agelopoulos. 1st ed., 38–48. London: Routledge. https://play.google.com/books

Goffman, Erving. 1959. *The Presentation of Self in Everyday Life*. Garden City, New York: Anchor Books.

Goffman, Erving. 1989. "On Fieldwork." *Journal of Ethnographic Research* 18 (2): 123–32. Transcribed and edited by Lofland, Lyn, H.

Gómez, Javier León. 2019. "Religiousness and Spirituality in the New Utopian Movements." *Religions* 10 (3): 166. https://doi.org/10.3390/rel10030166

Goodwin, Jeff, James M. Jasper, and Francesca Polletta. 2000. "The Return of the Repressed: The Fall and Rise of Emotions in Social Movement Theory." *Mobilization: An International Journal* 5 (1): 65–83.

Goodwin, Jeff, James M. Jasper, and Francesca Polletta, eds. 2001a. *Passionate Politics: Emotions and Social Movements*. Chicago, London: University of Chicago Press.

Goodwin, Jeff, James M. Jasper, and Francesca Polletta. 2001b. "Why Emotions Matter." In *Passionate Politics: Emotions and Social Movements*, edited by Jeff Goodwin, James M. Jasper, and Francesca Polletta, 1–24. Chicago, London: University of Chicago Press.

Gordon, Colin, ed. 1980. *Michel Foucault. Power/ Knowledge: Selected Interviews and Other Writings, 1972–1977*. Translated by Colin Gordon, Leo Marshall, John Mepham, Kate Soper. 1st ed. New York: Vintage Books.

Gouldner, Alvin Ward. 1976. *The Dialectic of Ideology and Technology: The Origins, Grammar and Future of Ideology*. New York: The Macmillan Press.

Gramsci, Antonio. 2005. *Οι Διανοούμενοι*. [The Intellectuals.] Translated by Thanos X. Papadopoulos. Athens: Stoxastis.

Gritzas, Giorgos, and Karolos I. Kavoulakos. 2016. "Diverse Economies and Alternative Spaces: An Overview of Approaches and Practices." European Urban and Regional Studies 23(4): 917–34. https://doi.org/10.1177/0969776415573778

Guibernau, Montserrat. 2013. *Belonging: Solidarity and Division in Modern Societies*. Cambridge: Polity.

Gupta, Akhil, and James Ferguson. 1992. "Beyond 'Culture': Space, Identity and the Politics of Difference." *Cultural Anthropology* 7 (1): 6–23.

Hadjimichalis, Costis. 2018. *Τοπία της Κρίσης στη Νότια Ευρώπη. Στα Μονοπάτια της Άνισης Γεωγραφικής Ανάπτυξης*. [Crisis Spaces in Southern Europe. On Uneven Geographical Development.] 1st ed. Athens: Alexandria Publications.

Hadjimichalis, Costis. 2020. *Crisis Spaces: Structures, Struggles and Solidarity in Southern Europe*. First published in paperback. Routledge Studies in Human Geography 72. London: Routledge.

Hall, Stuart, David Held, and Anthony McGrew, eds. 2003. *Η Νεωτερικότητα Σήμερα*. [Modernity and its Future.] Translated by Thanasis Tsakiris & Victoras Tsakiris. Athens: Savvalas.

Hansen, Linda Prueitt. 2010. "Where Have All the Utopias Gone? Ritual, Solidarity and Longevity in a Multifaith Commune in New Mexico." Master's Thesis, University of Denver. Accessed February 20, 2023. https://digitalcommons.du.edu/cgi/viewcontent.cgi?article=1265&context=etd

Haraway, Donna. 1988. "Situated Knowledge: The Science Question in Feminism and the Privilege of Partial Perspective." *Feminist Studies* 14 (3): 575–99.

Hastrup, Kirsten. 2005/1992. "Writing Ethnography: State of the Art." In *Anthropology and Autobiography*, edited by Judith Okely and Helen Callaway, 115–32. ASA monographs 29. London, New York: Routledge.

Henley, Jon, and Lizzy Davies. 2012. "Greece's Far-Right Golden Dawn Party Maintains Share of Vote." *The Guardian*, June 18, 2012. Accessed January 12, 2023. https://www.theguardian.com/world/2012/jun/18/greece-far-right-golden-dawn

Herzfeld, Michael. 2002a. *Πάλι Δικά Μας: Λαογραφία, Ιδεολογία και η Διαμόρφωση της Σύγχρονης Ελλάδας*. [Ours Once More: Folklore, Ideology and the Making of Modern Greece.] Translated by Marinos Sarigiannis. Athens: Alexandria Publications.

Herzfeld, Michael. 2002b. "The Absent Presence: Discourses of Crypto-Colonialism." *The South Atlantic Quarterly* 101 (4): 899–926.

Herzfeld, Michael. 2016a. "The Hypocrisy of European Moralism: Greece and the Politics of Cultural Aggression – Part 1." *Anthropology Today* 32 (1): 10–13. https://doi.org/10.1111/1467-8322.12224

Herzfeld, Michael. 2016b. "The Hypocrisy of European Moralism: Greece and the Politics of Cultural Aggression - Part 2." *Anthropology Today* 32 (2): 10–13. https://doi.org/10.1111/1467-8322.12238

Herzfeld, Michael. 2020. *Ours Once More: Folklore, Ideology, and the Making of Modern Greece*. Revised edition. New York: Berghahn. https://play.google.com/books

Hirai, Kyonosuke. 2015. "Social Movements and the Production of Knowledge: Body, Practice, and Society in East Asia." *Senri Ethnological Studies* 91: 1–22.

Hjelm, Titus. 2019. "Rethinking the Theoretical Base of Peter L. Berger's Sociology of Religion: Social Construction, Power, and Discourse." *Critical Research on Religion* 7 (3): 223–36. https://doi.org/10.1177/2050303219874392

Hoare, Quintin, and Geoffrey Nowell Smith, eds. 1986a. *Selections from the Prison Notebooks of Antonio Gramsci*. 11th ed. London, New York: Lawrences and Wishart; International Publishers.

Hoare, Quintin, and Geoffrey Nowell Smith. 1986b. "Introduction." In *Selections from the Prison Notebooks of Antonio Gramsci*, edited by Quintin Hoare and Geoffrey N. Smith. 11th ed., xvii–xcvi. London, New York: Lawrences and Wishart; International Publishers.

Hoelzl, Michael. 2004. "Recognising the Sacrificial Victim: The Problem of Solidarity for Critical Social Theory." *Journal for Cultural and Religious Theory* 6 (1): 45–64.

HumanRights360. Accessed November 06, 2020. https://www.humanrights360.org/articles/page/4/

Huss, Boaz. 2014. "Spirituality: The Emergence of a New Cultural Category and Its Challenge to the Religious and the Secular." *Journal of Contemporary Religion* 29 (1): 47–60. https://doi.org/10.1080/13537903.2014.864803

Jacoby, Russell. 1999. *The End of Utopia: Politics and Culture in an Age of Apathy.* New York, United Kingdom: Basic Books.

Jasper, James M. 1998. "The Emotions of Protest: Affective and Reactive Emotions In and Around Social Movements." *Sociological Forum* 13 (3): 397–424.

Jasper, James M. 2015/1997. *The Art of Moral Protest: Culture, Biography, and Creativity in Social Movements.* Chicago, London: The University of Chicago Press.

Jerrome, Dorothy. 1984. "Good Company: The Sociological Implications of Friendship." *The Sociological Review* 32 (4): 696–718.

Juris, Jeffrey S. 2008. "Performing Politics. Image, Embodiment, and Affective Solidarity during Anti-corporate Globalization Protests." *Ethnography* 9 (1): 61–97. https://doi.org/10.1177/1466138108088949

Kalantzis, Konstantinos. 2015a. "Από την «Παιδικότητα» στον «Ιθαγενισμό»: Κοσμολογία και Κοινωνικό Φαντασιακό εντός «Κρίσης.»" [From Infantilism to 'Nativism': Cosmology and the Social Imaginary in 'Crisis.'] In *Μεταπολίτευση. Η Ελλάδα στο Μεταίχμιο Δύο Αιώνων.* [Metapolitefsi: Greece on the Verge of Two Centuries], edited by Manos Avgeridis, Effi Gazi, and Kostis Kornetis, 367–92. Athens: Themelio.

Kalantzis, Konstantinos. 2015b. "'Fak Germani': Materialities of Nationhood and Transgression in the Greek Crisis." *Comparative Studies in Society and History* 57 (4): 1037–69. https://doi.org/10.1017/S0010417515000432

Kallianos, Ioannis. 2011. "December as an Event in Greek Radical Politics." In *Revolt and Crisis in Greece: Between a Present yet to Pass and a Future Still to Come*, edited by Antonis Vradis and Dimitris Dalakoglou, 151–65. Oakland, California, Edinburgh: AK Press & Occupied London.

Kallianos, Ioannis. 2012. "The Fall of the 'Purified' Community: Crisis, Transformation and Collective Action in Greece." *The Unfamiliar* 2 (2): 28–34. https://doi.org/10.2218/unfamiliar.v2i2.76

Kalyvas, Stathis N., and Nikos Marantzidis. 2003. "Greek Communism, 1968–2001." *East European Politics and Societies* 16 (3): 665–90.

Kanali. 2010. "16/12/1979. Η Νύχτα του Χημείου." [The Night in the Chemistry Department.] Accessed February 03, 2023. https://kanali.wordpress.com/2010/12/22/nyxtatouxhmeioy/

Kapetanyannis, Vasilis. 2014. "The Left in the 1980s: Too Little, Too Late." In *Greece 1981–89: The Populist Decade*, edited by Richard Clogg, 78–93. Studies in Russia and East Europe. Basingstoke, Hampshire and London: Palgrave Macmillan.

Karamanolakis, Vangelis D., Ioanna Papathanasiou, and Eudokia Olympitou, eds. 2010. *Η Ελληνική Νεολαία στον 20ο Αιώνα. Πολιτικές Διαδρομές, Κοινωνικές Πρακτικές και Πολιτιστικές Εκφράσεις.* [Greek Youth in the 20th Century: Political Pathways, Social Practices and Cultural Expressions.] 1st ed. Athens: Themelio.

Karapostolis, Vassilis. 1987. *Συμβίωση και Επικοινωνία στην Ελλάδα*. [Co-Existence and Communication in Greece.] Athens: Gnosi.

Karyotis, Georgios, and Stratos Patrikios. 2010. "Religion, Securitization and Anti-Immigration Attitudes: The Case of Greece." *Journal of Peace Research* 47 (1): 43–57. https://doi.org/10.1177/0022343309350021

Karyotis, Georgios, and Wolfgang Rüdig. 2018. "The Three Waves of Anti-Austerity Protest in Greece, 2010–2015." *Political Studies Review* 16 (2): 158–69. https://doi.org/10.1177/1478929916685728

Karyotis, Georgios, and Dimitris Skleparis. 2014. "Migrant Mobilization During the Economic Crisis: Identity Formation and Dilemmas." In *Remapping 'Crisis': A Guide to Athens*, edited by Myrto Tsilimpounidi and Aylwyn Walsh, 145–66. Winchester: Zero Books.

Kassimeris, George. 2005. "Junta by Another Name? The 1974 *Metapolitefsi* and the Greek Extra-Parliamentary Left." *Journal of Contemporary History* 40 (4): 745–62. https://doi.org/10.1177/0022009405056128

Kateb, George. 2000. "Political Action: Its Nature and Advantages." In *The Cambridge Companion to Hannah Arendt*, edited by Dana R. Villa, 130–50. Cambridge: Cambridge University Press.

Kathimerini. 2012. "Pangalos Stands by We All Ate Together Statement." *Kathimerini*, April 18, 2012. Accessed January 28, 2023. http://www.ekathimerini.com/140898/article/ekathimerini/news/pangalos-stands-by-we-all-ate-together-statement

Katz, Jack, and Thomas J. Csordas. 2003. "Phenomenological Ethnography in Sociology and Anthropology." *Ethnography* 4 (3): 275–88. https://doi.org/10.1177/146613810343001

Kaufmann, Walter. 1989/1967. "Editor's Introduction: On the Genealogy of Morals." In *On the Genealogy of Morals and Ecce Homo*, edited by Walter Kaufmann, 3–14. Translated by Walter Kaufmann & R.J. Hollingdale. New York: Vintage Books; Random House US.

Kaufmann, Walter, ed. 2015. *The Faith of a Heretic.* Updated edition. Princeton: Princeton University Press.

Kavoulakos, Karolos, I., and Gritzas George. 2015. *Εναλλακτικοί Οικονομικοί και Πολιτικοί Χώροι.* [Alternative Economic and Political Spaces.] Kallipos, Open Academic Editions. https://hdl.handle.net/11419/6131. Accessed January 21, 2023.

Kazantzakis, Nikos. 1960. *The Saviours of God: Spiritual Exercises*. Translated by Kimon Friar. New York: Simon and Schuster. https://play.google.com/books

Kazantzakis, Nikos, ed. 2007. *Ασκητική. Salvatores Dei*. Edited by Patroklos Stavrou. Athens: Kazantzaki Editions.

Kleinman, Sherryl. 1996. *Opposing Ambitions: Gender and Identity in an Alternative Organization*. Chicago, London: University of Chicago Press.

Knight, Daniel M., and Charles Stewart. 2016. "Ethnographies of Austerity. Temporality, Crisis and Affect in Southern Europe." *History and Anthropology* 27 (1): 1–18. https://doi.org/10.1080/02757206.2015.1114480

Kolakowski, Leszek. 1997. *Modernity on Endless Trial*. Chicago, London: The University of Chicago Press.

Koopman, Sara. 2015. "Decolonizing Solidarity." Accessed September 17, 2020. http://decolonizingsolidarity.blogspot.com/2015/04/inspring-solidarious-academic-strike.html

Koppa, Marilena. 1997. *Οι Μειονότητες στα Μετα-Κομμουνιστικά Βαλκάνια. Πολιτικές του Κέντρου και Μειονοτικές Απαντήσεις*. [Minorities in the Post-Communist Balkans. Politics of the Centre and Minority Responses.] Athens: Nea Synora, Livani.

Kornetis, Kostis. 2015a. "'Cuban Europe'? Greek and Iberian Tiersmondisme in the 'Long 1960s'." *Journal of Contemporary History* 50 (3): 486–515. https://doi.org/10.1177/0022009414556663

Kornetis, Kostis. 2015b. *Τα Παιδιά της Δικτατορίας. Φοιτητική Αντίσταση, Πολιτισμικές Πολιτικές και η Μακρά Δεκαετία του Εξήντα στην Ελλάδα*. [Children of Dictatorship: Student Resistance, Cultural Politics and the "Long 1960s" in Greece.] Translated by Pelagia Marketou. Athens: Polis.

Kouki, Hara, and Antonis Liakos. 2015. "Narrating the Story of a Failed National Transition: Discourses on the Greek Crisis, 2010–2014." *Historein* 15 (1): 49–61. Accessed 28 January, 2023. https://doi.org/10.12681/historein.318

Kountouri, Fani. 2016. "Ο Οικονομικός Μετανάστης στην Πολιτική Ατζέντα. Η Δημόσια Κατασκευή του Μεταναστευτικού στη Μεταπολίτευση." [The Economic Immigrant on the Political Agenda: The Public Construction of the Immigration Issue in Metapolitefsi.] *The Greek Review of Social Research* 128: 39–76. Accessed December 12, 2023. https://doi.org/10.12681/grsr.9882

Kourie, Celia. 2007. "The 'Turn' to Spirituality." *Acta Theologica* 27 (2): 19–38, Supplementum 8. 10.4314/actat.v27i2.52310

Kranioti, Ioanna. 2014. "Χαΐνηδες." [Chainides.] *Monopoli*, August 27, 2014. Accessed February 03, 2023. https://www.monopoli.gr/2014/08/27/people/130152/cha%CF%8A%CE%BDhdes/

Kristeva, Julia. 2011. *Αυτή η Απίστευτη Ανάγκη για Πίστη*. [Cet Incroyable Besoin De Croire.] Translated by Tzeni Konstantinou. Athens: Metaixmio.

Kurtz, Ernest, and William White. 2015. "Recovery Spirituality." *Religions* 6 (1): 58–81. https://doi.org/10.3390/rel6010058

Kyriakakis, Giannis. 2004. "Η Εθνογραφική Εμπειρία και η Κριτική της Κουλτούρας. Μια προσπάθεια Σκιαγράφησης της «Ανθρωπολογικής Οπτικής ως Ερμηνευτικής της Ανθρώπινης Συνθήκης." [Ethnographic Experience and The Critique of Culture: An Attempt at an Outline of the Anthropological Perspective as a Hermeneutics of the Human Condition.] In *Ανθρωπολογία, Κουλτούρα και Πολιτική*. [Antropology, Culture and Politics], edited by Christos Dermentzopoulos and Manos Spyridakis, 57–72. Athens: Metaixmio.

Kyriakakis, Giannis, and Martha Michailidou, eds. 2006. *Η Προσέγγιση του Άλλου. Ιδεολογία, Μεθοδολογία και Ερευνητική Πρακτική*. [Approaching the Other: Ideology, Methodology and Research Practice.] 1st ed. Athens: Metaixmio.

La Fuente, Eduardo de. 2016. "The Place of Culture in Sociology. Romanticism and Debates about the 'Cultural Turn.'" *Journal of Sociology* 43 (2): 115–30. https://doi.org/10.1177/1440783307076891

Labaree, Robert V. 2002. "The Risk of 'Going Observationalist': Negotiating the Hidden Dilemmas of Being an Insider Participant Observer." *Qualitative Research* 2 (1): 97–122. https://doi.org/10.1177/1468794102002001641

Ladkin, Donna. 2005. "'The Enigma of Subjectivity': How Might Phenomenology Help Action Researchers Negotiate the Relationship Between 'Self', 'Other' and 'Truth'?" *Action Research* 3 (1): 108–26. https://doi.org/10.1177/1476750305049968

Lasch, Christopher. 1979. *Η Κουλτούρα του Ναρκισσισμού*. [The Culture of Narcissism.] Translated by Vasilis Tomanas. Thessaloniki: Nisides.

Lasch, Christopher. 1991. *The Culture of Narcissism: American Life in an Age of Diminishing Expectations*. W.W. Norton & Company. https://play.google.com/store/books

Lather, Patti. 1993. "Fertile Obsession: Validity After Poststructuralism." *The Sociological Quarterly* 34 (4): 673–93.

LAW NO. 3386. 2005. "Entry, Residence and Social Integration of Third-Country Nationals in the Hellenic Territory." Accessed February 11, 2023. https://ec.europa.eu/migrant-integration/library-document/law-no-338605-entry-residence-and-social-integration-third-country-nationals_en

Lefebvre, Henri. 2005/1991. *Critique of Everyday Life. Volume 1*. Translated by John Moore. London: Verso.

Left Voice. 2008. "Social Revolt in Greece." *Left voice*, December 21, 2008. Accessed February 07, 2023. https://www.leftvoice.org/social-revolt-in-greece

Lekkas, Pantelis E. 1994. "Διανοούμενοι και Ιδεολογία." [Intellectuals and Ideology.] In *Επιστημονική Συνάντηση στη Μνήμη του Κ.Θ. Δημαρά*. [Scientific Meeting in Memory of K.Th. Demaras], edited by Triantafyllos Sklavenitis. Athens: Kentro Neoellinikon Ereunon/E.I.E.

Lekkas, Pantelis E. 1996. *Η Εθνικιστική Ιδεολογία. Πέντε Υποθέσεις Εργασίας στην Ιστορική Κοινωνιολογία.* [The Nationalist Ideology: Five Working Hypotheses in Historical Sociology.] 2nd ed. Athens: Katarti.

Lekkas, Pantelis E. 2012. *Αφαίρεση και Εμπειρία. Μια Φορμαλιστική Θεώρηση του Ιδεολογικού Φαινομένου.* [Abstraction and Experience: Toward a Formalist Theory of Ideology.] Athens: Topos.

Lekkas, Pantelis E. 2016. "Η Πολιτική Ιδεολογία ως Κοσμική Θρησκεία." [Political Ideology as Secular Religion.] In *Πολιτική Θεωρία. Αξιακές Επιλογές και Προσδοκίες.* [Political Theory. Value Choices and Expectations], edited by A-I.D. Metaxas. 2nd ed., 159–82. Athens: Idrima Themistokli & Dimitri Tsatsou; Sideris.

Lentin, Alana. 2004. *Racism and Anti-Racism in Europe.* London: Pluto.

Lentin, Alana, and Gavan Titley. 2011. *The Crises of Multiculturalism: Racism in a Neoliberal Age.* 1st ed. London: Zed Books.

Leontidou, Lila. 1996. "Alternatives to Modernism in (Southern) Urban Theory: Exploring In-Between Spaces." International Journal of Urban and Regional Research 20 (2):179-95.

Leontidou, Lila. 2010. "Urban Social Movements in 'Weak' Civil Societies: The Right to the City and Cosmopolitan Activism in Southern Europe." *Urban Studies* 47 (6): 1179–1203. https://doi.org/10.1177/0042098009360239

Leontidou, Lila. 2015. "'Smart Cities' of the Debt Crisis: Grassroots Creativity in Mediterranean Europe." *The Greek Review of Social Research* Special issue 144 A: 69–101. Accessed February 02, 2023. https://ejournals.epublishing.ekt.gr/index.php/ekke/article/viewFile/8626/8940.pdf

Lincoln, Yvonna S. 1995. "Emerging Criteria for Quality in Qualitative and Interpretive Research." *Qualitative Inquiry* 1 (3): 275–89. https://doi.org/10.1177/107780049500100301

Lincoln, Yvonna S., and Norman K. Denzin, eds. 1998. *The Landscape of Qualitative Research: Theories and Issues.* Thousand Oaks Calif., London: SAGE Publications.

Lipovats, Thanos. 1995. "Η Διχασμένη Ελληνική Ταυτότητα και το Πρόβλημα του Εθνικισμού." [The Divided Greek Identity and the Problem of Nationalism.] In *Η Ελληνική Πολιτική Κουλτούρα Σήμερα.* [The Greek Political Culture Today], edited by Nikos Demertzis, 115–131. Athens: Odysseas.

Lipovats, Thanos. 1996. *Ψυχανάλυση, Φιλοσοφία, Πολιτική Κουλτούρα. Διαπλεκόμενα Κείμενα.* [Psychoanalysis, Philosophy, Political Culture. Intertwined Texts.] Athens Plethron.

Löwy, Michael. 2002. *Λύτρωση και Ουτοπία.* [Redemption and Utopia.] Translated by Thanasis Papadopoulos. Athens: Psichogios.

Lyon, Margot L. 1997. "The Material Body, Social Processes and Emotion: 'Techniques of the Body' Revisited." *Body & Society* 3 (1): 83–101.

Lyrintzis, Christos, and Michalis Spourdalakis. 2017/1993. "Περί Λαϊκισμού: Μια Σύνδεση με Αφορμή την Ελληνική Βιβλιογραφία." [About Populism: A Synthesis

Concerning the Greek Bibliography.] *Greek Political Science Review* 1(2): 133–62. Accessed February 19, 2023. https://doi.org/10.12687/hpsa.1539

Macedo, Donaldo, and Panayota Gounari, eds. 2008. *Η Παγκοσμιοποίηση του Ρατσισμού*. [The Globalisation of Racism.] Translated by Paraskeyi Arapoglou. Athens: Epikentro.

Manuel, Frank Edward, ed. 1973/1966. *Utopias and Utopian Thought.* London: Souvenir Press.

Marvakis, Athanasios, Dimitris Parsanoglou, and Miltos Pavlou, eds. 2001. *Μετανάστες στην Ελλάδα.* [Migrants in Greece.] Athens: Ellinika Grammata.

Marvakis, Athanasios, and Ioanna Petritsi. 2014. "Solidarity, Not Adjustment: Activism Learning as (Self-)Transformation." In *Psychology in Education: Critical Theory~Practice*, edited by Tim Corcoran, 129–44. Rotterdam: SensePublishers.

Mavrogordatos, George Th. 2014. "Civil Society Under Populism." In *Greece 1981–89: The Populist Decade*, edited by Richard Clogg, 47–64. Studies in Russia and East Europe. Basingstoke, Hampshire and London: Palgrave Macmillan.

Mead, George Herbert. 2015. *Mind, Self, and Society.* Edited by Charles W. Morris. Annotated Edition by Daniel R. Huebner, and Hans Joas. The definitive edition. Chicago: The University of Chicago Press. https://play.google.com/books

Melucci, Alberto, ed. 1989. *Nomads of the Present: Social Movements and Individual Needs in Contemporary Society.* Edited by John Keane and Paul Mier. London: Hutchinson Radius.

Melucci, Alberto. 1996a. *Challenging Codes: Collective Action in the Information Age.* Cambridge: Cambridge University Press.

Melucci, Alberto. 1996b. *The Playing Self: Person and Meaning in the Planetary Society.* Cambridge: Cambridge University Press.

Melucci, Alberto. 1999. "Difference and Otherness in a Global Society." In *Racism*, edited by Martin Bulmer and John Solomos, 412–25. Oxford: Oxford University Press.

Melucci, Alberto. 2015. "Identity and Difference in a Globalised World." In *Debating Cultural Hybridity: Multicultural Identities and the Politics of Anti-Racism*, edited by Pnina Werbner and Tariq Modood, 58–69. London: Zed Books.

Metaxas, A-I D., ed. 2016. *Πολιτική Θεωρία. Αξιακές Επιλογές και Προσδοκίες* [Political Theory. Value Choices and Expectations.] 2nd ed. Athens: Idrima Themistokli & Dimitri Tsatsou; Sideris.

Michani tou Xronou. "«Η Μακεδονία Είναι Ελληνική.» Το Μαζικό Συλλαλητήριο Για Την Ονομασία Των Σκοπίων. Ποιοι Το Διοργάνωσαν Και Τι Αποφάσισε Η Πολιτική Ηγεσία Την Επόμενη Μέρα (Φωτο & Βίντεο)." ['Macedonia is Greek.' The Mass Demonstration for the Name of Skopje. Who Organised it and what Decisions Were Made by the Political Leadership in its Wake.] Accessed January 10, 2023. https://www.mixanitouxronou.gr/i-makedonia-einai-elliniki-to-maziko-syllalitirio-tou-1992-stin-thessaloniki-gia-tin-onomasia-ton-skopion-poi

oi-tin-diorganosan-kai-ti-apofasise-i-politiki-igesia-tin-epomeni-mera-foto-vinte/
Miles, Robert. 1999. "Racism as a Concept." In *Racism*, edited by Martin Bulmer and John Solomos, 344–54. Oxford: Oxford University Press.
Mills, C. Wright. 1999. *The Sociological Imagination.* New York: Oxford University Press.
Modood, Tariq. 2015. "'Difference', Cultural Racism and Anti-Racism." In *Debating Cultural Hybridity: Multicultural Identities and the Politics of Anti-Racism*, edited by Pnina Werbner and Tariq Modood, 154–72. London: Zed Books.
Mohanty, Satya P. 2001. "Can Our Values Be Objective? On Ethics, Aesthetics, and Progressive Politics." *New Literary History* 32 (4): 803–833.
Moshonas, Gerasimos. 1995. "Η Διαιρετική Τομή Δεξιάς-Αντιδεξιάς στη Μεταπολίτευση (1974–1990). Το Περιεχόμενο της Τομής και Όψεις της Στρατηγικής των Κομμάτων του «Αντιδεξιού Υποσυστήματος.»" [The Right -Anti-right Cleavage in the Post-Authoritarian Period in Greece (1974–1990). The Character of the Division and Aspects of the Strategy of the Parties of the Anti-Right-Wing Subsystem.] In *Η Ελληνική Πολιτική Κουλτούρα Σήμερα.* [The Greek Political Culture Today], edited by Nikos DemertzIs, 159–216. Athens: Odysseas.
Nietzsche, Friedrich. 1989/1967. "On the Genealogy of Morals." In *On the Genealogy of Morals and Ecce Homo*, edited and translated by Walter Kaufmann & R.J Hollingdale, 15–214. New York: Vintage Books; Random House US.
Nietzsche, Friedrich. 2019. *Beyond Good and Evil.* London: Arcturus Publishing Limited.
Nietzsche, Friedrich Wilhelm, and R. J. Hollingdale. 1969/1961. *Thus Spoke Zarathustra: A Book for Everyone and No One*. Edited, translated by and with an introduction by R.J. Hollingdale. The Penguin classics. Harmondsworth, England, New York.
Novick, Peter. 1991. "My Correct Views on Everything." *The American Historical Review* 96 (3): 699–703.
Pahl, Ray. 2000. *On Friendship.* Cambridge: Polity.
Paine, Robert. 1969. "In Search of Friendship: An Exploratory Analysis in 'Middle-Class' Culture." *Man, New Series* 4 (4): 505–24.
Paine, Robert. 1999. "Friendship: The Hazards of an Ideal Relationship." In *The Anthropology of Friendship*, edited by Sandra Bell and Simon Coleman, 39–58. Oxford: Berg.
Panagiotopoulos, Panayis. 2015. "Από την Προστατευόμενη στην Ανασφαλή Δημοκρατία. Κοινωνιολογία της Μεταπολίτευσης υπό το Φως της Κρίσης." [From Protected to Unsafe Democracy: The Sociology of the Metapolitefsi in the Light of the Crisis.] In *Μεταπολίτευση. Η Ελλάδα στο Μεταίχμιο Δύο Αιώνων.* [Metapolitefsi: Greece on the Verge of Two Centuries], edited by Manos Avgeridis, Effi Gazi, and Kostis Kornetis, 335–66. Athens: Themelio.

Panagiotopoulos, Panayis, and Pavlos Pantazis. 2010. "Νεολαία και Στρατιωτική Θητεία 1980–1987. Υποκειμενικότητα και Εκδημοκρατισμός των Θεσμών στην Κοινωνία της Επιθυμίας." [Youth and Military Service 1980–1987: Subjectivity and the Democratisation of Institutions in the Society of Desire.] In *Η Ελληνική Νεολαία στον 20ο Αιώνα. Πολιτικές Διαδρομές, Κοινωνικές Πρακτικές και Πολιτιστικές Εκφράσεις.* [Greek Youth in the 20th Century: Political Pathways, Social Practices and Cultural Expressions], edited by Vangelis D. Karamanolakis, Ioanna Papathanasiou, and Eudokia Olympitou. 1st ed., 369–75. Athens: Themelio.

Panagiotopoulos, Panayis, and Dimitris Sotiropoulos. 2020. *Political and Cultural Aspects of Greek Exoticism. Reform and Transition in the Mediterranean.* Basingstoke: Palgrave Macmillan/ Springer. https://play.google.com/books

Panagiotopoulos, Panayis, and Vassilis Vamvakas. 2014. "Acrobats on a Rope: Greek Society Between Contemporary European Demands and Archaic Cultural Reflexes." In *The Great Catalyst: European Union Project and Lessons from Greece and Turkey*, edited by Bülent Temel, 113–34. Lanham: Lexington Books.

Panourgia, Neni. 2009. *Dangerous Citizens: The Greek Left and the Terror of the State.* 1st ed. New York: Fordham University Press.

Pantazopoulos, Andreas. 2001. *Για το Λαό και το Έθνος. Η Στιγμή Ανδρέα Παπανδρέου, 1965–1989.* [For the People and the Nation: The Andreas Papandreou Moment, 1965–1989.] Athens: Polis.

Pantazopoulos, Andreas. 2011. *Λαϊκισμός και Εκσυγχρονισμός 1965–2005. Απορίες και Κίνδυνοι μιας Μαχητικής Συμβίωσης.* [Populism and Modernisation, 1965–2005. The Questions and Dangers Surrounding a Challenging Coexistence.] Athens: Vivliopolio tis Estias.

Pantazopoulos, Andreas. 2012. "Πολιτισμική Ανασφάλεια και Πολιτική Βία." [Cultural Insecurity and Political Violence.] Accessed November 28, 2023. https://politicalreviewgr.blogspot.com/2012/09/blog-post_3.html

Papadogiannis, Nikolaos. 2010. "Η Πολλαπλή Υποδοχή της Ροκ Μουσικής από τις Κομμουνιστικές Οργανώσεις Νεολαίας στην Ελλάδα στα Τέλη της Δεκαετίας του 1970." [The Multiple Reception of Rock Music in the Youth Communist Organisations in Greece in the End of 1970s.] In *Η Ελληνική Νεολαία στον 20ο Αιώνα. Πολιτικές Διαδρομές, Κοινωνικές Πρακτικές και Πολιτιστικές Εκφράσεις.* [Greek Youth in the 20th Century: Political Pathways, Social Practices and Cultural Expressions], edited by Vangelis D. Karamanolakis, Ioanna Papathanasiou, and Eudokia Olympitou. 1st ed., 318–44. Athens: Themelio.

Papadogiannis, Nikolaos. 2015a. *Militant Around the Clock? Left-Wing Youth Politics, Leisure, and Sexuality in Post-Dictatorship Greece, 1974–1981.* 1st ed. New York: Berghahn Books. https://play.google.com/books

Papadogiannis, Nikolaos. 2015b. "Νεανική Πολιτικοποίηση και «Πολιτισμός» στα Πρώτα Χρόνια της Μεταπολίτευσης." [Youth Politicisation and 'Culture' in the First Years of Metapolitefsi.] In *Μεταπολίτευση. Η Ελλάδα στο Μεταίχμιο Δύο*

Αιώνων. [Metapolitefsi: Greece on the Verge of Two Centuries], edited by Manos Avgeridis, Effi Gazi, and Kostis Kornetis, 133–50. Athens: Themelio.

Papataxiarchis, Evthymios. 2006. "Ο Κόσμος του Καφενείου: Ταυτότητα και Ανταλλαγή στον Ανδρικό Συμποσιασμό." [The World of the Coffeehouse: Identity and Exchange in Spaces of Male Interaction.] In *Ταυτότητες και Φύλο στη Σύγχρονη Ελλάδα. Ανθρωπολογικές Προσεγγίσεις*. [Identity and Gender in Modern Greece: Anthropological Approaches], edited by Evthymios Papataxiarchis and Theodoros Papadellis. 3rd ed., 209–50. Athens: Alexandria Publications.

Papataxiarchis, Evthymios. 2014. "Ο Αδιανόητος Ρατσισμός: Η Πολιτικοποίηση της Φιλοξενίας την Εποχή της Κρίσης." [The Inconceivable Racism: The Politicisation of Hospitality at the Age of Crisis.] *Sychrona Themata* 127: 46–62.

Papataxiarchis, Evthymios. 2015. *Περιπέτειες της Ετερότητας: Η Παραγωγή της Πολιτισμικής Διαφοράς στη Σημερινή Ελλάδα*. [Adventures of Alterity: The Production of Cultural Difference in Modern Greece.] 2nd ed. Athens: Alexandria Publications.

Papataxiarchis, Evthymios. 2016. "Unwrapping Solidarity: Society Reborn in Austerity." *Social Anthropology* 24 (2): 205–210. doi.10.1111/14698676.12309

Papataxiarchis, Evthymios. 2017. "Pragmatism Against Austerity: Greek Society, Politics and Ethnography in Times of Trouble." In *Critical Times in Greece: Anthropological Engagements with the Crisis*, edited by Dimitris Dalakoglou and Georgios Agelopoulos. 1st ed., 203–21. London: Routledge. https://play.google.com/book s

Pappas, Takis S. 2010. "The Causes of the Greek Crisis Are in Greek Politics." 29 November 2010, Accessed February 03, 2020. https://www.opendemocracy.ne t/en/openeconomy/causes-of-greek-crisis-are-in-greek-politics/

Passerini, Luisa. 2002. "'Utopia' and Desire." *Thesis Eleven* 68 (1): 11–30. https://doi.o rg/10.1177/0725513602068001002

Pavlou, Miltos. 2001. "Οι «Λαθρέμποροι του Φόβου»: Ρατσιστικός Λόγος και Μετανάστες στον Τύπο μιας Υποψήφιας Μητρόπολης." [Smugglers of Fear: Racist Discourse and Migrants in the Press of a Potential Metropolis.] In *Μετανάστες στην Ελλάδα*. [Migrants in Greece], edited by Athanasios Marvakis, Dimitris Parsanoglou, and Miltos Pavlou, 127–62. Athens: Ellinika Grammata.

Pavlou, Miltos. 2004. "Οι Μετανάστες «Σαν κι Εμάς»: Όψεις της Απόκρισης στο Μεταναστευτικό Φαινόμενο στην Ελλάδα και την Ευρώπη." [Migrants Like 'Us': Aspects of Response to the Migration Phenomena in Greece and Europe.] In *Η Ελλάδα της Μετανάστευσης. Κοινωνική Συμμετοχή, Δικαιώματα και Ιδιότητα του Πολίτη*. [Greece of Migration: Social Participation, Rights and Citizenship], edited by Miltos Pavlou and Dimitris Christopoulos, 39–87. Athens: Kritiki-Kemo.

Pavlou, Miltos. 2009. "Λόγος και Πολιτικές για τους Μετανάστες." [Discourse and Policies for Migrants.] In *Μετανάστες και Μειονότητες. Λόγος και Πολιτικές*. [Migrants and Minorities: Discourse and Policies], edited by Miltos Pavlou and Athina Skoulariki, 21–68. Seira meleton / KEMO 3. Athens: Bibliorama.

Pavlou, Miltos, and Dimitris Christopoulos, eds. 2004. *Η Ελλάδα της Μετανάστευσης. Κοινωνική Συμμετοχή, Δικαιώματα και Ιδιότητα του Πολίτη*. [Greece of Migration: Social Participation, Rights and Citizenship.] Athens: Kritiki-Kemo.

Pavlou, Miltos, and Athina Skoulariki, eds. 2009. *Μετανάστες και Μειονότητες. Λόγος και Πολιτικές*. [Migrants and Minorities: Discourse and Policies.] Seira meleton / KEMO 3. Athens: Bibliorama.

Però, Davide. 2007. *Inclusionary Rhetoric: Left-Wing Politics and Migrants in Italy*. Oxford: Berghahn.

Petmetzidou, Maria, ed. 1998. *Σύγχρονη Κοινωνιολογική Θεωρία I*. [Contemporary Sociological Theory I.] Translated by Giorgos Barouxis and Vasilis Kapetanyannis. 2nd ed. Herakleio: Panepistimiakes Ekdoseis Kritis.

Petrinioti, Xanthi. 1993. *Η Μετανάστευση προς την Ελλάδα. Μια Πρώτη Καταγραφή, Ταξινόμηση και Ανάλυση*. [Immigration to Greece: A First Description, Categorisation and Analysis.] Athens: Odysseas & Library of the Institution of International Relations.

Plummer, Kenneth. 2001. *Documents of Life 2: An Invitation to a Critical Humanism*. 2nd ed. London: SAGE.

Polletta, Francesca. 1999. "'Free Spaces' in Collective Action." *Theory and Society* 28 (1): 1–38.

Polletta, Francesca, and Jasper, James, M. 2001. "Collective Identity and Social Movements." *Annual Review of Sociology* 27: 283–305.

Portaliou, Eleni. 2007. "Anti-global Movements Reclaim the City." *City* 11 (2): 165–75. https://doi.org/10.1080/13604810701396009

Progressive All-Student Unionist Camp. 1980. "Σάλπισμα." Accessed December 28, 2023. https://kanali.files.wordpress.com/2009/10/salpisma_17_01_198012mb.pdf

Psaras, Dimitris. 28/01/18. "Σκληρό Μάθημα του 1992." [A Tough Lesson From 1992.] *Efimerida ton Syntakton*, 28 January 2018. Accessed 03 January 2023. http://www.efsyn.gr/arthro/skliro-mathima-toy-1992

Psimitis, Michalis. 2006. *Εισαγωγή στα Σύγχρονα Κοινωνικά Κινήματα*. [Introduction in the Modern Social Movements.] Athens: Atrapos.

Rabinow, Paul. 2010. "Representations Are Social Facts: Modernity and Postmodernity in Anthropology." In *Writing Culture: The Poetics and Politics of Ethnography*, edited by James Clifford and George E. Marcus. 25th ed., 234–61. Berkeley, California, London: University of California Press.

Rakopoulos, Theodoros. 2014a. "Resonance of Solidarity: Meanings of a Local Concept in Anti-Austerity Greece." *Journal of Modern Greek Studies* 32 (2): 313–37. https://doi.org/10.1353/mgs.2014.0040

Rakopoulos, Theodoros. 2014b. "The Crisis Seen from Below, Within, and Against: From Solidarity Economy to Food Distribution Cooperatives in Greece." *Dialectical Anthropology* 38 (2): 189–207. https://doi.org/10.1007/s10624-014-9342-5

Rakopoulos, Theodoros. 2015. "Solidarity's Tensions: Informality, Sociality, and the Greek Crisis." *Social Analysis* 59 (3): 85–104. https://doi.org/10.3167/sa.2015.590305

Rakopoulos, Theodoros. 2016. "Solidarity: The Egalitarian Tensions of a Bridge-Concept." *Social Anthropology* 24 (2): 142–51. https://doi.org/10.1111/1469-8676.12298

Rasmussen, Ulrik Houlind. 2009. "The Memory of God: Hans Blumenberg's Philosophy of Religion." Doctoral Thesis, Theological Faculty, University of Copenhagen.

Revault D'Allonnes, Myriam. 2013. *Ο Συμπονετικός Άνθρωπος.* [L' Homme Compassionnel.] Translated by Michalis Pagalos. 1st ed. Athens: Vivliopolio tis Estias.

Riboli, Diana. 2006. "Πλησιάζοντας τον Άλλο. Μύθοι και Αυταπάτες του Ανθρωπολόγου στην Προσπάθειά του να Αντιμετωπίσει την Ετερότητα στη Δύση και στην Ανατολή."[Approaching the Other. The Anthropologist's Myths and Illusions in His Attempt to Approach Otherness in the West and East.] In *Η Προσέγγιση του Άλλου. Ιδεολογία, Μεθοδολογία και Ερευνητική Πρακτική.* [Approaching the Other: Ideology, Methodology and Research Practice], edited by Giannis Kyriakakis and Martha Michailidou. 1st ed., 143–74. Athens: Metaixmio.

Ricœur, Paul. 1976. *Interpretation Theory: Discourse and the Surplus of Meaning.* Fort Worth, Texas: Texas Christian University Press.

Ricœur, Paul. 1978. "The Metaphorical Process as Cognition, Imagination and Feeling." *Critical Inquiry* 5 (1): 143–59.

Ricœur, Paul. 2003/1978. *The Rule of Metaphor: The Creation of Meaning in Language.* Translated by Robert Czerny with Kathleen McLaughlin and John Costello. London, New York: Routledge.

Riessman, Catherine Kohler. 2008. *Narrative Methods for the Human Sciences.* London: SAGE.

Ritzer, George. 1998. "Φαινομενολογική Κοινωνιολογία και Εθνομεθοδολογία." [Phenomenological Sociology and Ethnomethodology.] In *Σύγχρονη Κοινωνιολογική Θεωρία I.* [Contemporary Sociological Theory I], edited by Maria Petmetzidou. Translated by Giorgos Barouxis and Vasilis Kapetanyannis. 2nd ed., 281–329. Herakleio: Panepistimiakes Ekdoseis Kritis.

Rosaldo, Renato. 1993. *Culture & Truth: The Remaking of Social Analysis.* Boston: Beacon Press.

Rozakou, Katerina. 2016. "Socialities of Solidarity: Revisiting the Gift Taboo in Times of Crises." *Social Anthropology* 24 (2): 185–99. https://doi.org/10.1111/1469-8676.12305

Rozakou, Katerina. 2018. *Από «Αγάπη» και «Αλληλεγγύη». Εθελοντική Εργασία με Πρόσφυγες στην Αθήνα του Πρώιμου 21ου Αιώνα.* [Out of "Love" and "Solidarity": Voluntary Work with Refugees in Early 21st Century Greece.] Athens: Alexandria Publications.

Rudolf, Susanne Hoeber. 2005. "Presidential Address: The Imperialism of Categories: Situating Knowledge in a Globalising World." *Perspectives on Politics* 3 (1): 5–14.

Said, Edward W. 1996a. *Οριενταλισμός*. [*Orientalism*.] Translated by Fotis Terzakis. Athens: Nefeli.

Said, Edward W. 1996b. *Representations of the Intellectual: The Reith Lectures*. New York: Vintage Books, Random House US.

Sakellaropoulos, Spyros. 2014. *Κρίση και Κοινωνική Διαστρωμάτωση στην Ελλάδα του 21ου αιώνα*. [Crisis and Social Stratification in Greece of the 21st Century.] Athens: Topos.

Samartzis, Thanos. 2017. Ο Εκκλησιαστής. [Ecclesiastes.] Athens: Doma.

Sartre, Jean-Paul. 2007. *Existentialism and Humanism*. Translated by Phillip Mairet. London: Methuen.

Schiffauer, Werner. 1997. *Fremde in Der Stadt: Zehn Essays Über Kultur Und Differenz*. 1st ed. Frankfurt am Main: Suhrkamp.

Schiffauer, Werner. 2000. *Die Gottesmänner: Türkische Islamisten in Deutschland: Eine Studie Zur Herstellung Religiöser Evidenz*. 1st ed. Frankfurt am Main: Suhrkamp.

Schutz, Alfred. 1972. *The Phenomenology of the Social World*. Edited by John Wild. Translated by George Walsh and Frederick Lehnert.1 pbk. print. Evanston: Northwestern University Press.

Schutz, Alfred. 1976. *Collected Papers II. Studies in Social Theory*. Edited and introduced by Arvin Brodersen. Phaenomenologica 15. Netherlands: Martinus Nijhoff/The Hague.

Seidman, Steven, ed. 1994. *The Postmodern Turn: New Perspectives on Social Theory*. Cambridge: Cambridge University Press.

Seoane, José, and Emilio Taddei. 2002. "From Seattle to Porto Alegre: The Anti-Neoliberal Globalization Movement." *Current Sociology* 50 (1): 99–122. https://doi.org/10.1177/0011392102050001008

Seymour, Susan. 2006. "Resistance." *Anthropological Theory* 6 (3): 303–21. https://doi.org/10.1177/1463499606066890

Siani-Davies, Peter, and Stefanos Katsikas. 2009. "National Reconciliation After Civil War: The Case of Greece." *Journal of Peace Research* 46 (4): 559–75. https://doi.org/10.1177/0022343309334611

Silos, Jill Katherine. 2003. "'Everybody Get Together': The Sixties Counterculture and Public Space, 1964–1967." Doctoral Thesis, University of New hampshire, Durham. Accessed August 07, 2020. https://scholars.unh.edu/cgi/viewcontent.cgi?article=1169&context=dissertation

Silver, Allan. 1989. "Friendship and Trust as Moral Ideals: An Historical Approach." *European Journal of Sociology* 30 (2): 274–97. https://doi.org/10.1017/S0003975600005890

Silver, Allan. 1990. "Friendship in Commercial Society: Eighteenth-Century Social Theory and Modern Sociology." *American Journal of Sociology* 95 (6): 1474–1504. https://doi.org/10.1086/229461

Simiti, Marilena. 2016. "Rage and Protest: The Case of the Greek Indignant Movement." *Contention: The Multidisciplinary Journal of Social Protest* 3 (2): 33–50.

Skerrett, Karen. 2016. "We-Ness and the Cultivation of Wisdom in Couple Therapy." *Family Process* 55 (1): 48–61. https://doi.org/10.1111/famp.12162

Smith, Jonathan A., Michael Howard Larkin, and Paul Flowers. 2009. *Interpretative Phenomenological Analysis: Theory, Method and Research.* Los Angeles, London: SAGE.

Solidarity4all. "Solidarity Campaign." Accessed June 13, 2020. https://www.solidarity4all.gr/el/%CE%B1%CE%BB%CE%BB%CE%B7%CE%BB%CE%B5%CE%B3%CE%B3%CF%8D%CE%B7-%CE%B3%CE%B9%CE%B1-%CF%8C%CE%BB%CE%BF%CF%85%CF%82

Sotirakopoulos, Nikos. 2011. "No Politics Please, We're Trying to Protest!", June 15, 2011. Accessed January 15, 2023. https://www.spiked-online.com/2011/06/15/no-politics-please-were-trying-to-protest/

Sotiropoulos, Dimitris A. 2004. "Formal Weakness and Informal Strength: Civil Society in Contemporary Greece." Discussion Paper No. 16. February, London: The Hellenic Observatory, The European Institute, The London School of Economics and Political Science. Accessed January 25, 2023. https://www.researchgate.net/publication/30525520_Formal_weakness_and_informal_strength_civil_society_in_contemporary_Greece

Souliotis, Nikos. 2016. "Καταναλωτικές Λογικές στον Καιρό της Κρίσης: Αναστοχασμός και Προσαρμογή." [Consumption Logics in the Age of Crisis: Reflection and Adjustment.] In *Κοινωνικές Τάξεις και Κατανάλωση. Οικονομικές Τάξεις, Στρώματα Status και Πρότυπα Πολιτιστικής και Υλικής Κατανάλωσης στην Αθήνα.* [Social Classes and Consumption: Economic Classes, Status Strata and Patterns of Cultural and Material Consumption], edited by Dimitris Emmanouil. 1st ed., 277–306. Athens: Alexandria Publications.

Spivak, Gayatri Chakravorty, Donna Landry, and Gerald M. MacLean, eds. 1996. *The Spivak Reader: Selected Works of Gayatri Chakravorty Spivak.* Edited by Donna Landry and Gerald MacLean. New York, London: Routledge.

Srivastava, Sarita. 2006. "Tears, Fears and Careers: Anti-Racism and Emotion in Social Movement Organisations." *The Canadian Journal of Sociology* 31 (1): 55–90.

Suri, Jeremi. 2009. "AHR Forum the Rise and Fall of an International Counterculture, 1960–1975." *The American Historical Review* 114 (1): 45–68. https://doi.org/10.1086/ahr.114.1.45

Svolopoulos, Konstantinos, D. 2004. *Η Ελληνική Εξωτερική Πολιτική, 1945–1981.* [The Greek Foreign Policy, 1945–1981.] 4th ed. Vol. 2. Athens: Vivliopolio tis Estias.

SYN. 1992. "First Congress." Accessed October 09, 2020. http://www.syn.gr/gr/keimeno.php?id=13386

Taquieff, Pierre-Andre. 1999. "The New Cultural Racism in France." In *Racism*, edited by Martin Bulmer and John Solomos, 206–12. Oxford: Oxford University Press.

Taylor, Charles. 1997. *Πολυπολιτισμικότητα.* [Multiculturalism.] Edited by Amy Gutmann. Translated by Philimon Paionidis. Athens: Polis.

Taylor, Jodie. 2011. "The Intimate Insider: Negotiating the Ethics of Friendship When Doing Insider Research." *Qualitative Research* 11 (1): 3–22. https://doi.org/10.1177/1468794110384447

Teivainen, Teivo. 2002. "The World Social Forum and Global Democratisation: Learning from Porto Alegre." *Third World Quarterly* 23 (4): 621–32. https://doi.org/10.1080/0143659022000005300

Theodossopoulos, Dimitrios. 2013. "Infuriated with the Infuriated? Blaming Tactics and Discontent about the Greek Financial Crisis." *Current Anthropology* 54 (2): 200–221. https://doi.org/10.1086/669855

Theodossopoulos, Dimitrios. 2016. "Philanthropy or Solidarity? Ethical Dilemmas About Humanitarianism in Crisis-Afflicted Greece." *Social Anthropology* 24 (2): 167–84. https://doi.org/10.1111/1469-8676.12304

Tillich, Paul. 2000. *The Courage to Be*. Translated by Peter J. Gomes. 2nd ed. New Haven, London: Yale University Press and Nota Bene.

Tillmann-Healy, Lisa M. 2003. "Friendship as Method." *Qualitative Inquiry* 9 (5): 729–49. https://doi.org/10.1177/1077800403254894.

Todorova, Maria. 1996. "Τα Βαλκάνια: Από την Ανακάλυψη στην «Κατασκευή» τους." [The Balkans: From Discovery to Invention.] In *National Movement and the Balkans* [Εθνικό Κίνημα και Βαλκάνια], edited by Miroslav Hroch and Maria Todorova, 57–114. Translated by Matalas Paraskeyas, Potamianos Nikos & Chatzaroula Pothiti. Athens: Themelio.

Todorova, Maria Nikolaeva. 2009. *Imagining the Balkans.* Updated edition. Oxford: Oxford University Press.

Tönnies, Ferdinand. 1963. *Community and Society*. Translated by Charles, P. Loomis. New York: Harper Torchbooks; Harper and Row.

Triandafyllidou, Anna, and Mariangela Veikou. 2002. "The Hierarchy of Greekness: Ethnic and National Identity Considerations in Greek Immigration Policy." *Ethnicities* 2 (2): 189–208. https://doi.org/10.1177/1468796802002002656

Trouillot, Michel-Rolph. 2003. *Global Transformations: Anthropology and the Modern World.* New York, Basingstoke: Palgrave Macmillan.

Trumpeta, Sevasti. 2000. "Μερικές Σκέψεις Σχετικά με την Παράσταση του «Άλλου» και το Φαινόμενο του Ρατσισμού στην Ελληνική Κοινωνία." [Zur Darstellung Des 'Anderen' Und Zum Phänomen Des Rassismus in Der Griechischen Gesellschaft.] *The Greek Review of Social Research* (101–102): 137–76.

Tsakatika, Myrto, and Costas Eleftheriou. 2013. "The Radical Left's Turn Towards Civil Society in Greece: One Strategy, Two Paths." *South European Society and Politics* 18 (1): 81–99. https://doi.org/10.1080/13608746.2012.757455

Tsakiris, Thanasis. 2019. "Το Κίνημα των Καταλήψεων του 1979 που Κατάργησε το Νόμο 815/1978." [The Squatting Movevement in 1979 That Abolished the Law 815/1978.] *Avgi*, December 2, 2019. Accessed February 15, 2023. http://www.avgi.gr/article/10811/10462750/to-kinema-ton-katalepseon-tou-1979-pou-katargese-ton-nomo-815-1978

Tsiakalos, Georgios. 2006. *Απέναντι στα Εργαστήρια του Ρατσισμού.* [Facing the Laboratories of Racism.] 1st ed. Athens: Typothito.

Tsilimpounidi, Myrto. 2014. "Anti-Conclusions: The 'Uprising' Will Not Be Analysed." In *Remapping 'Crisis': A Guide to Athens*, edited by Myrto Tsilimpounidi and Aylwyn Walsh, 318–22. Winchester: Zero Books. https://play.google.com/books

Tsilimpounidi, Myrto, and Aylwyn Walsh, eds. 2014. *Remapping 'Crisis': A Guide to Athens.* Winchester: Zero Books. https://play.google.com/books

Tsoukalas, Konstantinos. 2017/1993. "«Τζαμπατζήδες» στη Χώρα των Θαυμάτων. Περί Ελλήνων στην Ελλάδα." ['Free Riders' in the Country of Miracles: About Greeks in Greece.] *Greek Political Science Review* 1(2): 9–52. Accessed January 10, 2023. dx.doi.org/10.12681/hpsa.15324

Turner, Victor W. 1977/1969. *The Ritual Process: Structure and Anti-Structure.* Cornell paperbacks. Ithaca, New York: Cornell University Press.

Uhl, Sarah. 1991. "Forbidden Friends: Cultural Veils of Female Friendship in Andalusia." *American Ethnologist* 18 (1): 90–105.

Vahabzadeh, Peyman. 2001. "A Critique of Ultimate Referentiality in the New Social Movement Theory of Alberto Melucci." *Canadian Journal of Sociology* 26 (4): 611–633. https://doi.org/10.2307/3341494

Vaiou-Hadjimichali, Ntina, and Costis Hadjimichalis. 2012. *Ο Χώρος στην Αριστερή Σκέψη.* [Space in Left Thought.] Athens: Nikos Poulantzas Institute & Nisos.

Vamvakas, Vasilis, and Panayis Panagiotopoulos, eds. 2014. *Η Ελλάδα στη Δεκαετία του '80. Κοινωνικό, Πολιτικό και Πολιτισμικό Λεξικό.* [Greece in the 1980s: Social, Political and Cultural Dictionary.] 2nd ed. Athens: Epikentro.

van der Veer, Peter. 2009. "Spirituality in Modern Society." *Social Research* 76 (4): 1097–1120.

van Gennep, Arnold. 2019. *The Rites of Passage*. Translated by Monika B. Vizedom & Gabrielle L. Caffee. With a new introduction by David I. Kertzer. 2nd ed. Chicago: The University of Chicago Press.

Vasilaki, Roza. 2017. "Πολυπολιτισμικότητα και Αντιεθνικός Λόγος στη Σύγχρονη Ελλάδα: Μια Κριτική Επισκόπηση." [Multiculturalism and Anti-National Discourse in Modern Greece: A Critical Overview.] *Greek Political Science Review* 36: 5–36. Accessed December 12, 2023. https://doi.org/10.12681/hpsa.14505

Venturas, Lina. 1994. *Μετανάστευση και Έθνος. Μετασχηματισμοί στις Συλλογικότητες και τις Κοινωνικές Θέσεις*. [Migration and Nation: Transformations of Collectivities and Social Positions.] Athens: Association for the Study of Modern Hellenism.

Venturas, Lina. 2004. "Εθνικισμός, Ρατσισμός και Μετανάστευση στη Σύγχρονη Ελλάδα." [Nationalism, Racism and Migration in Contemporary Greece.] In *Η Ελλάδα της Μετανάστευσης. Κοινωνική Συμμετοχή, Δικαιώματα και Ιδιότητα του Πολίτη*. [Greece of Migration: Social Participation, Rights and Citizenship], edited by Miltos Pavlou and Dimitris Christopoulos, 174–204. Athens: Kritiki-Kemo.

Venturas, Lina. 2009. "Κράτος, Έθνος και Ομοιογένεια: 1974–2001." [State, Nation and Homogeneity: 1974–2001.] In *Μετανάστες και Μειονότητες. Λόγος και Πολιτικές*. [Migrants and Minorities: Discourse and Policies], edited by Miltos Pavlou and Athina Skoulariki, 105–40. Seira meleton / KEMO 3. Athens: Bibliorama.

Veremis, Thanos. 2005. *Βαλκάνια από τον 19ο ως τον 21ο Αιώνα. Δόμηση και Αποδόμηση Κρατών*. [The Balkans from the 19th to the 21st Century. Structuring and De-structuring States.] 3rd ed. Athens: Patakis.

Villa, Dana Richard, ed. 2000. *The Cambridge Companion to Hannah Arendt*. Cambridge: Cambridge University Press.

Voulgaris, Giannis. 2002. *Η Ελλάδα της Μεταπολίτευσης 1974–1990. Σταθερή Δημοκρατία Σημαδεμένη από τη Μεταπολεμική Ιστορία*. [Greece in Post Regime Period 1974–1990. Stable Democracy Marked by Post WWII History.] Athens: Themelio.

Voulgaris, Giannis. 2008. *Η Ελλάδα από τη Μεταπολίτευση στην Παγκοσμιοποίηση*. [Greece from the Metapolitefsi to Globalization.] Athens: Polis.

Voulgaris, Giannis. 2019. *Ελλάδα: Μια Χώρα Παραδόξως Νεωτερική*. [Greece: A Paradoxically Modern Country.] Athens: Polis.

Vradis, Antonis, and Dimitris Dalakoglou, eds. 2011. *Revolt and Crisis in Greece: Between a Present yet to Pass and a Future Still to Come*. Oakland, California, Edinburgh: AK Press & Occupied London.

Vulliamy, Ed, and Helena Smith. 2009. "Children of the Revolution." *The Guardian*, February 22, 2009. Accessed January 17, 2023. https://www.theguardian.com/world/2009/feb/22/civil-unrest-athens

Walhof, Darren R. 2006. "Friendship, Otherness, and Gadamer's Politics of Solidarity." *Political Theory* 34 (5): 569–93. https://doi.org/10.1177/0090591706290515

Walldén, Sotiris. 2004. *Η Ελλάδα Στα Βαλκάνια Και Τον Κόσμο 1995–2003. Ο Δύσκολος Εκσυγχρονισμός Της Εξωτερικής Πολιτικής*. [Greece in the Balkans and the World, 1995–2003. The Difficult Modernisation of Foreign Policy.] Athens: Themelio.

Walsh, George. 1972. "Introduction." In *The Phenomenology of the Social World*. Edited by John Wild. Translated by George Walsh and Frederick Lehnert. 1 pbk. print, xv–xxix. Evanston: Northwestern University Press.

Walzer, Michael. 2001. *Περί Ανεκτικότητας. Για τον Εκπολιτισμό της Διαφοράς*. [On Toleration.] Translated by Katerina Mandelaki. Athens: Kastaniotis.

Weber, Max, ed. 1949. *The Methodology of the Social Sciences*. Edited and translated by E. A. Shils and H. A. Finch. Glencoe, Illinois: The Free Press.

Weber, Max. 2002. *The Protestant Ethic and the Spirit of Capitalism*. Translated by Talcott Parsons. With an Introduction by Antony Giddens. Routledge classics. London: Routledge.

Weber, Max. 2004a. "Politics as a Vocation." In *The Vocation Lectures*, edited by David S. Owen, and Tracy B. Strong, 32–94. Translated by Rodney Livingstone. Indianapolis: Hackett Publishing Company.

Weber, Max. 2004b. "Science as a Vocation." In *The Vocation Lectures*, edited by David S. Owen, and Tracy B. Strong, 1–31. Translated by Rodney Livingstone. Indianapolis: Hackett Publishing Company.

Weber, Max. 2005. *Οικονομία και Κοινωνία I. Κοινωνιολογικές Έννοιες*. [Wirtschaft und Gesellschaft. Soziologie. Begriffe.] Edited and translated by Thanasis Giouras. Athens: Savvalas.

Weber, Max. 2007a. *Οικονομία και Κοινωνία II. Κοινότητες*. [Wirtschaft und Gesellschaft. Gemeinschaften.] Edited and translated by Thanasis Giouras. Athens: Savvalas.

Weber, Max. 2007b. *Οικονομία και Κοινωνία III. Κοινωνιολογία της Θρησκείας. Θρησκευτικές Κοινότητες*. [Wirtschaft und Gesellschaft. Religiöse Gemeinschaften.] Edited and translated by Thanasis Giouras. Athens: Savvalas.

Weber, Max. 2013. *From Max Weber: Essays in Sociology*. Edited and translated by Hans Heinrich Gerth, and Charles Wright Mills. With a New Preface by Bryan S. Turner. New York: Routledge. https://play.google.com/books

Weber, Max. 2019. *Economy and Society I*. Edited and translated by Keith Tribe. Cambridge, Massachusetts: Harvard University Press.

Weiss, Anja. 2008. "Ο Ρατσισμός της Παγκοσμιοποίησης." [The Racism of Globalisation.] In *Η Παγκοσμιοποίηση του Ρατσισμού*. [The Globalisation of Racism], edited by Macedo, Donaldo, and Panayota Gounari. Translated by Paraskeyi Arapoglou. Athens: Epikentro.

Werbner, Pnina, and Tariq Modood, eds. 2015. *Debating Cultural Hybridity: Multicultural Identities and the Politics of Anti-Racism*. London: Zed Books.

Wolff, Kurt, H. 2012. *The Sociology of Georg Simmel*. United States: Nabu.

WSF Document. 2001. "Charter of Principles: World Social Forum." Accessed January 18, 2023. http://www.universidadepopular.org/site/media/documentos/WSF_-_charter_of_Principles.pdf

Yioka, Lia. 2006. "Επεισόδια της Ετερότητας." [Episodes in Alterity.] In *Η Προσέγγιση του Άλλου. Ιδεολογία, Μεθοδολογία και Ερευνητική Πρακτική*. [Approaching the Other: Ideology, Methodology and Research Practice], edited by Giannis Kyriakakis and Martha Michailidou. 1st ed., 257–80. Athens: Metaixmio.

Zaretsky, Eli. 1986. *Capitalism, the Family, and Personal Life.* 1 Perennial Library edition. New York: Perennial Library.

Zavos, Alexandra. 2006. "Moving Relationships/Shifting Alliances: Constructions of Migration in the Leftist Anti-Racist Movement in Athens." *Annual Review of Critical Psychology* 6: 89–109.

Zavos, Alexandra, and Barbara Biglia. 2009. "Embodying Feminist Research: Learning from Action Research, Political Practices, Diffractions, and Collective Knowledge." *Qualitative Research in Psychology* 6 (1–2): 153–72. https://doi.org/10.1080/14780880902901380

Social Sciences

kollektiv orangotango+ (ed.)
This Is Not an Atlas
A Global Collection of Counter-Cartographies

2018, 352 p., hardcover, col. ill.
34,99 € (DE), 978-3-8376-4519-4
E-Book: free available, ISBN 978-3-8394-4519-8

Gabriele Dietze, Julia Roth (eds.)
Right-Wing Populism and Gender
European Perspectives and Beyond

April 2020, 286 p., pb., ill.
35,00 € (DE), 978-3-8376-4980-2
E-Book: 34,99 € (DE), ISBN 978-3-8394-4980-6

Mozilla Foundation
Internet Health Report 2019

2019, 118 p., pb., ill.
19,99 € (DE), 978-3-8376-4946-8
E-Book: free available, ISBN 978-3-8394-4946-2

All print, e-book and open access versions of the titles in our list are available in our online shop www.transcript-publishing.com